3 1994 01412 2425

V09 PLC

SAN

D0438699

1/09 PLC

FIGHTING THE GREAT WAR

FIGHTING THE GREAT WAR

HARVARD UNIVERSITY PRESS
Cambridge, Massachusetts
London, England
2005

A Global History

MICHAEL S. NEIBERG

940.4 NEI
Neiberg, Michael S.
Fighting the Great War

$27.95
CENTRAL   31994014122425

Copyright © 2005 by the President and Fellows of Harvard College
All rights reserved
Printed in the United States of America

Designed by Dean Bornstein

Pages ii–iii: Australian troops charge a Turkish
trench in the Dardanelles, ca. 1915. © Corbis.

Library of Congress Cataloging-in-Publication Data

Neiberg, Michael S.

Fighting the Great War : a global history / Michael S. Neiberg.
p. cm.
Includes bibliographical references and index.
ISBN 0-674-01696-3 (alk. paper)
1. World War, 1914–1918—History. 2. History, Modern—20th century. I. Title.

D521.N44 2005
940.4—dc22   2004054330

For Dennis Showalter

CONTENTS

· CONTENTS ·

ILLUSTRATIONS

MAPS

FIGURES

TIMELINE OF MAJOR EVENTS

1914

June 28	Assassination of Archduke Franz Ferdinand
July 23	Delivery of the Austrian ultimatum to Serbia
August 4	German invasion of Belgium
August 6–24	Battles of the Frontiers
August 8	British invasion of Togoland and East Africa
August 20	Battle of Gumbinnen
August 26–30	Battle of Tannenberg
September 4–10	First Battle of the Marne
September 7–14	Battle of the Masurian Lakes
Sept. 17–Oct. 18	The Race to the Sea
Oct. 17–Nov. 24	First Battle of Ypres/Battle of the Yser
Dec. 10–May 25	French offensive in Champagne

1915

Feb. 19–Dec. 20	Dardanelles/Gallipoli campaign
March 8–15	Battle of Neuve Chapelle
April 22–May 25	Second Battle of Ypres
May 2–13	Gorlice-Tarnow offensive
May 7	German sinking of the *Lusitania*
May 23	Italian entry into the war
June 29–July 7	First Battle of the Isonzo
July 9	British conquest of German Southwest Africa
August 5	German capture of Warsaw
Sept. 21–Nov. 6	Battles of Artois and Loos
October 3–5	Landing of Allied troops at Salonika

1916

January 18	Allied capture of Cameroon
Feb. 21–Dec. 15	Battle of Verdun
April 29	Surrender of British garrison at Kut
May 31–June 1	Battle of Jutland
June 4–August 11	Brusilov offensive
June 6	Start of the Arab Revolt
July 1–Nov. 18	Battle of the Somme
August 27	Romanian entry into the war
September 4	Allied capture of Dar es Salaam
September 15	Introduction of the first tanks (Somme)
November 28	First air raid on London

1917

February 1	German resumption of USW
March 11	British capture of Baghdad
March 15	Abdication of Tsar Nicholas II
April 6	United States entry into the war
April 9	Canadian capture of Vimy Ridge
April 16	Start of the Nivelle offensive
July 1–18	Kerensky offensive
July 31–Nov. 10	Third Battle of Ypres (Passchendaele)
September 1–5	German capture of Riga
Oct. 24–Nov. 10	Battle of Caporetto
November 16	Bolshevik government formed in Russia
Nov. 20–Dec. 4	Battle of Cambrai
December 9	British capture of Jerusalem

1918

January 8	Announcement of Wilson's Fourteen Points
March 3	Signing of Treaty of Brest-Litovsk
March 21	Start of German spring offensives

Mar. 26	Foch named Allied Supreme Commander
June 2–24	Battles of Château-Thierry and Belleau Wood
July 15–Aug. 4	Second Battle of the Marne
August 8–12	Battle of Amiens
September 12–16	American capture of St. Mihiel
Sept. 26–Nov. 11	Battle of the Meuse-Argonne
October 3	Hindenburg Line breached
October 30	Surrender of Ottoman Empire and Austria-Hungary
November 11	Armistice signed with Germany

IMPORTANT PEOPLE

Albert I	King of the Belgians
Alekseev, Mikhail	Russian general
Allenby, Edmund	British field marshal
Asquith, Herbert H.	British prime minister
Baker, Newton	American politician
Beatty, David	British admiral
Bernstorff, Johann	German diplomat
Bethmann Hollweg, Theobald von	German chancellor
Birdwood, William	British general
Böhm-Ermolli, Eduard	Austro-Hungarian general
Boroević, Svetozar	Austro-Hungarian field marshal
Botha, Louis	South African general
Bruchmüller, Georg	German colonel
Brusilov, Alexei	Russian general
Byng, Julian	British general
Cadorna, Luigi	Italian general
Capello, Luigi	Italian general
Casement, Roger	Irish nationalist
Castelnau, Edouard Noël de	French general
Cavell, Edith	British nurse
Churchill, Winston	British politician
Clemenceau, Georges	French prime minister
Conrad von Hötzendorf, Franz	Austrian general
Currie, Arthur	Canadian general
Diaz, Armando	Italian general
Driant, Emile	French soldier and deputy
Duchêne, Denis	French general

Enver Pasha	Ottoman general and statesman
Erzberger, Matthias	German politician
Faisal, Emir	Arabian prince
Falkenhayn, Erich von	German general
Foch, Ferdinand	French marshal
Fokker, Anthony	Dutch aircraft designer
Franchet d'Esperey, Louis	French general
François, Hermann von	German general
Franz Ferdinand	Assassinated Austrian archduke
Franz Joseph I	Austro-Hungarian emperor
French, John	British field marshal
Gallieni, Joseph	French general
Gibbs, Philip	British journalist
Goltz, Colmar von der	German/Ottoman field marshal
Gough, Hubert	British general
Grey, Edward	British statesman
Haig, Douglas	British field marshal
Hamilton, Ian	British general
Harrington, Charles	British general
Hindenburg, Paul von	German field marshal
Hipper, Franz	German admiral
Hoffmann, Max	German general
Holtzendorf, Henning von	German admiral
Hughes, William	Australian prime minister
Hutier, Oskar von	German general
Jellicoe, John	British admiral
Joffre, Joseph	French marshal
Kemal, Mustapha	Ottoman general and statesman
Kerensky, Alexander	Russian politician
Kitchener, Horatio	British field marshal
Kluck, Alexander von	German general
Kornilov, Lavr	Russian general

Lanrezac, Charles	French general
Lawrence, T. E.	British soldier
Lenin, Vladimir	Russian revolutionary
Lettow-Vorbeck, Paul von	German general
Liman von Sanders, Otto	German general
Lloyd George, David	British prime minister
Ludendorff, Erich	German general
Mackensen, August von	German field marshal
Mangin, Charles	French general
Max of Baden, Prince	German statesman
Mitchell, William "Billy"	American general
Moltke, Helmuth von	German general
Monash, John	Australian general
Nicholas II	Tsar of Russia
Nikolai Nikolaevich	Russian duke, army commander
Nivelle, Robert	French general
Painlevé, Paul	French politician
Pershing, John	American general
Pétain, Henri Philippe	French marshal
Plumer, Herbert	British general
Poincaré, Raymond	French president
Princip, Gavrilo	Serbian assassin
Putnik, Radomir	Serbian field marshal
Rawlinson, Henry	British general
Rennenkampf, Pavel	Russian general
Robertson, William	British field marshal
Samsonov, Alexander	Russian general
Sarrail, Maurice	French general
Scheer, Reinhard	German admiral
Sims, William	American admiral
Skoropadsky, Pavlo	Ukrainian statesman

Smith-Dorrien, Horace	British general
Smuts, Jan	South African general
Swinton, Ernest	British tank developer
Townshend, Charles	British general
Trotsky, Leon	Russian revolutionary
Venizelos, Eleutherios	Greek prime minister
Wilhelm II	German kaiser
Wilhelm, Crown Prince	German general
Wilson, Henry	British field marshal
Wilson, Woodrow	American president
Zhilinsky, Yakov	Russian general

INTRODUCTION

An Exchange of Telegrams

On July 29, 1914, Tsar Nicholas II of Russia sent a telegram to his cousin, Kaiser Wilhelm II of Germany, seeking his aid:

> In this serious moment, I appeal to you to help me. An ignoble war has been declared to a weak country. The indignation in Russia, shared fully by me, is enormous. I foresee that very soon I shall be overwhelmed by the pressure forced upon me and be forced to take extreme measures which will lead to war. To try and avoid such a calamity as a European war I beg you in the name of our old friendship to do what you can to stop your allies from going too far.

This telegram was the first in a series of ten exchanged by the two European monarchs in the tense days between July 29 and August 1. The crisis that the two men were discussing had resulted not from the assassination of Austro-Hungarian Archduke Franz Ferdinand in Sarajevo on June 28, but from the delivery of an ultimatum by Austria-Hungary to Serbia on July 23. Few Europeans had thought that the assassination would lead to war. The archduke's political views were unpopular in the Viennese court, and the royals of Europe had often snubbed Franz Ferdinand because he had married a woman of inferior social status. Although she had died at the same assassin's hand, and had left behind three small children, the Habsburg monarchy refused to place her body alongside her husband's in the royal family's crypt.

None of Europe's major military or political figures thought the assassination a significant enough event to attend the funeral or to cancel their summer vacation plans. The Austro-Hungarian Empire at first downplayed the significance; the emperor himself did not even attend his nephew's funeral. The mood of indifference seemed to be reflected throughout the continent. Russian General Alexei Brusilov, vacationing in Germany at the time of the assassination, noted that people at his spa "remained unperturbed" by the events in Sarajevo.[1] It appeared for a time that Europe might yet survive another crisis—or, if there was to be war, that it might be contained to the Balkans.

The ultimatum, however, changed the situation in Europe dramatically. It set harsh conditions against Serbia, the nation that most Austro-Hungarians believed had precipitated the assassination. Its terms included the demand that Serbia allow Austro-Hungarian officials to participate in Serbia's own investigation of the assassination. The terms were a slap in the face both to Serbia and to Russia, Serbia's self-anointed protector. Hoping that Serbia would reject the terms and therefore give them an excuse for war, the Austro-Hungarians had begun to mobilize even before the deadline for a Serbian response to the ultimatum had passed. Brusilov thought the ultimatum had changed the situation sufficiently to cause him to end his vacation early and return to his unit. On passing through Berlin he found crowds gathered, demanding war with Russia.

Tensions continued to rise as crowds in Serbia and Bosnia burned Austro-Hungarian flags and Viennese crowds burned Serbian flags. In Vienna, a mob estimated at 1,000 people tried to storm the Serbian legation. As a precautionary measure, Great Britain's Royal Navy, fortuitously on a scheduled practice mobilization, went to sea on July 29. The international crisis had an impact as far away as New York. On July 30, the New York Stock Exchange made its first unscheduled closing in forty years. The same day, Great Britain cut its telegraph links to Germany, and the German government demanded that Russia declare its intentions within twenty-four hours. Now the situation had become sufficiently tense to prompt statesmen and officers across Europe to change plans and return to work as quickly as possible. Troops were confined to barracks, leaves canceled, and reservists advised to remain close to home. Anything might happen.

The assassination of Archduke Franz Ferdinand and the subsequent Austro-Hungarian ultimatum need not have been a trigger for war. Cooler heads had prevailed during two incidents in Morocco (1905 and 1911), the Austro-Hungarian annexation of Bosnia in 1908, and two wars in the Balkans (1912–1913). Any of these crises could have led to a general war, but all had passed peacefully. By 1914, however, both the Germans and the Austro-Hungarians had determined that war served their interests more than peace. The previous year French ambassador to Germany Jules Cambon had noted a change in German attitudes. He reported to his government that "Wilhelm II has been brought to think that war with France is inevitable, and that it will have to come one day or the other. . . . [Chief of Staff] General [Helmuth von] Moltke spoke in exactly the same strain as his sovereign. He also declared that war was necessary and inevitable."[2]

By 1914, Germany and Austria-Hungary concluded that the time for the war that they believed to be inevitable had arrived. Both nations feared the ongoing modernization of the Russian army, scheduled to be completed in 1917. If assured of German support, Austria-Hungary thought that war could increase its influence in the Balkans and end the pan-Slavic threat posed by Serbia. Germany hoped to reduce one of its principal continental rivals, most likely France, to second-rate status; but France, too, had made recent military reforms. The most notable one, enacted in 1913 in response to the second Moroccan crisis, extended the period of time for military service in France from two years to three. The three-year law, once fully implemented, promised to increase the number of French soldiers on active duty by nearly one-third.

German officials had therefore given their Austro-Hungarian allies their full support as early as July 5, even though such a course threatened war with Russia. Even as the sovereigns of Rus-

*German reservists head to the front in 1914 amid cheers from the crowd.
German war planning relied on using reserves in offensive operations in
order to place as many men as possible in Belgium and France
in the war's early weeks. (National Archives)*

sia and Germany sought a way to avoid war via their telegram correspondence, their nations' militaries prepared for armed conflict.
Kaiser Wilhelm met with his senior general, Helmuth von Moltke,
nephew of the legendary general who had led Prussian armies to
lightning victories over Denmark, Austria, and France between
1864 and 1871. The kaiser asked Moltke to prepare for the possibility of war with Russia. Moltke informed the kaiser that a war
with Russia alone was not possible because German war planning
called for a war against France first, in order to eliminate Russia's
principal ally. The plan also called for a strike through Belgium to
outflank French defenses, thus threatening war with Great Britain, which was anxious to keep the English Channel coastline free
of German shipping.

Germany's global aspirations and the kaiser's clumsy diplomacy had placed Moltke and his predecessors in the difficult position of having to face a multifront war against superior numbers on land and at sea. Previous Prussian and German war fighting had benefited from its generals setting limited goals and winning quickly. Under Wilhelm II Germany had grown powerful, but its ambitions had outpaced its power. The signing of the Triple Entente (Russia, France, and Britain) in 1907 had bound Germany's three most powerful rivals together. Moltke had therefore assumed that war with one meant war with all. As a result, he told the kaiser, he could not plan only for war with Russia, nor could he even redirect the bulk of German forces to the east to fight the Russians first. If Germany were to go to war, it would need to fight first in Belgium and France. The kaiser responded by telling Moltke, "Your uncle would have given me a different answer." His rebuke led Moltke to confide to his wife that he felt "like a broken man, and [I] shed tears of despair. . . . My confidence and self-reliance were destroyed."[3] In such an emotional state, Moltke set off to the field in command of German armies.

In Russia, the kaiser's cousin faced a similar dilemma. The tsar had ordered his generals to prepare for the mobilization of only the four military districts opposite the Austro-Hungarian frontier. Nicholas hoped that the optimism in the kaiser's telegrams might lead to negotiations or, at worst, war between Austria-Hungary and Russia only. Russian War Minister Alexander Sazonov quickly shattered these illusions. He warned the tsar that a partial mobilization would create a dangerous and confusing situation. Russia needed time to organize across its enormous land mass and had limited rail assets compared to Germany. If Russia did not order a complete mobilization, it might soon find its frontiers with Germany indefensible. The tsar reluctantly agreed and ordered a general mobilization on July 30.

Although neither man fully understood the consequences of his actions, the tsar and the kaiser had taken the first steps toward

Paris, the goal of German operations in 1914, sat largely unable to defend itself. French planners, expecting to assume the offensive, had made inadequate preparations for the defense of the capital. (United States Air Force Academy McDermott Library Special Collections)

their own demise. In direct contrast to its own successful military history, Germany was about to embark on a general war against the combined might of three powerful enemies. Its only allies were the shaky Austro-Hungarian Empire, on its way to termination itself, and an unreliable Italy, which was soon to switch sides. Germany's high command knew that the longer the war lasted, the more the odds of winning leaned against them. They would need to win the war in Belgium and France quickly or risk not winning at all.

By November 1918 both Nicholas and Wilhelm had paid dearly for the war they had started. In March 1917 revolution and military defeat led Nicholas to abdicate the throne; in July 1918 the

Bolsheviks murdered him and his family. Wilhelm's reign lasted just a few months longer. On November 10, 1918, just hours before a new German government signed an armistice ending the war he had begun, Wilhelm abdicated his throne and crossed into exile in the Netherlands. Monarchs in Austria-Hungary and the Ottoman Empire met similar fates.

The victors of World War I were the democratic states of Great Britain, France, and the United States. These nations, while suffering from their own structural shortcomings, depended less on the authority of antiquated monarchical systems. They were therefore able to modify or change governments as situations demanded without having simultaneously to discard entire systems. As a result, they did not experience revolutions, and they were able to develop governments that could work with generals to achieve victory. When one system of organization failed, they created another until they finally found the formula for success.

Ironically, none of the three most powerful victors of World War I had sought war in 1914. The French government, anxious to avoid war unless its own territory were threatened, ordered French units to back away six miles from the frontier with Germany and to stay there unless Germany actually invaded France. Although some French nationalists believed that war with Germany could avenge the loss of the Franco-Prussian War in 1870–1871 and recover the provinces taken from France after that war, France had long ruled out an offensive war to achieve those aims. France would defend its borders, but would not start a war of its own.

Great Britain's most important military asset, its powerful navy, would play a small role if the war were to be as short as most experts predicted. Its small professional army was not designed to fight a major continental war, despite the formation of a British Expeditionary Force (BEF) in 1907 to facilitate its rapid deployment. The Germans disdained the British army and made no attempt to sink the transports that took Britain's troops to France and Belgium. Better, Moltke and his colleagues believed, to de-

In August 1914 British officers led their small army into the teeth of the German advance into France and Belgium, incurring tremendous casualties in the process. One journalist commented in 1916 that the prewar British army had become nothing but a "heroic memory." (© Corbis)

stroy the army once it arrived on the continent, if the British government actually dared to send it.

Neither Britain nor France in 1914 fully understood its war aims or how to implement them. Brusilov believed that France was "far from being ready" for war in 1914.[4] Douglas Porch's description of the French army as "unable to decide in which historical epoch it lived" could apply to Britain as well.[5] Elite units of the

Lieutenant Benjamin Foulois (left) and an instructor from Wright Aviation steer the United States Army's only airplane in 1910. Within a decade these humble beginnings had given way to a new method of waging war, and Foulois had become chief of the Air Service in the American Expeditionary Force. (United States Air Force Academy McDermott Library Special Collections)

French army went to war in 1914 wearing brightly colored uniforms more reminiscent of their African colonies than the modern war of steel. The British, for their part, were still led by colonial heroes who had little understanding of the intricacies of continental politics, like Secretary of State for War Horatio Kitchener and Sir William Robertson, who spoke six Indian languages, but neither French nor German. The British army had not fought on the continent since the Crimean War of 1854 to 1856. Both the British and the French paid heavy prices for the steep learning curves that they experienced from 1914 to 1917.

By the end of 1917, however, that learning curve was nearly complete. France, Britain, and the United States had developed industrial, political, and military structures that saw them through the crisis of 1918. Victory resulted from a combination of improved military prowess and the evolution of an administrative, economic, and social support system that drove battlefield success. Both nations had come far from August 1914, when British General Henry Wilson observed the meeting at which Britain's senior leadership had decided upon war. He described it as a "historic meeting of men mostly entirely ignorant of their subject."[6] By 1917–1918 his description no longer fit the senior civilian and military leaders of the Allied powers.[7] They oversaw massive military machines with the infrastructure to support them. Because of the allied creation of a joint civil-military system, French Marshal Ferdinand Foch directed representatives of the new German government to a forest clearing near Compiègne in November 1918. In a railway car in that clearing, the German government surrendered, thereby ending the war that they had played such a large role in beginning.

[1]

A CRUEL DISILLUSION

The German Invasion and the Miracle of the Marne

The French soldier has lost none of the military qualities of his race;
he retains all of his courage and all of his offensive ardor, but these
same qualities need to be wisely directed on the modern battlefield or
they will lead to a rapid wearing out of forces.

—French *Bulletin des Opérations* from General Joffre's
headquarters to commanders, September 21, 1914

BECAUSE German war planning assumed that war with one
member of the Triple Entente meant war with them all, the first
major German operations moved west against Belgium and France,
two nations only indirectly involved in the crisis precipitated by
the Austro-Hungarian ultimatum. Belgium's only offense to Germany was its unfortunate geographic position, and the terms of
the Triple Entente obligated France to mobilize only in the event
of a German mobilization and to declare war only if Germany attacked Russia. France need not have been involved in the July crisis at all. Ironically Russia, the main diplomatic problem for Germany during the July crisis, began the war as a secondary German
concern. While seven German armies headed west, only the German Eighth Army headed east.

FIGHTING ACCORDING TO PLAN

German war planning remains the subject of intense historical
controversy, but scholars have reached general consensus on three
points. First, the Germans assumed the need to defeat France
before defeating Russia because they guessed that France would

mobilize more quickly than Russia would. Second, Germany assumed the need to outflank the French fortifications by violating the neutrality of Belgium if it were to defeat France quickly enough to turn east and face the Russians. Third, Germany guessed that either Great Britain would not fight for Belgian neutrality (with the kaiser famously referring to the 1839 treaty as a "scrap of paper") or, if it did fight, the Germans would annihilate the small British Expeditionary Force (BEF) somewhere on the continent. The possible intervention of the British army therefore did not pose a major challenge to German planners.

To achieve this lightning strike on Belgium and France, the Germans deployed seven of their eight armies westward beginning on August 2. The units principally responsible for the movement through Belgium were the German First and Second Armies, with 320,000 and 260,000 men respectively. Two more German armies, the Third and Fourth, offered support by moving through Luxembourg and southern Belgium, while the Fifth, Sixth, and Seventh Armies defended Alsace and Lorraine. Moltke set up his headquarters in Luxembourg, which turned out to be too far from his armies to exercise real control over them and too far from Berlin to maintain a firm grasp on the larger picture.

Although it violated a treaty that Germany had signed, an attack through neutral Belgium offered several important advantages. France's strongest line of fortifications ran along the German border from Verdun to Toul and from Epinal to Belfort. Except for Maubeuge, the forts that existed in northeastern France had fallen into general disrepair, as the French concentrated defense spending on offensive weapons. Furthermore, French forces were concentrated along the border with Alsace and Lorraine. If the Germans could move quickly, the French armies might be too far from Paris to prevent a German capture or encirclement of the capital.

Belgium appeared ripe for the taking. It had a small military force, numbering just 117,000 men, less than half the size of the

German Second Army alone. It was short of many of the modern weapons of warfare, and its staff work and support services fell far below the standards of its more powerful neighbors. Jealous to guard its neutrality, it had not conducted extensive talks with either France or Britain before the war. Some Germans had even hoped that the Belgians might permit the German army free movement through their nation rather than try to resist.

Contrary to these expectations, the Belgians did plan to resist despite the overwhelming odds they faced. Their hopes turned on a series of fortified cities that guarded the nation's major rivers, roads, and rail lines. Among the strongest was Liège, with twelve separate forts, 400 pieces of artillery, and the capacity to maintain a garrison of 20,000 men. Namur, to the southwest of Liège, had nine forts that Belgian commanders believed could hold out for six months without reinforcement. Both Liège and Namur sat on the German Second Army's line of advance. The most impressive of all the Belgian fortifications sat further north and guarded the port city of Antwerp. The defenses there included twenty-seven miles of outer lines, seventeen separate forts, and eight miles of inner ramparts.

The Germans did not intend to besiege the Belgian garrisons; they planned to obliterate them with modern artillery custombuilt for the purpose. German 28cm howitzers could fire shells from as far as six miles away, too far for the Belgian fortress guns to reply. The shells these howitzers fired weighed 748 pounds and traveled at a speed of 1,133 feet per second, yielding a striking energy of more than 6,000 tons. A skilled German battery could fire as many as twenty such shells per minute.

Liège guarded the approaches across the Meuse River and was the first major obstacle to German progress across Belgium. It also sat along the trunk railroad line from Cologne to Brussels and was therefore critical to German supply routes toward France. Its position held such strategic significance that the German chief of the mobilization staff had visited the region in 1909, dressed as a

German soldiers move through Belgium. Tight timetables and fears of partisan activity unnerved young German soldiers, leading to atrocities and reprisals against Belgian civilians. (Library of Congress)

tourist. Five years later, General Erich Ludendorff put the information he had learned on that tour to good use as commander of the 14th Brigade, which was charged with taking the fort. Ludendorff boasted that his artillery could force Liège's surrender within forty-eight hours. In addition to the 28cm howitzers, he had at his disposal five 42cm guns, built specifically to destroy the forts of Liège, and four batteries of 305mm high-angle mortars. Zeppelins added to this firepower, making Liège the first city in Europe to be bombarded from the air.[1]

Ludendorff almost fulfilled his promise as his men infiltrated Liège in a series of daring attacks. He led several of the charges himself, banging on the main doors of the Liège citadel with the hilt of his sword and demanding its surrender on August 7. As a result of his success in Liège, Ludendorff became an overnight hero in Germany, setting him on a meteoric rise that soon led to much larger responsibilities. But Germany's immediate problem remained. Loss of the Liège citadel notwithstanding, forts on both sides of the Meuse River remained in Belgian hands, although the intense German artillery fire caused enormous damage to the forts and tremendous casualties to the Belgian garrisons. The final fortress around Liège did not surrender until August 16. Namur posed less of a problem, surrendering in just two days.

Of greater concern to the speed-conscious Germans, the Belgian army and irregular forces (called *franc tireurs,* meaning "free shooters") refused to submit to the larger and more powerful Germans. The actions of the *franc tireurs* especially enraged German commanders, who recalled the tremendous problems that French irregulars had caused for them in the Franco-Prussian War of 1870–1871. Young German conscripts, terrified at the rifle fire coming from all angles and at the most unexpected times, grew frightened and edgy. Afraid of the impact on their men and the disruptions to their precious timetable, the German army reacted with a premeditated campaign of *Schrecklichkeit,* or frightfulness, against Belgian civilians, a policy that had been approved by leaders of both the army and the government.[2]

The city of Louvain felt the full weight of *Schrecklichkeit.* The Germans shot the burgomaster, the university rector, and all of the town's police officers. Then they set fire to the university's library, destroying the precious buildings and the irreplaceable Gothic and Renaissance manuscripts contained within. The Germans deported thousands of Belgian civilians to work camps and shot thousands more, most on only the slightest provocation. In late August, the Germans arrested an English nurse, Edith Cavell, and accused her of espionage, a charge that appeared manifestly unjust, even to many Germans. German officials refused to release the evidence on which they had arrested her and denied requests to have English lawyers or observers present at her trial. In

*Germany's execution of English nurse Edith Cavell in October 1915
produced a surge in British enlistments and provided the Allies with an
important tool in the propaganda war. (Imperial War Museum, Crown
Copyright, 86/28/2)*

October 1915 the Germans executed her, outraging Entente and
neutral opinion and leading to the largest increase in British re-
cruitment since the outbreak of the war. German attempts to ra-
tionalize their actions as self-defense rang hollow. "We are in a position of necessity," proclaimed German Chancellor Theobald von
Bethmann Hollweg, "and necessity knows no law."[3]

The British government declared war on Germany as soon as
German forces entered Belgium. The callousness with which Germany had violated the neutrality of a nation that posed no con-
ceivable threat to it shocked the British. On a more practical level,
fears of Germany seizing control of the southern edge of the English Channel drove the British to act. As stories (both real and ex-
aggerated) of German actions in Belgium spread, the cause of Belgium soon became, as one writer put it, "shorthand for the moral

issues of the war."⁴ Standing up for the rights of Belgium soon became equated with the honor of Britain and, for the first few months of the war at least, led thousands of young Britons to volunteer for military service.

While young men across Britain were enlisting, 100,000 professional soldiers and reservists of the BEF landed on the continent between August 11 and 17, although the Germans did not become fully aware of their presence until August 22. Private Reeve of the British Royal Field Artillery later recalled that while marching along the roads of northern France, British soldiers "got a frantic welcome all the way[,] people going mad with delight. Had flags, cigarettes, tobacco, fruit, and wine at every station [at] which we were decorated."⁵ This enthusiasm notwithstanding, the integration of the French and British armies proved to be an extremely difficult process. There had been little prewar planning between the British and the French and much mutual suspicion between the commanders of the respective armies. The commander of the northernmost French army (the Fifth), Charles Lanrezac, distrusted the British almost as much as BEF commander Sir John French distrusted the French. Upon the BEF's arrival, Lanrezac's chief of staff greeted Sir John's chief of staff coldly, saying, "At last you are here. . . . If we are beaten we will owe it all to you."⁶

Such problems notwithstanding, the BEF advanced toward Belgium from a line based between the French fortress of Maubeuge and the town of Le Cateau. The men of the BEF were tough, well-trained, and expert marksmen. They had all volunteered for military service; and they came from a British regimental tradition that stressed loyalty to the unit, assuring that the men would fight, and fight hard. By all measures, they were some of the best soldiers in Europe. The kaiser soon came to regret his casual dismissal of the BEF as a "contemptible little army."

The BEF's most important weakness came from the top. Field Marshal Sir John French had been named commander more for his principled resignation during a threatened army mutiny in Ulster than for any competence to handle such a serious assignment. Most of his senior colleagues thought Sir John woefully ill suited for such a command. One of them, General Douglas Haig, had unsuccessfully protested the appointment directly to the king. A dashing colonial cavalry officer in his youth, Sir John was sixty-four years old in 1914 and had been in military service since joining the Royal Navy as a midshipman in 1866. Now he had come to France with an army whose corps and division commanders did not fully believe in him in order to fight alongside an ally that did not trust him.

By August 22, the French Fifth Army held the Belgian towns of Dinant and Charleroi, the remnants of the Belgian army sat south of Namur, and the BEF had advanced to the town of Mons. The next day, the II Corps of the BEF, comprising 30,000 men, found itself directly in the line of advance of the entire German First Army in an area that left one brigade commander "not favorably impressed by its possibility for defense."[7] The II Corps commander in charge of this sector, Horace Smith-Dorrien, had been one of just five officers to survive the massacre of 1,750 Europeans at the 1879 Battle of Isandhlwana during the Zulu War. He had risen to become one of the British Army's most respected field commanders, and at Mons he did not panic. Neither did his soldiers. Despite the odds against them at Mons, the British professionals of the II Corps used their rifles skillfully and took 1,500 casualties, but held the line.

Despite these heroics, the BEF found itself in a dangerous position. Early the next morning, Sir John learned that Lanrezac's Fifth Army to his right was beginning a retreat. The retirement left the II Corps' right flank dangerously exposed. Furious at Lanrezac and growing despondent about the future of his army, Sir John ordered the II Corps to retreat. At the same time, German First Army commander Alexander von Kluck attempted to encircle British forces and cut Smith-Dorrien off from Douglas Haig's nearby I Corps. The movement almost succeeded. Sir John saw the threat to the II Corps and ordered Smith-Dorrien to withdraw. By the time the order arrived, however, the II Corps found itself desperately fighting for survival. Smith-Dorrien's men, already exhausted from Mons, found themselves in an area with poor defensive terrain and no reserves able to come to their rescue. Unable to disengage himself from the Germans opposite him, he disobeyed French's order and fought.

The resulting Battle of Le Cateau, fought on August 26, became the largest battle the British army had fought since Waterloo a century earlier. In a driving rain, the men of the II Corps fought a tough rear-guard action against 140,000 Germans. The British lost 8,000 men—few by later World War I standards, but enormous for an army that totaled less than 100,000 men and had already been bloodied at Mons. The hard combat at Le Cateau permitted the remaining elements of the BEF to retreat back into France and reorganize. Smith-Dorrien's decision to stand and fight very likely saved the BEF, although his commander never fully forgave him for disobeying an order.

The British then began a long retreat back toward Paris. Private Reeve, the field artillerist who had noted the ecstatic reaction of the French civilians to the British arrival, wrote one week later that "nearly all the places that welcomed us going up are now deserted."[8] Another British soldier, an Irish veteran of wars in India and South Africa, recorded the tragic sight of an army retreating up to seventeen miles a day without rations, subsisting on potatoes found along the way. Most soldiers were wearing the same clothes they had worn upon their departure from Britain. Adding to the oddity of the scene, many of the long-service veterans in his unit had discarded their coats and hats and had managed to acquire ladies' sun hats to protect them from the unusually intense August heat. Still, wrote the soldier, "on the notable occasions

The German advance displaced thousands of families unfortunate enough to be caught in the path of the German armies. These French children were among the refugees. (National Archives)

when these same weary men had to turn and fight they pushed themselves and did well."[9] The British Army was wounded, but it was not beaten.

Lanrezac's failure to inform the British of his withdrawal strained Allied relations for months, but the withdrawal itself made perfect military sense in light of French failures to the southeast. French war planning has received great condemnation from historians, and with good reason. French planners, however, faced much greater political and social obstacles than their German counterparts did. French politicians forbade the army from violating Belgian neutrality until Germany had done so. Moreover, France lacked the continental ambition of Germany and therefore had no obvious war aims other than self-defense and the reconquest of Alsace and Lorraine, the two provinces Germany had seized in 1871.

Although French war aims were essentially defensive, France's generals had no intention of executing a defensive war plan. Their study of the debacle of 1870–1871 had concluded that France's defensive stand in the early weeks of the war had yielded the initiative to the enemy and therefore had been a primary cause of defeat. Accordingly, France's Plan XVII called for a concentration of French forces south of the Belgian border along a line from Sedan to Belfort. While such a plan left Picardy and Artois exposed, it offered French commander Joseph Joffre the choice of advancing into Alsace-Lorraine or, if the Germans did indeed violate Belgian neutrality, advancing northeast into Belgium to cut off the Germans from behind.[10]

Political, cultural, and economic motivations made an advance into Alsace-Lorraine the most obvious French option. The return of these two "Lost Provinces" was the only war aim, other than the obvious one of self-defense, that unified the French citizenry. In addition, more than one-third of Germany's iron ore came from Alsace and Lorraine; capturing the iron mines could cripple German war production. From a military standpoint, control of Alsace-Lorraine would bring French forces to the Rhine River, thereby interfering with German abilities to reinforce and resupply its armies. It also accorded with prewar agreements made with the Russians to pressure Germany by launching simultaneous offensives from the east and the west.

Between August 7 and 14, as German forces were moving through Belgium, the French completed their own concentrations. By August 14, Joffre and his staff still did not think that they had enough information to judge German intentions in Belgium accurately. They believed that the situation appeared to lean in their favor. They could not—or did not want to—rule out the possibility that the German advance in Belgium was just a feint. They also believed that the Germans did not have enough strength to advance through Belgium, defend against a major attack in Alsace-Lorraine, and hold off the Russians in the east all at the same time. Moreover, at that point some of the fortresses at Liège were continuing to hold out, and the Germans had not yet attempted to attack Namur. Joffre therefore underestimated the significance of operations in Belgium and ordered his forces into Alsace-Lorraine.

Expecting to liberate Alsace-Lorraine, France's finest soldiers concentrated in four armies opposite the German Sixth and Seventh Armies. Cadets from the French military academy at St. Cyr reported for battle in full dress uniforms, prepared to sacrifice their lives for France. As they advanced into Alsace, locals showered them with wine and flowers. Joffre issued a proclamation to the people of Alsace that read:

> After forty-four years of sorrowful waiting French soldiers once more tread the soil of our noble country. They are the pioneers in the great work of revenge. . . . The French nation unanimously urged them on, and in the folds of their flags are inscribed the magic words, "Right and Liberty." Long live Alsace! Long live France![11]

The four separate engagements that followed between August 14 and 27, collectively known as the Battle of the Frontiers, began hopefully for France, but ended in abject disaster. The German Sixth and Seventh Armies had expected to defend in this sector and had prepared the ground accordingly. The hills, mountains, and forests of Alsace provided excellent positions for the German defenders. Nevertheless, the French advanced courageously. One-armed General Paul-Marie Pau's Army of Alsace advanced as far as Mulhouse. To his north the strongest French formations, the First and Second Armies, with one-third of France's total manpower, advanced northeast from positions astride the Moselle River. The French Third and Fourth Armies prepared to strike the presumably weak German center in the Ardennes Forest.

For the first week, the French believed that their offensive was showing signs of success. Much of this success, however, was illusory because French forces had not yet reached the main German positions. They did so on August 20 in two places. The French Second Army struck the heights of Morhange northeast of Nancy as the French First Army met strong German positions near Sarrebourg between Nancy and Strasbourg. No soldiers ever fought harder; but, as on so many battlefields to follow in this war, their enthusiasm could not compensate for the challenges they faced. In the hills and valleys of Alsace, units became separated from one another and communications quickly broke down. Inexperienced soldiers, many in bright uniforms ill suited to modern warfare, charged camouflaged machine-gun nests with predictable results.

Having been thrown back from Morhange and Sarrebourg, the French next faced determined counterattacks from the German Sixth and Seventh Armies. The Germans sought to exploit French losses, seize the critical city of Nancy, and rush through the Trouée de Charmes, a lightly fortified region southwest of Nancy between Toul and Epinal. Joffre had to manage this crisis as well as the one developing in Belgium, where the Germans were preparing to cross the Meuse River and advance on Mons. The situation had grown desperate.

On August 24, the same day that the BEF held its lines at Mons, the Germans charged the Trouée de Charmes, which Joffre ordered held at all costs. Second Army Commander Edouard-Noël de Castelnau turned over the defense of Nancy to his intelligent and aggressive XX Corps commander, Ferdinand Foch. Foch had left school in 1870 and volunteered to fight as a private in the Franco-Prussian War, although he saw no combat. After the war he returned to school in Nancy, where he had studied for his French officer corps entrance exams while German occupation bands taunted the residents by playing "Retreat" every day. He knew the terrain around Nancy well, and he burned at the chance for revenge.[12] Foch also benefited from excellent relations with Joffre, who willingly overlooked many of Foch's shortcomings. At

The enormous casualties of the early weeks severely taxed medical systems utterly unprepared for war. This French church served as a makeshift military hospital. (National Archives)

the beginning of August 1914 Foch had ignored the government's order to move his units six miles away from the frontier, and at Morhange he had pressed forward when Castelnau had ordered him to retreat. As a result, Castelnau largely blamed him for the dismal situation in which his Second Army now stood.

Foch reorganized the retreating French units around a chain of wooded hills 300 to 400 meters high northeast of Nancy collectively known as the Grand Couronné. The French First and Second Armies then reestablished contact and prepared to meet the German attack. On August 25, the Germans came close to breaking the French lines, but Foch responded. He ordered his XX

Corps to counterattack, hoping that the confusion his attack generated would disrupt German planning. His maneuver worked: the French managed to hold Nancy and the Trouée de Charmes through bloody fighting that lasted until September 12.

Despite this success, the French had failed to recapture Alsace-Lorraine and had paid an enormous human price at the Battle of the Frontiers. French officers, imbued with the belief that leadership meant the willingness to attack and die with one's boots on, conducted bloody attack after bloody attack. French offensive doctrine collapsed in the face of German field artillery and machine guns. French losses are estimated at 200,000 men and 4,700 of its 44,500 prewar officers. The best men of the French army had sacrificed their lives in an attempt to recover Alsace and Lorraine, only to discover that the real threat lay elsewhere.

THE MIRACLE OF THE MARNE

Joffre responded to the overlapping series of emergencies he faced without panicking. A massive man with a soldier's presence and an almost inhuman calm, he took stock of the simultaneous crises that had developed in Belgium and Alsace without missing his enormous lunches or his daily naps. Belatedly realizing that the main threat came from the German right wing advancing toward Paris from the northeast, he ordered French forces to remain on the defensive from Verdun to Belfort. He ruthlessly replaced dozens of officers that he believed had not met the challenge of the war's first weeks, including Lanrezac and Pau. He disbanded Pau's Army of Alsace and sent most of its men to Paris, where they contributed to the formation of a new Sixth Army to guard the northeast approaches to the capital. He also reassigned Foch to the command of another new unit, the Ninth Army, which was being formed east of Paris between the Fourth and Fifth Armies.

The Germans were tantalizingly close to a victory in the west on schedule. On August 31 a German pilot dared to drop a flag over Paris's Les Halles market carrying the words "The Germans will be in Paris in three days."[13] Even so, the French capital was figuring less and less in the Germans' plans. Believing that he had crushed the BEF, Kluck decided to switch strategies. He opted not to move to the north and west of Paris as planned. Instead, he changed his axis of attack to the south and east of the capital in order to crush the French Fifth Army, which he erroneously believed to be the last capable Allied army near Paris. French air reconnaissance and cavalry patrols soon reported the change in Kluck's movements.

The German shift was welcome news to Paris's military governor, General Joseph Gallieni, a hero of the French colonial wars who had been returned to active service in spite of his rapidly declining health. On September 1, Gallieni had informed Joffre that Paris could not defend itself with the resources on hand. But the news of the German movement to the southeast that Gallieni received on September 3 meant that the main battle could be fought outside Paris and the capital would not have to suffer a siege for which it was woefully unprepared. Joffre and Gallieni both saw an opportunity to smash the now exposed German right flank, although Joffre still recommended that the French government evacuate to Bordeaux, 360 miles to the southwest.

At the same time, Sir John had grown despondent and considered moving the BEF in the direction of the channel port of Le Havre, whence it could be evacuated by the Royal Navy. On August 31, he telegraphed British Secretary of State for War Lord Kitchener, admitting, "My confidence in the ability of the leaders of the French Army to carry this campaign to a successful conclusion is fast waning."[14] Kitchener, a soldier of legendary proportions, immediately understood that if the BEF followed Sir John's proposed retreat a dangerous gap would open between the French Fifth and Sixth Armies, leaving Paris precariously exposed. He therefore took the unusual step of rushing to France personally to convince Sir John to stay. Although he was then serving in government as a civilian, he came to France in his field marshal's uniform to impress upon Sir John his own view of the chain of command. Kitchener succeeded in changing Sir John's mind, and the BEF assumed defensive positions east of Paris.

By September 4, the opposing armies were spread out, like taut elastic bands, across a 200-mile front from Paris to Verdun. The revised German plan envisioned rolling up the two flanks of the Allied line and pushing the Allied armies in against each other. The maneuver promised to destroy the Allied forces in front of Paris, but it demanded a great deal from German soldiers who had been on the march and engaged in combat for a month. The First, Second, and Third Armies were thousands of men below the strength with which they had begun the war. Many units had outmarched their supplies and were living off the land. The men were tired, hungry, and short of ammunition.

Joffre's own men were as tired as their German enemies were, but they were closer to their supply lines, and reinforcements from the French provinces were on their way to Paris. With Paris no longer the target of the German First Army, Joffre and Gallieni gambled: on September 4 they ordered the men of the Paris garrison to "maintain contact with the German army and prepare to participate in the battle now developing."[15] Gallieni then met with Sir John's Chief of Staff and agreed on a plan to act together, the details of which Joffre and Sir John soon confirmed. The change of direction reenergized the men of the BEF, who were glad to move forward instead of backward. "Only those who had actually taken part in the retreat [from Mons]," recalled one British officer, "can fully appreciate what it felt like when we were told that we were to make up our deficiencies and be prepared to *advance*."[16] Despite their fatigue, the men of the BEF had not lost the will to fight.

The resulting Battle of the Marne stretched across the entire front from the Ourcq River to Verdun. It was at the time the largest battle ever fought, with one million men engaged on each side.

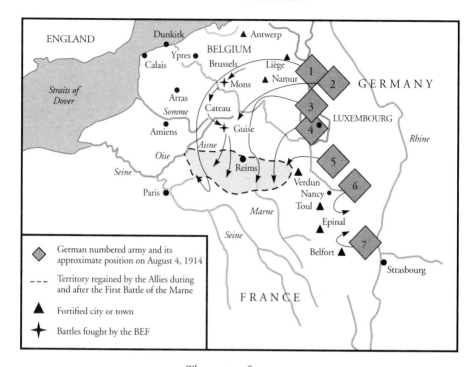

The western front, 1914

The stakes were enormous. If the Germans succeeded in enveloping the Allied armies, it could lead to disaster on an unprecedented scale. If they failed, the Germans would be forced to retreat across the Marne River and Paris would be safe. The Fifth Army general order of the day on September 5 conveyed the sense of urgency: "Every soldier must know before this battle that the honor of France and the health of the Fatherland rests on the energy that he brings into tomorrow's battle. The nation counts on every man to do his duty."[17] The future of France hung in the balance.

On Sunday morning, September 6, the Allied armies advanced all along the line. On the German left, the kaiser himself had appeared, hoping to lead a triumphal march into Nancy. In continued combat on the Grand Couronné, the French denied him the opportunity. Having learned a lesson from Belgium, French forces abandoned their fortifications and fought from trenches and earthworks as deep as eighteen feet. Vigorous attacks by German forces led them within just six miles of Nancy, but the French held, despite an overwhelming German advantage in both men and artillery pieces. The setback in front of Nancy not only humiliated the kaiser, it also meant that the eastern pincer in the German double envelopment had failed to do its job.

The key to the battle occurred further to the west, near Paris. Kluck's German First Army had lost contact with General Bülow's Second Army, resulting in an exposed gap of twelve miles between them. Moltke, isolated in Luxembourg, could not receive information quickly enough to manage the situation. Joffre, closer to the front, could. He assigned Foch's Ninth Army to hold the German Second Army in place while the French Fifth Army and the BEF drove into the gap between the two German armies. The fate of Paris, and perhaps the war itself, would be determined the next morning, Monday, September 7.

At dawn the Allied armies advanced. Kluck saw the danger and counterattacked to the west, inflicting enormous casualties on the French. The French Sixth Army commander, Michel Joseph Manoury, considered retreating, but Gallieni's planning saved him. On September 1 the military governor had ordered all Parisian taxicabs and chauffeurs to stand ready for potential service, and on September 6 he had ordered the 1,200 cabs and their drivers to assemble at Paris's train stations. In what became known as the "Miracle of the Marne," Gallieni used those cabs to rush 5,000 recently arrived reinforcements to Manoury in time to stop Kluck's counterattack, forever earning Gallieni the title "Savior of Paris."

At the same time that Gallieni's reinforcements were saving Paris, the BEF was threatening Kluck's left flank. I Corps commander Douglas Haig drove the BEF forward almost eight miles into the gap that had opened between the German First and Second armies. Although the events of September 7 had not yet won the battle, they had changed the situation dramatically. The Allies threatened the German First Army with encirclement. The kaiser's playboy son, German Fifth Army commander Crown Prince Wilhelm, shelved his plans for a triumphal march down the Champs Elysées reminiscent of the one the Prussian army had taken in 1871. Paris was safe.

Back in Luxembourg, Moltke understood as well as the Crown Prince that the battle was not leaning in his favor. Far from the front lines, he had a much less clear picture of events than did Joffre or Sir John. German General Erich von Falkenhayn, soon to replace Moltke, caustically noted that "our General Staff has completely lost its head. Schlieffen's notes do not help any further and so Moltke's wits come to an end."[18] To gain a better grasp of the situation, Moltke sent one of his ablest staff officers, Lieutenant Colonel Richard Hentsch, to the front. While touring the front on September 8 and 9, Hentsch found Bülow and Kluck engaged in blaming each other for the existence of the gap between them. The Germans had no reserves to fill the gap and admitted their inability to force the French out of their positions in the east. On September 9, a determined attack on the Allied center failed when Foch's Ninth Army held its ground. Foch then surprised the Germans by counterattacking. Bülow decided to retreat behind the Marne River, widening the gap between himself and Kluck. Hentsch, on Moltke's authority, then ordered Kluck to retreat as well.

For the next two days, Allied armies advanced slowly and cautiously across the Marne River. Joffre and Sir John were not yet ready to believe that the Germans had admitted defeat and were indeed retreating instead of reorganizing for another offensive. Critics later blamed Joffre for not pursuing the retreating Germans, but those critics failed to take into account the tremendous

E. R. Heaton shown in a photograph taken shortly after he volunteered to serve in the New Armies. He and almost 20,000 other Britons died on the first day of the Battle of the Somme, July 1, 1916. (Imperial War Museum, Crown Copyright, E. R. Heaton)

losses that the Allies had suffered. In just over three weeks of active combat, the Allies and the Germans had each lost more than 500,000 men. Both armies were exhausted, short of supplies, and uncertain about what they should do next. Joffre and the Allied armies had halted the Germans and saved Paris. To have asked them to do more was beyond the capabilities of men who had suffered so much already.

Moltke immediately grasped the significance of the German setback. He presciently wrote to his wife, "The war which began with such good hopes will in the end go against us. . . . We shall be crushed in the fight against East and West. . . . Our campaign is a cruel disillusion. And we shall have to pay for all the destruction which we have done."[19] The defeat at the Marne also meant the end of Moltke's command. He suffered a nervous breakdown and was replaced by Falkenhayn on September 13. The war that the generals had planned for was over. The war of improvisation was about to begin.

THE RACE TO THE SEA

As occurred so often in the First World War, the advantages in the days after the Battle of the Marne lay with the defender. The Aisne and Oise Rivers to the north of the Marne ran unusually deep that September as a result of heavy summer rains, thus creating a solid natural line of defense for the Germans. As they retreated, the Germans enacted a scorched-earth policy leaving the ground behind them bereft of water wells, food, and communications links. The Germans had the luxury of entrenching on ground of their own choosing, and they selected excellent defensive positions.

In mid-September, Joffre attempted to attack and turn the right of the German line, which lay exposed near the town of Noyon. The idea of a flanking maneuver such as this one is to move forces around the enemy's line and cut its communications. Once this is accomplished, the enemy's forces can be neither reinforced nor resupplied. Tired French soldiers once again answered their commander's call and attacked. At the First Battle of the Aisne (September 14 to 18) the French got a taste of the difficulty faced by attackers who attempted to advance against established trench lines. The attack failed with heavy losses, forcing Joffre to improvise another approach.

During the remainder of September and into October, the two sides stretched their forces to the north, probing for weaknesses in their enemy's flank while struggling simultaneously to defend their own flanks. By October 8 the opposing armies had extended their lines as far as Lille and the Franco-Belgian border. This series of maneuvers, somewhat inaccurately known as the "Race to the [North] Sea," created a gigantic bulge, known in military terms as a salient, in the line. At about the same time, fighting in northern Belgium had virtually ended. Throughout the early weeks of the war, Antwerp's formidable defenses had withstood German sieges. On October 1, however, the outer line of the city's defenses fell. Two days later, 12,000 British marines arrived to help the garrison. The operation's mastermind, the young and brash First Lord of the Admiralty, Winston Churchill, arrived at Antwerp himself, determined that the city should hold out. It did not. On October 9, Antwerp finally surrendered, with most of the British marines leaving the city by sea, just as they had arrived. The remnants of the Belgian army retreated west, followed closely by five German infantry divisions and the awesome siege guns the Germans had used to destroy the port's defenses.

The focus of operations soon fell to a small sliver of Belgian territory on the North Sea based around the town of Ypres behind the Yser River. There an Allied salient pushed into German lines. Falkenhayn planned to push in the face of the salient and drive onto the English Channel ports of Dunkirk, Calais, and

Boulogne, the BEF's main supply port. Once again the kaiser came to the front lines, this time expecting to lead his men into Ypres. Once again, he would be disappointed.

To defend the Ypres/Yser area, Joffre sent Foch north to take command of what became known as Army Group North. It consisted of the disorganized remains of the Belgian Army, the BEF, and the French Tenth Army. Foch was in fact junior to both Sir John, a field marshal, and the commander of the Belgian Army, King Albert I. Nevertheless, France had the most men in the sector, and Foch knew the terrain well. He quickly divined that the Allied position required the retention of the French cities of Lille and Dunkirk and the Belgian town of Dixmude, north of Ypres. He rushed reinforcement to all three and ordered them defended at all costs.

Getting three armies to work together posed a significant challenge. The British and Belgian positions differed substantially. Sir John was naturally concerned with securing the Channel ports and wanted to evacuate the Ypres sector in order to concentrate along the coast. King Albert, however, determined to hold on to the last strip of his nation's territory not under German control, whatever the cost. On October 17, as Foch was reorganizing the Allied forces in and around Ypres, Falkenhayn's forces struck. The chance to destroy the tired British, whom Prince Rupprecht of Bavaria called "our most detested enemy," added fuel to the German drive.[20]

The resulting campaign involved two overlapping battles, the First Battle of Ypres and the Battle of the Yser (October 17 to November 12). The relatively flat, featureless terrain of the Ypres sector favored the German attackers because the presence of water tables just under the surface made digging in futile. Foch understood that his forces lacked the power to counterattack. They would have to stand, fight, and somehow survive. The most desperate fighting occurred from October 21 to 29. The situation looked so bad that at one point Sir John turned to Foch and said,

"There is nothing left for me to do but go up and be killed with the I Corps."[21] Foch himself, usually a paragon of optimism, grew pessimistic as well because of the imminent arrival of German forces from the Antwerp sector, the low morale of many Belgian units, and what the French saw as a slow concentration of British forces in the region.

The Allied position held in large part due to the courage of a group of Belgian sappers. On October 29, they moved toward the hydraulic works at Nieuport, on the North Sea coastline. They advanced close enough to the German lines to be able to hear their enemy's movements. At 7:30 that evening, they opened the sluice gates that kept the North Sea out of Flanders. In a matter of just a few hours, more than 700,000 cubic meters of water flooded into Flanders, covering an area twenty-two miles long. The sappers stayed long enough to close the gates before the ebb tides sent the water out again. Their daring act created a temporary line of defense that the Allies needed in order to regroup and hold their line.[22]

Mid-November brought winter weather and mutual exhaustion. The two sides took the opportunity to assess where they stood. Their war plans, which had been so carefully prepared by the best military minds over many years, had failed to yield the quick victories their authors had promised. The enormous casualties of the first year of the war effectively destroyed the cores of the prewar European armies. New armies of volunteers and conscripts would need to be formed, trained, and sent into battle. This realization was most painful for Great Britain, which had for so long resisted the general trend of mass-conscript armies in place of a small, professional force. That force no longer existed. In its place came new armies of volunteers that closely linked the nation's army and its society.

For France, the year ended with a German occupation of most of the country's industrial northeast. The region included one-tenth of France's population, 70 percent of its coal fields, and 90

French soldiers dig in near Reims in Champagne. Note the damaged building in the background, a victim of artillery fire. (Library of Congress)

percent of its iron ore mines. To end the occupation, France would have to assume the offensive in 1915, a prospect that the past several months had demonstrated would not be easy. The damage to France, both moral and material, was already high. The city of Reims, in the heart of Champagne, had already had 300 buildings destroyed and 700 civilians killed by German shelling. By the end of 1914 the city, which had 110,000 residents before the war, was a virtual ghost town. Its magnificent cathedral, coronation site of twenty-six French kings, had been badly damaged by shelling, much of it intentional. Between 1914 and 1918 the Germans fired more than 100,000 shells at Reims.

For all of their operational success, Germany sat in an equally inopportune position. Its entire strategy had depended on winning quickly in the west. As Moltke himself realized, the Germans' failure to do so required them to fight the industrial powers of Britain and France on one side while having to fend off the massive Russians in the east. A long war, moreover, would enable the British to institute a blockade and thereby attack the German economy. As a result, all three nations were committed to fighting on in 1915, even if few people could remember exactly how the assassination of an unpopular Austrian archduke had put them in such a predicament.

2

LOOSED LIKE WILD BEASTS

The War in Eastern Europe

There is no village which does not bear the mark of wanton destruction of life and property—houses burned, others pillaged, and the contents dragged into the street and there smashed. Churches have been invariably gutted and defiled.

—London *Daily Chronicle* correspondent Percival Gibbon
reporting from Poland, October 1914

THE movement of the great powers in eastern Europe in 1914 depended in large measure on the speed with which the Russian army completed mobilization. Simply put, mobilization is the time between a nation's decision to prepare its armed forces for war and its completion of those preparations. Russia had an immense army of more than 6 million men, but it was stretched out across the landmass of the largest state in the world. Prewar investments (much of it by French firms) to improve the Russian railway network had helped to increase its speed and efficiency, but the Russian transportation infrastructure remained woefully inadequate for the task of mobilization.

Once organized, the Russian army still faced myriad problems. Its leadership was riven by ideological, social, and personal fissures; several of its senior military officers were barely on speaking terms. In addition, the same transportation difficulties that delayed mobilization ensured that even when the Russians had the materiel they needed, the right weapons rarely reached the right units at the right times. Most of Russia's fortresses were obsolete, and the nation retained such a faith in cavalry (a faith soon shown to be anachronistic) that in the early days of the war, wrote one historian, "railways that might have sent infantrymen speedily to the front were loaded, instead, with horses and fodder for them."[1]

Russia had many impressive soldiers, but it had many more who owed their positions to court intrigue or personal connections. Alexei Brusilov, one of Russia's most competent officers, noted that in the years leading up to the war the promotion system did not value "independence, initiative, strong views and [strong] personalities." The average Russian infantryman's worldview had not prepared him to understand the war or his place in it. Brusilov noted that the Russian draftees from the interior of the country had no idea why they were fighting. "Practically no one knew who these Serbians [on whose behalf Russia had ostensibly entered the war] were; they were equally doubtful as to what a Slav was."[2] Despite some anti-German sentiment in the Cabinet, few Russian soldiers thought much about Germans, and fewer still hated them. Members of the upper strata of society had little anti-German sentiment, as the tsar's friendly exchange of telegrams with his cousin the kaiser reflected. Several members of the Russian court, including the tsarina, were demonstrably pro-German.

The Germans, for their part, feared nothing about the Russian army except its size. Dennis Showalter's characterization of the Russian army as a clumsy heavyweight boxer with neither fancy footwork nor timing is apt. The Germans saw themselves as a skilled middleweight capable of taking advantage of their larger, but slower, opponent.[3] Even their allies questioned the ability of the Russians to provide any meaningful military assistance in the event of war. Most prewar French and British observers of the Russians thought their ally's operations primitive and their support structure insufficient for the demands of modern warfare.

The Russian army also suffered from immense problems on the home front. The Russo-Japanese War of 1904–1905 had resulted in the creation of an elected parliament, but had done little to compensate for the fragility of the Russian state. While few people in 1914 predicted the magnitude of the revolution that assailed the country in 1917, many believed that the structure of the Russian state was far too weak to survive a prolonged war. Ironically, this weakness led many members of the Russian aristocracy to support the war in the hopes that a national emergency might rally the Russian people around the tsar and the status quo.

All of these problems notwithstanding, Russia surprised even itself with a vigorous effort in the days and weeks following the tsar's mobilization order of July 30. Hundreds of thousands of Russians, disproportionately from the cities, volunteered for military service, and the number of reservists who failed to report to their units as ordered was substantially lower than the Russians had estimated. One week after issuing the mobilization order, the tsar received leaders of the parliament's major political parties, many of whom had been openly hostile to him. They agreed to set aside political differences and join together to support the war. Even Russia's most vicious anti-Semites praised the nation's Jews as fellow subjects with a common interest in winning the war.

Geographically, Russia sat in a position that offered both challenges and opportunities. Russia's western border included the Polish salient, a 100-mile-long bulge that stuck out into the German border with Austria-Hungary. It therefore sat exposed to a joint enemy attack, but it also gave Russian planners the option of attacking north into the German province of East Prussia, the traditional home of the German aristocracy, or south over the Carpathian Mountains into the agricultural heartland of Hungary. Russian planners were divided over which option offered the better chance of success. Almost all Russians thought the Austro-Hungarians would be easier to defeat, but the mountainous terrain of the Carpathians was a drawback. An attack into Germany, however, would provide the most help to France; and if Germany were defeated, Austria-Hungary would likely have no choice but to surrender.

Unable to decide between the two options, the Russians chose a flexible war plan, called Plan 19. It contained two variants: an "A" variant against Austria; and a "G" variant, which involved an attack into East Prussia. The key to Plan 19 lay in a staged mobilization. Unlike the Germans, the Russians chose not to wait until all their units had mobilized before beginning offensive operations. Twenty-seven Russian divisions were ready for combat within fifteen days; another twenty-five divisions prepared to join them eight days later. Less than two months after the decision to mobilize, the Russian army had ninety divisions in the Polish salient and twenty more in Trans-Caucasia to guard against the contingency of the Ottoman Empire's entering the war.

The success of the mobilization notwithstanding, Russian efforts in East Prussia faced problems before they even began. The tsar had convinced his uncle, Grand Duke Nikolai, to assume command of the Russian armies. Nikolai had an impressive military career that dated to the Russo-Turkish War of 1877–1878. He had been responsible for many of the important military reforms that the Russian military had implemented in the wake of the disaster in 1904–1905. In 1909, however, as the result of another of the innumerable Russian inner-circle rivalries, the new War Minister, V. A. Sukhomlinov, had relegated Nikolai to a secondary role. His marginalization had been so complete that when Nikolai accepted the job of commander-in-chief on August 2, he had to be briefed about Plan 19, because he was not familiar with its details. Although he felt unable to decline his nephew's request, he felt completely overwhelmed by his new responsibilities.

Nikolai ordered Russian armies into the field before mobilization had been completed, placing immediate pressure on both Germany and Austria-Hungary. The Russian First and Second Armies were charged with invading East Prussia. The First Army's commander, Pavel Rennenkampf, was a Baltic German by ethnicity; his ancestry later led to misguided charges that he had pro-German sympathies and that his failures had resulted from treason rather than bad leadership. Rennenkampf had been promoted through the Russian General Staff system and had ties to both the tsar and Nikolai. Second Army commander Alexander Samsonov, by contrast, had been a protégé of Nikolai's adversary, Sukhomlinov. The rivalry between Nikolai and Sukhomlinov had filtered down to their protégés and had grown so deep that it became standard Russian practice to assign a second in command from the General Staff to an army commander from the War Ministry and vice versa, to minimize the negative consequences of the rivalry between the factions. A widely circulated story that Rennenkampf and Samsonov had exchanged blows on a railway platform during the Russo-Japanese War was not true, but the mutual dislike between the men was intense enough that people who knew the two men easily believed it.

The man most directly responsible for overcoming these problems, Northwest Front Commander Yakov Zhilinski, could hardly have been less well suited to the task. An aggressive advocate of Plan 19's G option, he had more ambition than aptitude. He owed his position in large measure to his understanding of French plans and needs. He was, however, a difficult man to work with and held the remarkable distinction of being unpopular with both the Sukhomlinov and the Nikolai cliques. Throughout the campaign in East Prussia, he failed to coordinate the movements of the First and Second Armies, with disastrous results.

These disasters likely would have come even earlier than they did if the Germans had not sent seven of their eight armies west instead of east. Facing a numerical inferiority of four to one, German Eighth Army commander Max von Prittwitz decided to lure Rennenkampf into East Prussia and attempt to destroy his First Army. Fighting in East Prussia put the Germans on familiar terrain and allowed them to be supplied by German trains; Russian rail lines used a different gauge. The existence of a sixty-mile chain of lakes known as the Masurian Lakes limited the avenues of Russian approach, forcing Rennenkampf to go around the lakes to the north while Samsonov went to the south, thus neutralizing

*German soldiers set up a firing line in East Prussia in 1914. Crushing
German victories in the east partially compensated for the failures in
the west, but were not enough to force Russia out of the war.*
(© Hulton-Deutsch Collection/Corbis)

the Russians' numerical superiority. The Germans had planned
and rehearsed an active defense in East Prussia for years; Prittwitz's
staff knew exactly what it was supposed to do.

The plan was sensible enough, but the improbably named
German I Corps commander Hermann von François did not care
for it. His hatred of Slavs overrode his sense of obedience and on
August 17, 1914, he disobeyed his superior and advanced toward
the Russian border. Rennenkampf had by then crossed into East
Prussia but, short of supplies and with his men weary from a
week of marching, had ordered a halt for August 20. François's
staff intercepted a radio transmission carrying the order to halt,
which the Russians had not bothered to encode, and convinced
Prittwitz to allow him to attack the resting Russians at the town of

Gumbinnen, about twenty-five miles west of the Russo-German border.

The fourteen-hour battle that resulted provided Russia with an early, if short-lived, boost of confidence. Although Russian artillery support was crude and infantry tactics even cruder, Rennenkampf's superior numbers forced François to admit that he lacked the strength to force the Russians back across the border. Samsonov's Second Army, meanwhile, continued its advance south of the Masurian Lakes, threatening the German Eighth Army with envelopment. Prittwitz thought the situation serious enough to contact Moltke, who was then engaged with the German advance through Belgium. He told Moltke that to prevent envelopment he was ordering a general retreat of the Eighth Army almost seventy miles to secure positions behind the Vistula River.

While many of Moltke's decisions in August 1914 appear mistaken in retrospect, his reaction to Prittwitz's call does not. He immediately relieved Prittwitz of his duties and called upon sixty-seven-year-old Paul von Hindenburg, then in retirement after completing an impressive fifty-one-year army career. Hindenburg had spent much of his retirement on his estate in East Prussia, occupying himself with the details of various Russian invasion scenarios of his homeland. Enthusiastic, intelligent, and physically imposing, he had been impatiently waiting for an assignment since the outbreak of the war. He was the perfect choice to assume command of the Eighth Army. In another inspired move, Moltke ordered Erich Ludendorff, the hero of Liège, to join Hindenburg as his chief of staff. The two met for the first time on an eastbound train from Hanover on August 23.

VICTORY AT TANNENBERG

Hindenburg and Ludendorff were of one mind concerning the situation facing the Eighth Army. Even before meeting Hindenburg, Ludendorff had taken the responsibility of ordering the Eighth Army to begin a concentration against Samsonov's Second Army. Only a solitary German cavalry division sat opposite Rennenkampf's First Army, which Ludendorff believed had been bloodied badly enough by the Battle of Gumbinnen to keep it from moving quickly in the near future. Hindenburg quickly approved the new dispositions, and upon arriving at Eighth Army headquarters the two generals discovered that the army's operations chief, Lt. Col. Max Hoffmann, had independently divined the same general strategy and had begun preparations for a concentration against Samsonov.

Moltke made one other decision, and this one has remained controversial ever since. Believing that he had more than enough strength to take Paris, he removed two corps from the right wing of the German approach in France and sent them east. These two corps would serve as protection for East Prussia in the event that the Eighth Army's bold offensive operations against the Russians failed. The two corps, however, spent late August in transit from west to east. As a result, they were unavailable for either the Battle of the Marne or the developing battle against Samsonov.

Samsonov, for his part, was almost entirely in the dark about developments in front of him. Russian communications were so primitive that Zhilinski had to send many of his messages via telegraph to Warsaw, where they were decoded and driven by automobile north over uneven roads to Samsonov's headquarters. On August 24, as the British were holding at Mons in Belgium, Zhilinski told Samsonov that only "insignificant forces" were in his sector.[4] Samsonov therefore pushed the center of his line forward, dangerously exposing his flanks to a peril he did not know existed.

The German high command sensed that the geographic and personal fissures between the Russian armies presented a golden opportunity. After some initial hesitation, the aggressive François led the attack on August 27, cutting off the lines of retreat for the Second Army's left and center. He continued his attack on the

Russian rear the next day, again disobeying an order, this one from Ludendorff to help a threatened German reserve unit. With little solid information on his situation, Samsonov moved slowly and failed to check the alarm growing in Russian ranks. By August 29, the Second Army was entirely encircled. Realizing the calamity he now faced, Samsonov broke down. After telling his staff, "The emperor trusted me. How can I face him after such a disaster?" he disappeared into the woods and committed suicide.

Leaderless, surrounded, and without hope of reinforcement, the Russians panicked. In many places, the German ring was too thin to resist a determined Russian attack, but none materialized. Of the 135,000 Russians trapped in the pocket, only 10,000 escaped. More than 100,000 Russians surrendered, along with 500 of their precious artillery pieces. Despite its numerical superiority, the Russian Second Army had performed miserably and suffered a crushing defeat. The size of the immense Russian Army meant that the rout only affected four of the nation's thirty-seven corps, but the psychological ramifications of the loss far outweighed the material ramifications. The Russians grew pessimistic, believing that they could not beat the more skillful Germans, a conclusion that many in France and Britain shared.

The German Eighth Army high command suggested calling the battle Tannenberg, after the nearby site of a battle half a millennium earlier in which Polish and Lithuanian knights had defeated the Teutonic knights. Hindenburg, Ludendorff, and Hoffmann believed that the Germans had reversed the humiliation that their ancestors had suffered against the Slavs. None of the three men lacked for self-confidence. They boasted that they had planned and executed one of the greatest victories in military history. They soon grew secure in the dominance of German methods and organization over those of a foe for whom they had neither professional respect nor humanitarian sentiment. Perhaps most important, Russia's size no longer intimidated them.

The eastern front, 1914

"We have a feeling of absolute superiority over the Russians," Hoffmann said that fall. "We must win, and we will."[5]

Flush with their great success, the Germans decided to turn north and perform the same trick again, this time against Rennenkampf's First Army. Uncertain about what was happening to his south and with his supply lines threatened by the German garrison at the fortress of Königsberg to his north, Rennenkampf moved slowly and cautiously. Zhilinski informed him on August 30 of the magnitude of Samsonov's defeat, but Russian headquarters incorrectly guessed that the Germans would next move south toward Warsaw. To spoil that effort, Zhilinski directed Rennenkampf to move forward into East Prussia.

An offensive disposition temporarily exposed Rennenkampf's flanks. For the third time in less than a month, François's aggressive, almost reckless, behavior placed him in the center of events. Marching his men seventy-five miles in four days, he surprised the Russian left and drove it back. Rennenkampf, however, did not panic as Samsonov had. A veteran of the Boxer Rebellion who gained favor with the tsar in 1905 by brutally seizing parts of the Trans-Siberian Railroad from revolutionaries, Rennenkampf had survived several personal bankruptcies and four failed marriages. He was not a stranger to crisis, and he kept his head despite the increasing deterioration of his strategic position.

Anxious to avoid Samsonov's fate, he directed two divisions to fight a rear-guard action in order to allow the remainder of his army to get away safely. From September 10 to 12, his army retreated more than fifty miles back into Russia. In what became known as the Battle of the Masurian Lakes, the First Army lost almost 150,000 men and 150 guns. The Germans pursued the retreating First Army into Russia, losing the advantage of railways on the German gauge. Heavy rains soon gave Russia some breathing room, allowing Rennenkampf to regroup and counterattack at the Augustowo forest on October 1, driving the German forces out of Russia. The kaiser's bad luck continued. He had joined the

Eighth Army too late to witness the victories of Tannenberg and the Masurian Lakes, but arrived at Augustowo just in time to escape a Russian cavalry charge.

The opening moves in the east had bloodied the Russians, but their massive human reserves remained. The Germans had inflicted two great defeats on them, but by the time winter set in, the Russians had managed to redeem themselves by clearing their homeland of German troops. This achievement was small comfort to their British and French allies, who increasingly saw the Russians as incurably incompetent. If the Allies wanted to keep the Russian front active, they would have to provide the Russian army with direct material assistance and as much advice as the Russians would accept. According to an old Russian proverb, Russia is never as strong as she looks, but Russia is never as weak as she looks. That maxim accurately reflected both Russia's dire situation in the north at the end of the 1914 and its ability to withstand more punishment.

THE CAMPAIGN IN SERBIA

The Russians expected more success against the Austro-Hungarian army than against Germany. The Austro-Hungarian Empire suffered from so many problems that even its emperor, the eighty-four-year-old Franz Joseph, harbored doubts about its survival. The brother of the ill-fated Emperor Maximillian of Mexico, Franz Joseph had been on his throne since 1848, making him the longest-reigning monarch in Europe. He presided over a multiethnic empire, with three bureaucracies using three languages: German, Hungarian, and Croatian. The army had to use eleven languages to accommodate all of the empire's major ethnic minorities, many of whose members actively hoped for the empire's dissolution. The antihero of Czech veteran Jaroslav Hašek's *The Good Soldier Schweik* (written in the 1920s) reacted to the news of Ferdinand's assassination by telling his charwoman that he knew two

Count Franz Conrad von Hötzendorf, the chief of the Austro-Hungarian General Staff, had urged his government to fight a preemptive war against Serbia for years. The failure of his war plan to achieve any Austrian state aims led to his demotion at the end of 1916. (© Corbis)

Ferdinands, one who had accidentally drunk a bottle of hair oil and another who collected manure. "They wouldn't be any great loss," he said, "either of 'em." Hašek's satire captured the ambivalence of so many Austro-Hungarians toward the war and to the empire itself.[6]

The largely agricultural economy of the Austro-Hungarian Empire forced it to keep military expenditures to a minimum. Its per capita spending on defense was the lowest of any of the great powers. This lack of funding combined with the need for farm laborers meant that it also had the smallest percentage of men under arms of any of the continental powers. The empire trained just 22 percent of its eligible males for military service annually, compared with Germany's 40 percent and France's 86 percent.[7] Napoleon's famous jibe at the Austrians as being always one army, one year, and one idea too late still applied to their empire in 1914.

These shortcomings notwithstanding, the members of Austria-Hungary's ruling elite had ambitions to increase their power, especially in the Balkans. In 1908 the empire had annexed the province of Bosnia-Herzegovina from the waning Ottoman Empire. The addition of three hundred miles of coastline on the Adriatic Sea gave the Austro-Hungarian Empire additional naval bases and a finger of territory that threatened Serbia. Not coincidentally, it also left Serbia landlocked. Austria-Hungary's Army Chief of Staff General Franz Conrad von Hötzendorf believed that the empire should have gone on to conquer Serbia in its entirety. Thereafter he presented the emperor with annual plans for a preemptive war against Serbia "with the regularity of an almanac."[8]

The Balkan Wars of 1912 and 1913 resulted in the Serbian conquest of two former Ottoman provinces, Novibazar and Macedonia. Serbia thereby doubled in size and grew in confidence. Its calls for the unification of all Slavs into one Serbian-dominated state grew increasingly shrill. Such rhetoric threatened the internal viability of Austria-Hungary, where Slavs represented one of the largest ethnic minorities. The army depended heavily on Slavs in its enlisted ranks, although Germans and Magyars dominated the officer corps. Thus the Austrians believed that the assassination of the archduke by a group of Slavs presumed to have links to Serbian officials could not go unanswered.

Conrad and other Austro-Hungarian hard-liners saw the assassination as a chance to settle scores with Serbia. Conrad was an intelligent and capable staff officer, but he had never learned the famous Clausewitzian dictum that war is an extension of policy by other means. For him, war was, or should have been, the guiding force of state policy. Only the army, he had repeatedly argued, could weld the empire's many mutually antagonistic nationalities into a loyal whole. By making war on some combination of Serbia, Russia, and Italy, he hoped to repeat the great success of Otto von Bismarck during the Wars of German Unification and create a powerful empire that would return Austria to the rank of first-rate powers.

In July 1914 Conrad calculated that his chances were fading, as Austria's relative power in Europe would only decline further in the coming years. Many Germans agreed with him. The more time they gave the Russians to modernize their army and build rail lines, the harder Austria's task would become. Better, many believed, to fight in 1914 than in 1917, when the Russian modernization program was scheduled to reach fruition. The latest Balkan crisis caused by the assassination gave Austro-Hungarian leaders an opportunity to set the conditions for war. Serbia's rejection of their harsh ultimatum gave them the veneer of justification they needed to take the final steps. Conrad therefore had a chance to enact his latest plan for the war that he wanted more than almost anyone else in Europe.

On paper at least, the plan was rather elegant and solved a contradiction in Austro-Hungarian thinking. Conrad's heart and soul burned to send his army south to conquer and subdue the detested Serbians. He knew, however, that he had to guard against the possibility of a massive Russian movement across the

Antipathy between Austria-Hungary and Serbia provided the proximate cause for the war and fueled a bitter campaign in the Balkans. Austro-Hungarian soldiers, like those shown here, rarely took Serbian prisoners. (National Archives)

Carpathian Mountains. He had hoped that Germany might accept primary responsibility for guarding against this possibility while he moved against Serbia. But talks between the military staffs of the two allies were limited in the years before the war; the two did not meet at all between 1897 and 1907. Discussions thereafter remained limited because the Germans suspected that Russian spies had infiltrated the Austrian general staff. As a result, Germany and Austria-Hungary each assumed that the other would engage the Russian giant while their own army hunted their primary prey. The very existence of such an enormous misunderstanding underscores the problematic nature of the German-Austrian alliance.

Given his inability to predict either Russian movements or German assistance, Conrad developed a plan that allowed him to attack Serbia whether Russia threatened Austria-Hungary or not. The plan divided the army into three groups. *Minimalgruppe Balkan,* nine divisions strong, was to advance on the Serbian capital of Belgrade and capture it, thereby neutralizing the Serbs. *A-Staffel,* with twenty-seven divisions, would advance into southern Poland, presumably with significant German help, to forestall Russian operations there. The final group, *B-Staffel,* contained ten divisions. If the Russians deployed quickly, it would join *A-Staffel* to defend the Carpathians; otherwise it could either join in the war against Serbia or redeploy against Italy in the expected event of that country's reneging on its Triple Alliance commitments to Germany and Austria.

With this plan, the shaky Austro-Hungarian Empire went to war. *Minimalgruppe Balkan* ominously marched toward Serbia under the command of General Oskar von Potiorek, the man who had been responsible for Archduke Franz Ferdinand's security detail in Sarajevo. As it happened, the vanguard of the Austro-Hungarian forces was the mostly Czech VIII Corps, whose soldiers the Austrian high command suspected of "treasonous tendencies."[9] The Czechs had long sought greater autonomy within the empire, and their loyalty remained questionable throughout the war. Nevertheless, they had the lead in Potiorek's 200,000-man force as it entered Serbia simultaneously from the west and northwest. Its ultimate goal, Belgrade, sat close to the Austro-Hungarian border and had not been properly fortified, leading Potiorek to predict an easy victory.

Opposing the Austro-Hungarian army were 250,000 hardy soldiers of the Serbian army and 50,000 more men from their tiny Balkan ally, Montenegro. Unlike the Austro-Hungarians, the Serbian soldiers had experienced recent battlefield successes in the Balkan Wars and therefore better understood the nature of modern warfare. Its commander, Radomir Putnik, had been largely responsible for the great victories of the Balkan Wars through his role as Serbia's Minister of War. After the Second Balkan War, however, his health had begun to deteriorate rapidly. When the July crisis began he was receiving treatment in an Austrian spa. Austro-Hungarian authorities temporarily arrested him, but both Franz Joseph and Conrad authorized his release, apparently on the assumption that at his age (sixty-seven) and in his debilitated condition he posed no threat.

They guessed wrong. Putnik still had plenty of fight left in him. He organized his forces into an impressive series of field defenses. He allowed the Austrians to advance, extending their supply lines and exposing their flanks. Although Belgrade itself suffered the destruction of 700 buildings due to Austrian artillery and air raids, Putnik succeeded in driving the invaders back in an engagement known as the Battle of the Jadar, fought from August 16 to 23. Putnik had managed to defend Serbian territory despite a numerical inferiority and virtually no modern heavy artillery pieces. He then made the rash decision to cross into Austrian-controlled Bosnia, expecting to fulfill Serbian rhetoric about fighting a war to free Slavs and hoping to inspire a local revolt.

Potiorek took advantage of the forward deployment of Serbian forces to attack again. For ten bitter days (September 7 to 17) the two armies fought for control of the Austrian bridgeheads across the Save and Drina Rivers. Had the Serbians not run low of ammunition they likely would have repeated the success of their operations the previous month. Instead Putnik had to admit that he lacked the strength to push the Austrians back. He wisely retired to defensive positions in the mountains, hoping to force the enemy to wear itself out in difficult terrain. When the opportunity presented itself Putnik planned to counterattack and once again chase Austro-Hungarian forces out of Serbia.

Meanwhile, Conrad's plan collapsed in the reality of modern

*Radomir Putnik, chief of the Serbian General Staff, modernized the
Serbian Army in the years before the war and led it to victory in
the Balkan Wars. He also led well in the war's early months, but was
relieved of command when Serbian forces fled to Corfu.*
(Library of Congress)

warfare. In order to provide for maximum flexibility and the
shortest movement times, his staff decided to organize the men assigned to *B-Staffel* in Galicia. The region had sufficiently well
developed railway networks to allow for the deployment of large
formations to almost any place in the empire. That decision

forced *B-Staffel*'s subordinate formations to move to the extreme north of the empire, only to organize and be transported south when Potiorek's failures necessitated their presence in Serbia. By the end of August, they were still trying to organize in Galicia. The fog and friction of war impeded the complicated timetables upon which Conrad had depended. As a result, *B-Staffel,* designed to fight in either the north or the south, spent its time in transit and did not fight at all at a time when it was needed in both places.

Despite his best efforts, Putnik could not hold Belgrade, which the Austrians finally entered on December 2. The Austrians had achieved an objective that might have ended the war had Germany and Russia stayed neutral. Now the capture of Belgrade meant little in the war's rapidly expanding larger picture. Nevertheless, to Austro-Hungarian commanders the capture of the Serbian capital represented a chance at catharsis. Belgrade was the home of Austria-Hungary's most implacable enemies. As a result, Austro-Hungarian officers singled Belgrade out for special punishment. An American war correspondent, who went on to write a famous account of the Bolshevik Revolution, was in Serbia that December. He wrote:

> The [Austrian] soldiers were loosed like wild beasts in the city, burning, pillaging, raping. We saw the gutted Hotel d'Europe and the blackened and mutilated church where three thousand men, women and children were penned together without food or water for four days, and then divided into two groups—one sent back to Austria as prisoners of war, the others driven ahead of the army as it marched south against the Serbians.[10]

It was the beginning of a terrible ordeal for Serbia. The nation had just 350 fully trained doctors in 1914, and more than 100 of them had served and died with the army. Medicines and properly equipped hospitals were both in short supply. Sanitation and

Serbian suffering engendered tremendous sympathy in the Allied and neutral nations. As this poster demonstrates, sympathy for the Serbian plight extended from France to the United States despite American neutrality. (Library of Congress)

public health, already precarious, broke down entirely. Typhus, cholera, and other diseases soon grew out of control. By one contemporary's estimate, 65 percent of Serbia suffered from typhus alone.[11]

But if the Austrians thought they had eliminated the Serbians, they soon learned otherwise. France and Britain rushed ammunition and hundreds of nurses and doctors to Serbia to stem the military defeats and ease the civilian suffering. Putnik waited until the Kolubra River behind the Austrians began to flood; then, on December 3, he struck savagely into their lines. With the swollen river behind them preventing an orderly retreat and winter weather complicating resupply, the Austrians fought desperately for six days, suffering terrible casualties. On December 15, Serbian forces reentered Belgrade as the Austrians finally found their way across the rivers to relative safety. Conrad's plan to annihilate his most hated enemy had failed.

The campaign in Serbia serves as a vivid example of the demodernization of warfare. Away from the western front, combat in World War I resembled that of the eighteenth and nineteenth centuries much more than it did the mechanized war of the western front. Disease, long marches, and savage hand-to-hand combat dominated this campaign, as they would much of the eastern front. Fluid front lines meant increased hardships for civilians, who could neither run nor hide from the war. Villages changed hands frequently and ill-supplied soldiers took what they needed, even from the people they were supposed to be defending.

Austrian losses in what was supposed to be the easier of their two war options were appalling. Recent estimates list Austrian casualties in the 1914 Serbian campaign at 227,000 men, or five times Austria's losses in the entire 1866 war with Prussia. Conrad replaced Potiorek with Archduke Eugen, who settled into winter quarters and attempted to reorganize his new army. Conrad reluctantly decided that his forces would have to remain on the defensive against Serbia and seek a decision against Russia, where his *A-Staffel* had fared little better than *Minimalgruppe Balkan.*

THE CARPATHIAN AND POLISH CAMPAIGNS

By mid-August the Russians had assembled more than 400,000 men in the south in four separate armies under the overall command of southwest front commander Nikolai Ivanov. He owed his position to his successful repression of a naval mutiny at the Baltic Sea base of Kronstadt in 1906. Despite his lackluster service in the Russo-Japanese War and his evident lack of ideas or enthusiasm, he retained his command. Of the four army commanders underneath him, three were, to be generous, of inconsistent ability. Fortunately for Ivanov and for Russia's early fortunes, the southwest front also included Russia's best wartime general, Alexei Brusilov, in command of the southernmost army, the Eighth.

Russia's plan involved an advance on the Austrian line of fortifications north of the Carpathian Mountains in Galicia. The Galician defenses were based around four major outposts. From east to west they were Lemberg, Przemysl, Tarnow, and Cracow. If the Russians could reach Cracow in force, they would have two enticing options. They could move southwest along the western foothills of the Carpathian Mountains into the Oder River valley between Austria and Hungary. Doing so would threaten the harvests of Austria-Hungary's breadbasket and impose tremendous hardship on their enemy. Alternatively, they could move northwest into the low ground of mineral-rich Silesia toward Breslau. Such a movement would imperil the smooth operation of German industry and place immediate pressure on Germany to defend Berlin from a direction where there were few forts and few natural defenses.

To achieve this goal, the Russians first had to capture Lemberg. The capital of Galicia and one of the largest cities in the Austro-Hungarian Empire, Lemberg was protected by an impressive series of fortifications amply supplied with artillery and linked to Austria by four separate rail lines, the most important of which for the supply of the garrison ran west to Przemysl. Lemberg had also been one of the assembly points for the Austro-Hungarian Fourth Army. The presence of Russian troops in the area forced yet another change in Austro-Hungarian war planning.

To forestall a Russian advance on the Carpathians, Conrad ordered an offensive into Russian Poland. Between August 23 and September 1, the Austrian First and Fourth Armies succeeded in driving the Russians back almost 100 miles in places. Farther to the south, however, the advance fared less well, forcing the Austrians to retire back toward the presumed safety of Lemberg. Leaving a garrison behind to hold the fortress, the Austrian Second and Third Armies conducted a retreat of almost 100 miles of their own, leaving them with their backs literally resting upon the Carpathians.

Surrounded and badly outnumbered, the Austrian garrison at Lemberg shocked Austro-Hungarian commanders by surrendering without firing a shot in its own defense. Estimates of the size of Austrian losses vary widely; contemporary sources indicated that 60,000 Austro-Hungarian soldiers became prisoners of war and that the Russians captured the garrison's 637 heavy artillery pieces. For the Russians, Lemberg was an ideal base from which to conduct operations to the west because its rail lines connected it to the Russian supply centers of Kiev and Warsaw. Przemysl, the next fortress on the Russian axis of advance, lay just 70 miles to the west.

The Russian victory at Lemberg was one of the first major Allied successes in the war, providing Russia with a modicum of confidence in the aftermath of Tannenberg. The Russians reinstated the city's Slavic name of Lvov, symbolically removing traces of its German connections. In a similar move, the Russians renamed St. Petersburg, giving it the Russian name of Petrograd. Most of the residents of Lvov welcomed the Russians as liberators

Russian Cossacks in the Austrian fortress city of Lemberg in 1915, one of the first clear Allied victories of the war. Russian pressure on the Austrians forced Germany to come to the aid of its beleaguered allies.
(© Hulton-Deutsch Collection/Corbis)

because eastern Galicia had a large population of Ruthenes, most of whom held pro-Russian sympathies.

The campaign in the Carpathians took an especially heavy toll on civilians. The region's many Jews supported Austria-Hungary, which, alone among the major powers, permitted Jews to serve in the army's senior ranks. The Jews of Galicia feared falling under the virulent anti-Semitism of the tsar's regime, which had only recently committed terrible atrocities against Jews during the notorious pogroms. The largest ethnic group in Galicia, the Poles, had no state after the three great powers of the eastern front had divided Poland among them at the end of the eighteenth century. Poles therefore served in all of their armies, often reluctantly. The tsar's August 1914 declaration of autonomy for Poland within the Russian empire in exchange for Polish loyalty swayed some of the less cynical Poles. The more cynical among the Polish leaders struggled to find a way in which the victory of one side might lead to the return of Polish independence. They therefore worked with and against both sides, often suffering heavy reprisals as villages and towns changed hands.

After the fall of Lemberg/Lvov, both sides turned their attention to Przemysl. Brusilov's Eighth Army advanced halfway to Przemysl, securing the town of Grodek by September 12. The Germans rushed reinforcements to Przemysl and Cracow to bolster the collapsing Austrians and prevent a Russian breakthrough. Austrian and German forces continued to retreat almost 100 more miles. They left the fortresses at Przemysl with 120,000 men and enough food to last into the spring. Although surrounded and holding out little hope of relief, Przemysl held out through the winter, threatening Russian supply lines and tying down tens of thousands of Russian soldiers. By March 1915 one British observer wrote of the fortress's defenders: "a more hopeless, dejected crowd I have never seen."[12] Przemysl finally surrendered to the Russians on March 22, 1915.

To the west of Przemysl, the Russian offensive quickly slowed down. Russian and Austrian trains used different gauges (the Austrians logically shared the German gauge), causing tremendous supply problems for the advancing Russians. Most units ran short of artillery shells and small arms. A lack of winter clothing ruled out a maneuver through the Carpathian Mountain passes into Hungary. Magyar soldiers defending their homeland, moreover, fought with increasing ardor. Illness, frostbite, and privation quickly became the lot of both armies. The Russian offensive ground to a halt in October, with Russian cavalry patrols coming as close as twenty miles to the outskirts of Cracow.

The campaign in the Carpathians destroyed both Russia and Austria-Hungary's prewar professional armies. Thousands of trained officers and, more importantly, noncommissioned officers were gone and could not be replaced. Austrian losses are estimated at 250,000 dead (many from disease) and wounded and nearly 100,000 prisoners of war in 1914 alone. Although no consensus figure for Russian losses exists, they were at least equivalent. Brusilov spoke for both armies when he described the men who replaced the prewar soldiers as "more and more like a sort of badly trained militia. . . . Many soldiers could not even load their rifles; as for their shooting, the less said about it the better."[13]

Fighting also raged in the heart of the Polish salient. In mid-September, Hindenburg moved part of the Eighth Army south of Warsaw and reformed it as the German Ninth Army. By September 28, it was ready to advance despite being outnumbered by the Russian forces opposite it. Hindenburg had hoped to drive the Russians away from Warsaw, which he wanted to occupy as winter quarters for his Ninth Army. His advance met the more numerous Russians in mid-October, and Hindenburg wisely decided to make an orderly retreat to the northwest. The Germans left Poland devastated, scorching the ground behind them as they had done in France after the setback at the Marne.

The obvious contrast between German military performance, skillful even in retreat, and the chaotic opening moves of the Austrians led to the creation of a joint command on November 1. Hindenburg assumed the role of Commander-in-Chief of German and Austrian forces on the eastern front. The move led one Russian officer to inform a British counterpart that the Austro-Hungarian Army "ceased to exist as an independent force."[14] The fusion of the two armies hurt Austro-Hungarian pride, but improved their staff work and preparation immeasurably. Hindenburg turned over command of the Ninth Army to August von Mackensen, a consummate professional and favorite of the kaiser who had served with distinction at Tannenberg and the Masurian Lakes.

With this new organization, Hindenburg planned one last push in the east for 1914. On November 11, he ordered the Ninth Army to strike between the Russian First and Second Armies, then re-fitting in the aftermath of their drubbings in August and September. The Russians were at that time planning to resume the offensive and had left flanks exposed. The unfortunate Pavel Rennenkampf once again saw his army imperiled as the Germans enveloped the Second Army to his south. Once again his units sat too far to the north to offer any meaningful assistance.

On November 15, the Russians fell back toward the supply center of Lódz, approximately 120 miles southwest of Warsaw. Hard marching and fast thinking allowed the Russians to assemble seven corps around the city before the Germans could arrive in force. Ludendorff mistakenly believed that the Russians were in headlong retreat toward Warsaw and ordered his units to move in behind them and cut off their avenues of retreat. This decision left German forces strung out, tired, and far from lines of supply. For a time it looked as if the Russians might win a great victory.

Quick thinking by a German reserve corps commander, Reinhard von Scheffer-Boyadel, changed the situation. Realizing that the Russians were moving to encircle him, not retreating to Warsaw, he attacked where the Russian line was held by two tired, second-rate units. In a driving snowstorm his corps fought for nine days, not only avoiding encirclement, but capturing 16,000 Russian prisoners and 64 artillery pieces as he fought his way to safety. The Russian First and Second Armies had again suffered monumental defeats, losing 100,000 men between them. The Russians abandoned Lódz on November 18 and retired toward Warsaw. The Germans were frustrated in their effort to take Warsaw, but they had chased the Russians far enough from the border to secure their homeland. Although no one knew it at the time, Russian forces would never again come so close to Germany. Two crushing defeats also spelled the end for Rennenkampf. Placed on trial for improprieties involving war contracts, he used his connections to avoid jail time and even became governor of Petrograd, but he never led troops again. The Bolsheviks later offered him command of the Red Army. When he refused, they executed him for treason.

The events of 1914 devastated Poland. A bitterly cold winter contributed to the country's misery. Ten of Poland's eleven districts saw sustained fighting. Contemporary estimates listed the number of towns destroyed at 200 and the number of villages destroyed at 9,000. More than 200,000 Poles were made homeless, and the loss of more than 2 million head of cattle virtually removed milk and meat from the peasants' diet.[15] The large spaces of Poland meant that the trench systems were not as dense as those in France, but the more fluid lines resulted in tremendous civilian suffering. As in the west, 1914 ended with the generals' carefully crafted plans having failed to produce victory.

3

THE COUNTRY OF DEATH

Stalemate on the Western Front

The result of the fighting here [in Artois] is to show that the Germans
can be driven back at the cost of an enormous effort, but that the
thing is possible. . . . People in England must be prepared for a long
war and I am afraid there are no brilliant or sudden victories to be expected—the best stayers will win in the end.

—Letter from British General Sir Charles Grant
to his father-in-law, April 15, 1915

As 1914 ended, the problem facing the Allied armies was at once
deceptively simple and immensely complicated. The simple part
lay in the obvious need to push the Germans out of those parts of
France and Belgium that they occupied. The British, French, and
Belgians all agreed on this war aim, unifying them at least on this
one level. The complication came from the immense operational
and tactical challenges posed by the new style of war. By the end
of the year, a solid line of German defenses reached from the
North Sea to the impassable terrain of the Alps. There were no
longer any flanks to turn; consequently, strategic envelopments,
like the one the Germans had so daringly executed at Tannenberg,
were virtually impossible. To make the problem even more complicated, in 1914 and 1915 the Allies could not count on any significant superiority in manpower, nor did they have access to any
weapons that the Germans did not also possess.

The Germans had decided to conduct their main offensive for
1915 in the east and therefore determined to fortify their defensive
positions in the west. They connected and improved the haphazard system of field entrenchments that had developed during the

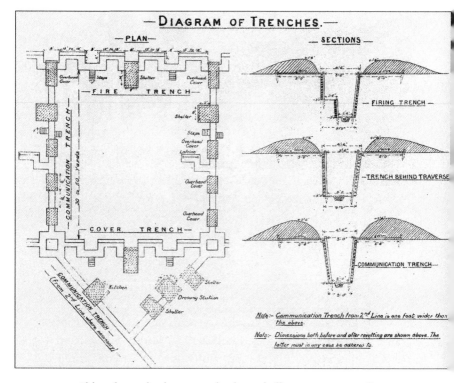

Although trenches began as a haphazard effort to protect men from the elements and enemy fire, they rapidly became sophisticated, as this diagram of an ideal trench system shows. (Imperial War Museum, Crown Copyright, E. R. Heaton)

Race to the Sea and protected them with thick tangles of barbed wire. They added concrete in places and buried telephone and telegraph lines to protect them from enemy artillery fire. The typical trench system zigzagged, both to prevent enfilading attacks and to create interlocking fields of fire whereby any given point could be covered by more than one machine gun, rifle, or artillery piece. Thus the ground between the two trench systems, known as No Man's Land, could be constantly observed and any point fired upon simultaneously by multiple weapons. Front-line defenses often contained as many as three separate parallel lines of trenches, connected by communications trenches running roughly perpendicular to the front.

The war on the western front did not represent the first use of trench warfare, nor were most Europeans entirely ignorant of it. Both the American Civil War, in its later phases, and the Russo-Japanese War had witnessed extensive static field trench systems. The latter conflict especially preyed on the minds of farsighted officers in the Great War, some of whom had been observers during the earlier war. Most senior commanders, however, thought that trench warfare was a temporary aberration, not the normal condition of warfare. For the men, the trenches in early 1915 were not yet the squalid, muddy, rat- and lice-ridden places that later became symbolic of the war. In 1914 and early 1915, trenches offered vital protection from machine guns, artillery, and the elements. One German soldier noted in the war's early weeks that trench life was "more agreeable than a long march; one gets used to this existence if the bodies of men and horses don't smell too bad."[1] In early 1915, trenches were not yet associated with indefinite stalemate. Even in the Russo-Japanese War, where defensive firepower often dominated, determined infantry frequently took enemy trenches and fieldworks, albeit with heavy losses.

In the early days of trench warfare on the western front, therefore, many officers saw trenches as a problem to be overcome, but certainly not an insurmountable one. Once the enemy's trenches had been neutralized or bypassed, they fully expected the return to a war of maneuver. Throughout the war, operational plans repeatedly called for the massing of cavalry to exploit any gaps that the artillery and infantry would open in the enemy's trench systems. Only in very rare instances did cavalry actually play a significant pursuit role on the western front, but the continued call for its preparation testifies to the persistence of the belief that trench systems could be broken. Indeed, there were just enough successes and near-successes to convince generals to keep trying.

One should not, therefore, criticize the generals of the western front without first fully appreciating the problems that they faced. Few Allied generals could expect to keep their jobs for very long if they remained a firm advocate of defensive warfare. The peoples and governments of the Allied nations expected their military minds, most of whom they still held in high esteem, to find a solution to the stalemate and liberate occupied regions. Trench warfare placed these men in increasingly unfamiliar intellectual terrain. Many of them failed to make the necessary adjustments, and many ineffectual generals kept their jobs much longer than they should have. That they remained in command despite their failings was often a function of there being no one with any obviously better solutions to take their place.

Historians have recently worked hard to debunk the conventional stereotype of the unfeeling general, safe behind lines, blithely ignoring the casualty figures presented to him.[2] Like any war, World War I had its share of effective generals and ineffective generals. Those that succeeded often had to relearn everything they thought they knew about modern warfare. Those few whose formative experiences had been in the Wars of German Unification (1864–1871) found themselves dealing with entirely new technologies, doctrines, and scales of operation. As for those too young to have fought in those wars, many had made their name in colonial operations in Africa or Asia, hardly adequate preparation for the western front. Several had reached the rank of general without ever having heard a shot fired in anger.

French commander Joseph Joffre was one of those generals whose military experiences in Madagascar and Indochina had shaped his outlook. His plan to fight a war of maneuver in 1914 had led his army to the position of deadlock in which it found itself at the end of the year. Not one to sit idly by while the enemy occupied a large swath of his nation's territory, Joffre sought a place on the line where an offensive stood the best chance of changing the situation in France's favor. The greatest danger to France, Joffre believed, lay in the giant salient stretching from Arras to Craonne that bulged toward Compiègne and sat just sixty miles from Paris at its westernmost extreme. The face of the salient sat between the towns of Noyon, on the German side of the line, and Soissons, on the Allied side.

THE CHAMPAGNE OFFENSIVE AND NEUVE CHAPELLE

On December 20, 1914, Joffre ordered attacks on the salient in the hope of achieving a breakthrough. The northern attacks struck Noyon, while the southern attacks pressured the line between Reims and Verdun. These attacks, which amounted to ill-coordinated advances against heavily defended positions, resembled the frustrations of the Battle of the Frontiers more than the fluidity of the Battle of the Marne. They failed, demonstrating that frontal assaults not only cost exposed infantry units tremendous casualties, but also stood little chance of creating an opening in the enemy line.

On January 8, the Germans learned a similar lesson when they sought their own rupture in an offensive toward Soissons. Although they gained some small bridgeheads south of the Aisne River and held Soissons until September, they could not achieve a breakthrough any more than the French could. Once again, the ill-fated kaiser had been invited by his staff to come to the front and witness the capture of a major objective, this time the Champagne capital of Reims. Once again, he had to look on as German forces failed to complete their mission. In both the French attack and the German counterattack, the defense had held supreme, underscoring the tactical disadvantage that modern weapons gave to the attackers.

A French Spad II aircraft patrols the western front. Note the machine gunner aiming his weapon behind the plane. In 1916 the Germans introduced a machine gun with an interrupter gear that allowed pilots to fire through the arc of the propeller, giving birth to the true fighter. (United States Air Force Academy McDermott Library Special Collections)

The impact that the war was having on nature and on the men who fought emerges from a letter written by a French soldier to a friend in February 1915:

When we arrived here in the month of November, this plain was magnificent with its fields as far as the eye can see full of beets, strewn with rich farms and filled with wheat. Now it is the country of death. All of its fields are upset, trampled, the farms are burned and ruined and another crop is born: tiny hills topped with a cross or simply a bottle turned upside down in which someone has placed papers of the man who lies there. Many times death has brushed its wings against me when I run sunken along

72

the trenches or paths to avoid the "shrapnel" or the tac-tac of the machine guns.[3]

This writer was one of the lucky ones. He survived the war.

The Champagne offensive demonstrated beyond any doubt the difficulty of offense. "The existence of the front continues to impede all maneuver," concluded an internal French study on the campaign. "Only frontal attacks remain possible. To prepare them and to put them in place requires crude work." Defensive firepower, most notably from machine guns, made almost any advance suicidal. "If a single machine gun remains in action [after the artillery phase]," concluded the same study, "losses can be great."[4] The great Napoleonic charges that the generals had studied in classrooms and emulated during war games simply did not work in the age of automatic weapons. The remainder of the war saw vigorous efforts by all sides, especially the Allies, to neutralize or bypass that firepower.

As this process of doctrinal change began, other processes reformed the armies, which became instruments of the generals' experimentation. In August 1914 British Secretary of State for War Horatio Kitchener had called for volunteers for the New Armies, men who would replace the professional soldiers of the BEF. Kitchener and the British government hoped to enlist 100,000 men. Instead, 1,186,000 men joined the colors in Great Britain within five months. By the end of 1915 2,466,719 Britons had volunteered for military service, complemented by 458,000 more from Canada and 332,000 from Australia.[5] Because Great Britain did not have universal military service before the war, few of these men knew even the most rudimentary details of military life; many did not know how to fire a rifle.

What these men lacked in experience, they more than made up for in cold determination. Journalist Philip Gibbs described their attitude as less of militarism than of resignation. Few of the men that Gibbs interviewed claimed to understand the diplomatic chain of events that had led Britain to war, and several had almost as many suspicions about the French as they had about the Germans. Nevertheless, they understood on a deep personal level that their nation was in danger and had called them to the colors. The thought of the British Empire in peril was, Gibbs noted, the "real call" that drove men to enlist. Gibbs summarized their attitude as "I hate the idea, but it's got to be done."[6]

Even though they did not see much action until the fall, the mere creation of the New Armies radically changed the British military system. Britain's wars had traditionally been the responsibility of volunteer professionals, who always stood apart from British society. Now the army was a mass citizen force with intimate links to the larger society. As such, the citizenry demanded changes in the nature of the army's operations. In 1914, Kitchener had succeeded in keeping journalists away from the army. But virtually everyone in Britain had a friend or relative in the New Armies, and they wanted to stay informed about the activities of their loved ones. Consequently, in March 1915 the British Army reluctantly accredited its first five war correspondents. Although Gibbs noted that British headquarters saw the reporters as "hardly better than spies," the generals had no choice but to accept this link between the army and the society that supported it.[7]

While the New Armies trained and prepared, the professionals tried once again. The British made good the BEF's 1914 losses with transfers from India, temporarily providing needed reinforcements while the new recruits trained. Using these reinforcements, Douglas Haig's First Army designed a meticulous plan to seize the area around the town of Neuve Chapelle. The First Army staff prepared detailed maps of the area for officers to study and complemented these maps with accurate aerial photographs of the topography and German defenses. The British preparations so impressed Joffre that he ordered the plan translated and distributed to his own staffs as a model. Indeed, the quality of British preparations should put to rest the persistent stereotype that World War I officers were manifest incompetents.

Haig's plan envisioned creating a breakthrough not, as Joffre had done in Champagne, with brute force, but with as much finesse as military operations in 1915 permitted. Haig planned to make a virtue out of necessity by limiting his pre-attack artillery barrage to just thirty-five minutes. A brief bombardment would give the Germans limited time to reinforce the sector; in any case, shortages of high explosive artillery ammunition forbade the barrage from being much longer. Haig planned diversionary attacks to the north and south of Neuve Chapelle in order to disguise his true intentions. British aircraft would clear the sky of German pilots, guaranteeing that the Germans would not be able to observe British movements. The main British strike was to come over a narrow 2,000-yard front by a mass of 45,000 men with cavalry in reserve. By concealing the true intention of his plan, Haig hoped to concentrate his forces in a small part of the front, thereby achieving a local numerical superiority at the point of attack. His men were to move through Neuve Chapelle, then to the southeast, passing along the southern face of high ground known as the Aubers Ridge.

The strength of the Neuve Chapelle operation lay in its goals. Haig did not plan to smash in the face of the salient with the intention of killing as many Germans as he could. Instead, he hoped that his breakthrough would menace and ultimately cut the north-south rail lines to the east of Neuve Chapelle. The entire German position in this sector depended on the supplies that came over those rail lines. By cutting German communications to the supply centers of Lille and Douai, Haig hoped to force a general retirement of his enemy without massive casualties.

The plan very nearly worked, in large part because the British First Army still had a large enough complement of professionals to follow such a carefully crafted, and therefore complex, series of arrangements. Although limited to just thirty-five minutes, the British artillery barrage was intense. The British fired more artillery shells in those thirty-five minutes than they had fired in the

Reconnaissance balloons like this one could both monitor movements of enemy units and help to correct the accuracy of artillery fire. They quickly became targets for enemy fighters. (National Archives)

entirety of the Boer War, demonstrating how much modern war had come to rely on industry. At 7:30 on the morning of March 10, 1915, British infantry began to advance, hoping that the artillery had destroyed the German barbed wire in front of them and interdicted German attempts to reinforce the Neuve Chapelle sector.

At first, all signs indicated that Haig and his staff had designed a masterpiece. As Haig had hoped, his preparations completely surprised the German defenders, forcing them into a headlong retreat. The town of Neuve Chapelle fell into British hands in just thirty minutes, a remarkable achievement by any standard of this war. East of the town, surprised and outnumbered German units retreated faster than the British could pursue them.

Despite this early success, however, the battle soon deteriorated. The elegance of the plan for Neuve Chapelle soon began to work against itself. The relative paucity of artillery shells led Haig and his staff to centralize their use at First Army headquarters. Thus local commanders could not redirect artillery fire where they needed it. The lack of field radios led to an overly rigid plan that set goals for unit commanders but did not let them advance further without instructions from higher headquarters. In many places, British units had advanced so quickly that they had to wait for their own prearranged artillery barrages to lift before moving forward. In other areas, they faced no opposition at all, but could not receive authorization to advance quickly enough to exploit the opportunities in front of them.

While the British delayed, the Germans responded. Moving men, artillery, and machine guns into the Neuve Chapelle sector by 5:30 that afternoon, they effectively stopped the British drive midway between Neuve Chapelle and the Aubers Ridge. British forces now sat exposed in an area without trenches, leaving them vulnerable to German counterattacks on March 11 and 12. These attacks drove the British back almost to the original starting line. For 13,000 casualties (more than 4,000 of them Indian) the British had nearly achieved their aims, but instead were left with gains amounting to a strip of insignificant territory 1,000 yards deep by 3,000 yards long. German casualties were slightly higher, at approximately 15,000.

Neuve Chapelle was both a "glorious victory" and a "bloody fiasco" for the British.[8] It had shown what careful preparations could accomplish, but it also showed how quickly success could deteriorate into failure. It helped to end the illusion that the war might end after one large battle like Sadowa, Sedan, or Waterloo. The war, many came to believe, would not end soon. One of the generals on Haig's staff concluded from the battle, "I am afraid that England will have to accustom herself to far greater losses than those of Neuve Chapelle before we finally crush the German Army."[9] However subtle the plan for Neuve Chapelle, it had not resulted in the victory that Haig had sought.

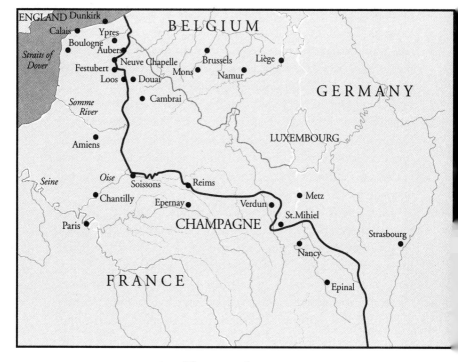

The western front, 1915

Nevertheless, Haig and his staff concluded, with some justification, that their plan had not gone awry. "We looked upon the operation as a success," recalled one of its planners, "and thought that but for bad luck and little mistakes, we would have gone forward."[10] The failure to accomplish more at Neuve Chapelle, many staff officers alleged, had been due to inadequate supplies of artillery shells. Such an analysis ignored Haig's centralization of his artillery once the infantry phase began, but it did point out a problem in British supply. In just three days along a narrow front, the British had fired one-sixth of their total stock of artillery ammunition. By the beginning of May, British industry had provided only 2 million of the 6 million shells it had promised to replace those

78

used in the war's first months. Sir John French expressed his frustration with British politicians, whom he blamed for the shortages and the low quality of the shells that the BEF did receive, to Charles Repington, the influential war correspondent of the London *Times*. Repington published the charges, coining the phrase "shell crisis," which contributed to a crisis in confidence in the British government.

STALEMATE AND THE BEGINNINGS OF GAS WARFARE

Farther to the north, in Flanders, the British believed that they had the situation well in hand. Events in 1915 thus far seemed to demonstrate that the Germans would hold on the defensive all across the western front. The British took advantage of this seeming inactivity to improve their position. They tripled the number of soldiers they had in the Ypres area and seized nearby Hill 60 (so named because it was 60 meters high), one of the few high points in Flanders.

These preparations made the Ypres salient stronger, but Horace Smith-Dorrien still thought it unwise to base British defenses there. The salient bulged out into the German lines in a particularly well-defined backward "C." It therefore sat exposed to attacks from the north, east, and south. Smith-Dorrien proposed retreating behind the Ypres canal, which sat at the British Second Army's back, thereby straightening out the line and offering the Germans fewer attack options. Sir John, still angry at Smith-Dorrien for his disobedience at Le Cateau the previous summer, refused to consider this idea.

Believing that the Germans would remain on the defensive in Flanders, Foch spent much of his time in March and early April planning an attack on Vimy Ridge, a series of hills north of Arras from which the Germans could observe all Allied movements in the area. German forces had also used the ridge to bombard Arras, virtually destroying its two magnificent town squares. If the Allies could relieve the pressure on the city, they could use it as a reliable supply and communications base for operations to the east. Foch became obsessed with capturing Vimy Ridge and the nearby Notre Dame de Lorette ridge; this view caused him to ignore threats in other sectors.

Allied focus on Arras proved costly. Evidence soon began to trickle in that the Germans might not sit idle in Flanders. During a small-scale raid of German trenches, French soldiers had captured a German soldier with a crude respirator. Other prisoners had told French interrogators that the respirators were designed to protect German forces from poison gas, which the Germans had been concentrating in the Ypres area. A British trench raid even uncovered cylinders that the Germans planned to use to project the gas. Still, British and French headquarters issued only vague warnings of the possibility of gas weapons being used in the Ypres sector.

Allied commanders likely interpreted the information regarding gas as a feint. Gas weapons stood in contravention of international laws regarding war. Although all of the great powers had some chemical stockpiles, the British and French had no plans to use them and likely assumed that out of humanity the Germans would not use theirs. Operationally, the only method of delivering poison gas involved opening the gas from cylinders placed inside one's own lines and trusting a favorable wind to carry it over. The Germans suffered from the disadvantage of being to the east, which placed them in the face of the normally prevailing westerly winds.[11] For whatever reason, the Allies badly misjudged German intentions regarding the new weapons. Their mistake cost them thousands of casualties and nearly cost them the entire Ypres sector.

German commander Erich von Falkenhayn had three goals for the offensive. First, he hoped to reduce the Ypres salient that bulged into his lines and impeded his lines of communication. Second, he sought to divert attention from his movement of four corps to the east to participate in the great German eastern offensive at Gorlice-Tarnow. Third, he wanted to inflict heavy casualties on the British Army defending Ypres. Falkenhayn, like many in the German elite, saw Britain as Germany's most implacable foe in the arenas of imperialism and international trade. He blamed Britain for, in the words of Chancellor Bernhard von Bülow, denying Germany her place in the sun.

Like Haig's plan for Neuve Chapelle, Falkenhayn's preparations for what became known as the Second Battle of Ypres showed some dexterity, but had some flaws as well. Falkenhayn decided to attain the critical element of surprise by not amassing large reserves in the Ypres sector. As a result, British and French reconnaissance aircraft flying over enemy lines did not notice any unusual activity. He hoped to use gas in coordination with an intense artillery bombardment to open gaps in the enemy line. The greater the shock and panic caused by the novelty of gas warfare, the greater the chance to expose and exploit the enemy's position.

The attack began with a conventional artillery barrage on April 22, 1915. Later that day, when the winds began to blow east to west, German soldiers opened 5,000 canisters filled with chlorine gas. The green cloud caused a unit of French African Territorials to panic, opening a four-mile gap in the Allied line to the north of Ypres. The Germans moved forward cautiously, not wanting to move into the gas cloud themselves and fearful of a change of wind that might blow the gas back on them. Still, within twenty-four hours they had captured the northern one-third of the salient and sat just three miles from Ypres itself.

Falkenhayn's plan, like Haig's, carried the seeds of its own failure. The German decision not to mass reserves in the Ypres sector had produced the surprise he sought. The lack of reserves, however, limited Falkenhayn's power to exploit the gap caused by the gas. British soldiers soon learned to improvise temporary gas masks by soaking pieces of cloth in any liquid available. The First Canadian Division, with failed real estate salesman Arthur Currie

*Gas attacks, like this one observed from the air, depended upon
favorable weather conditions. Unpredictable winds limited the utility
and lethality of gas, although it still caused tremendous suffering.
(National Archives)*

as one of its brigade commanders, deployed to the north of Ypres
and slowed the German advance. In June 1917 Currie became
commander of the Canadian Corps and went on to lead it to
spectacular victories. Under his leadership the Canadian Corps
became, in Dennis Showalter's estimation, "the finest large fighting unit relative to its circumstances in modern history."[12]

Foch and Sir John ordered counterattacks that led to high casualties, but that managed to slow the momentum of German attacks. Renewed attacks in May led to the German seizure of the
eastern third of the salient, but the town remained in Allied
hands. The Second Battle of Ypres had been a victory for the

Allies only in the sense that they had held on. But it had been bloody (approximately 15,000 casualties for each side), and the embarrassing failure of the Allies to prepare for the gas cloud called for a scapegoat. Not surprisingly, Sir John offered up Smith-Dorrien, who was informed of his dismissal by telegram.

In his place, Sir John, whose own days were numbered, promoted Herbert Plumer. Portly and distinctly unmilitary in appearance, Plumer had a sharp mind and a knack for planning. Almost all observers of the British Army then and since have singled out him and Tim Harrington, his talented chief of staff, for special praise. Even Philip Gibbs, who spent much of the war as a journalist observing and criticizing the inner workings of the British generals, thought them a fine team. The promotion of Plumer partly counterbalanced the injustice done to Smith-Dorrien.

Neither Plumer nor most other British officers saw the tragic irony contained in the near-success at Neuve Chapelle: that it had been successful enough to lead to more frontal assaults on prepared enemy positions. This lesson posed the least challenge to traditional military thinking and therefore became the standard interpretation of the senior Allied generals. The most aggressive among them wanted to repeat the Neuve Chapelle operational plan, with some adjustments in the size of the artillery preparation, at another point in the line. With the Second Battle of Ypres over, Foch set his sights once again on Vimy Ridge.

As at Neuve Chapelle, the Allied staffs planned to interdict the German lateral lines of supply that ran parallel to the western front. Without these lines of supply, the Allies hoped, the Germans might be forced to retreat into open country where cavalry could pursue them. This time, the British and French planned to coordinate two offensives at the same general time in the same general area, thereby impeding the German ability to concentrate reinforcements. While Foch and the French attacked Vimy Ridge, the British would attack near Neuve Chapelle again, this time opposite the town of Festubert.

The British made one other adjustment to their thinking. Having seen the difficulty of attacking, the British developed the idea of "bite and hold" attacks. The notion involved seizing a piece of easily defensible territory, then enticing the enemy to counterattack it. This ingenious tactic placed the burden of attack on the enemy if he fell for the bait. Although many officers worked on the idea, General Henry Rawlinson deserves the most credit for it. Another general whom Sir John despised, Rawlinson had commanded one of the corps involved at Neuve Chapelle. Festubert thus represented a chance to begin a shift in British doctrinal thinking.

At Festubert Rawlinson commanded a corps under the overall direction of Haig. Although the two men had disagreements, they shared a disdain for Sir John's leadership thus far and therefore had grown closer professionally. Having concluded that the setback at Neuve Chapelle had resulted from inadequate artillery, Haig and Rawlinson did not want to make the same mistake twice. They still, however, faced the problem of low shell stocks, especially of the high-explosive shells needed to damage German trenches and wire. Instead, the British had a disproportionate amount of shrapnel, effective for killing men in the open, but virtually useless for killing them in trenches and dugouts. For Festubert, the British had just 71 guns larger than five inches in caliber; 92 percent of the shells they fired were shrapnel.[13] Shortages of ammunition limited their pre-attack shelling to just forty minutes, scarcely better than what they had used at Neuve Chapelle.

May 9, 1915, saw the French and British armies each advance on their respective targets. (Coincidentally, it was also the day when the first men of the New Armies embarked for France.) Neither attack proceeded well. The British soon found that their low shell stocks were only part of the problem. Many artillery pieces had fired more shells in the first months of the war then they had been designed to fire in a lifetime; as a result, many of their tubes were warped and fired shells inaccurately. Many of the shells, moreover, turned out to be duds. One report claimed that soldiers saw shells filled with sawdust rather than explosives, although this story was likely just battlefield rumor that shifted the blame for the defeats of 1915 to saboteurs or war profiteers.

As a result of the poor quality of the artillery support, the infantry advance was unable to repeat the initial success of Neuve Chapelle. The Germans had learned from their experience as well and had dug in more deeply to protect themselves from enemy artillery. British and Indian soldiers advanced in such dense formations that German commanders gave the order "Fire until the [machine gun] barrels burst." During the battle, Rawlinson demanded of a brigade commander why his men were not advancing. The general replied, "They are lying out in No-Man's Land, sir, and most of them will never stand again." Aerial reconnaissance reports indicating that the Germans were reinforcing the sector led Haig to call the battle off. The British Army suffered almost 12,000 casualties in one day. They had gained nothing to make good the sacrifice.[14]

Farther to the south, near Arras, the French had fared even worse despite much more plentiful artillery stocks. Forgoing the element of surprise, Foch ordered a six-day artillery bombardment. French artillerists fired more than 300,000 shells at German positions. Foch confidently predicted that the artillery would cut the German wire, allowing French infantry to break the German lines. He told Joffre that the success of his Vimy Ridge operation would end the war on the western front in three months.

The French made some advances, temporarily capturing one of the three principal hills of Vimy Ridge and advancing up the near slope of another. By May 15, Foch's forces had moved the line three miles, but at tremendous human cost. The British failure at Festubert allowed the Germans to move reinforcements to Vimy Ridge, greatly strengthening the line. Still, Foch believed that the German line was ready to break and ordered another attack. He

*Unlike their brightly clad mainland counterparts, African soldiers in the
French Army went to war in khaki uniforms. Designed for war in
Africa, they proved to be well suited to the war on the western front.
(© Bettmann/Corbis)*

continued the offensive into June with diminishing gains. In all,
France suffered an astonishing 102,000 casualties while inflicting
less than half of that number on their German foes.

With all sides low on ammunition and human reserves, the
summer passed relatively quietly. Both sides needed to restock
their ammunition and train replacements. They also had to take
serious stock of their own ideas. Although the plans for 1915 represented significant advances from the rather crude approaches of
1914, they had failed to achieve the promised results. Allied generals, who had theretofore largely managed to avoid serious ques-
tioning of their handling of the war, came under increased scru-
tiny. Sir John, Joffre, and Foch all lost the air of competence that
had seen them through earlier disasters. For their part, the generals blamed inadequate artillery. In the fall of 1915, British daily

shell production equaled just 22,000 shells. The Germans were producing more than ten times that number.[15] The "shell crisis" soon became the most important subject of conversation in Allied headquarters staffs and in its capitals.

Shell and artillery problems affected France as well. The mainstay of the French army had been its 75mm field artillery piece. Agile, accurate, and capable of rapid fire, it fit perfectly into prewar French offensive doctrine. Its 75mm flat trajectory shell, however, could not damage the deep defenses of the German lines. In January 1915 France had just seventeen guns that fired shells larger than 155mm. Joffre and his generals blamed the lack of large guns for their early failures in 1915, although politicians rightly pointed out that Joffre himself had supported France's reliance on the 75mm gun in the years leading up to the war. Joffre's repeated arguments that lack of munitions prevented him from winning the war quickly grew thin. French Prime Minister René Viviani told President Raymond Poincaré that Joffre "wants to make us believe that it is our fault his offensive failed. When he began the [Champagne] offensive he knew full well what we had for munitions. He wants to throw back on the government the errors he himself has committed."[16]

The fever pitch that grew in the face of the shell crises contributed to shake-ups in both the British and French governments. The British formed a coalition government on May 9 and a Ministry of Munitions one month later. At its head sat the Chancellor of the Exchequer, David Lloyd George, a former opponent of the Boer War. As a stopgap measure, the energetic Lloyd George dramatically increased shell orders from factories in the United States, and he began to reorganize industry at home, relying on female labor to replace the men who had left for the front.

At the beginning of the war, virtually all elected legislatures made public shows of solidarity to help their governments operate more smoothly. The truces eliminated partisan debate but effectively removed the legislatures from the decision-making process

The departure of male factory workers to the front, combined with the expanded need for munitions, led to changes in the wartime workforce. All sides relied on female munitions workers, like these women in a British factory. (National Archives)

in the early years of the war. Executive authority also began to diminish, in large measure because few senior politicians understood the intricate workings of the military. Neither British Prime Minister Herbert Asquith (prime minister from 1908 to 1916) nor French President Raymond Poincaré held a firm grasp of the economic, social, and political changes taking place around him. Prime Minister René Viviani played almost no role in high-level decision-making, resigning in favor of Foreign Minister Aristide Briand in October 1915.

The monarchical states suffered even more deeply from the developing vacuum of authority. Kaiser Wilhelm II believed that he knew much more about the military than he actually did. The prewar custom of the general staff of rigging war games so that the kaiser's side always won did not help the monarch to understand the army as it was, not as he wished it to be. Beginning with the mobilization process, the kaiser's limited knowledge led to his increasing marginalization. With the German Reichstag having effectively rendered itself irrelevant, the military stepped in. Consequently, as the war dragged on the German Army came perforce to assume more and more responsibility for the political and economic direction of the war.

THE BATTLES OF ARTOIS AND LOOS

By early autumn, the Allies believed that they were ready to attack again. Their plan called for the largest operation yet. The main attack would come against the Noyon salient in Champagne, with thirty-five French infantry divisions totaling more than 500,000 men. As diversions, Foch would resume his attacks near Vimy Ridge and the British would attack just to the north near the vital mining town of Lens. The Allies hoped that their attacks in this sector would lead the Germans to believe that the Vimy Ridge–Lens area was again the main target and thus might leave the Champagne region less strongly defended.

Haig and several other BEF generals argued against the plan. They contended that if attacks of this nature had failed in this same region in the spring, they could only fail again given stronger German positions and lower Allied shell stocks. Many Allied artillery batteries had just half of their authorized allotment of shells, and the British still depended too much on shrapnel. Nevertheless, Joffre insisted that the British launch their offensive in order to support his own in Champagne and to bring some relief to the Russians, who were then in a desperate condition. Not for the last time in the war, an army launched an offensive not of its choosing in the interests of helping a struggling ally.

Their reservations notwithstanding, Sir John and his generals concluded that they had little choice but to attack. To launch the offensive with the artillery they had, however, would be to leave the infantry without adequate fire support, thus condemning their army to certain slaughter. The offensive would also see the first large-scale appearance in battle of the New Armies. The British did not expect much tactical sophistication from these men, so adequate support became all the more critical. To square this circle and to avenge the Second Battle of Ypres, the British turned to asphyxiating gas. The surprise of gas, they hoped, would provide the cover for the infantry that the unsatisfactory artillery could not.

The coordinated Allied offensives began on September 25. At the Battle of Loos, the British used poison gas for the first time. As the Germans had done at Ypres, the British launched most of their gas from cylinders. Where conditions were favorable, gas forced many Germans out of their positions. Fickle winds and technical difficulties, however, led to a high number of friendly casualties. Because the British had used gas in place of large-scale artillery attacks, the German wire and trench systems remained only lightly damaged. The British suffered more than 60,000 casualties at Loos, more than twice what they inflicted.

The British never again used gas released from cylinders. Both sides appreciated the devastating effect that poison gas had on those exposed to it. Men not killed by the gas often panicked and ran away. Both sides quickly began to invest in chemical warfare. They developed projectors capable of launching gas over long distances, thus reducing the risk of exposing one's own troops to gas. They also began a deadly cat-and-mouse game, producing gases capable of passing through existing respirators. When one side upgraded its respirators to meet the challenge, the game began again.

Joffre's Champagne offensive did not depend heavily on cylinder gas as Loos had, but it failed as well. The French Army had prepared the ground with what was then the heaviest concentration of artillery fire in history. By releasing industrial workers from military service, French industry had augmented its number of heavy guns and increased shell production from 3,000 rounds of

This soldier is wearing a gas mask while peeling potatoes in an obviously posed photograph. Armies fought a cat-and-mouse war to develop better gas masks while simultaneously introducing new gases capable of passing through the enemy's masks. (National Archives)

heavy ammunition per day in December 1914 to 52,000 rounds per day one year later. As a result, Joffre had ample stocks for the more than 900 heavy artillery pieces and 1,600 field guns that pounded the German front lines. Joffre confidently assembled his cavalry divisions to exploit the gaps he expected the artillery to create. The Germans responded by moving back to their second and third trench lines, as far as three miles to the rear. They effectively surrendered their first line, but in pulling back they rendered much of the French bombardment useless. As French troops advanced they saw a sign in the abandoned first line of German trenches that read (in French) "Land for sale, but at high price."[17]

In places, the French did open gaps in the German lines, but heavy rains complicated the rapid movement of both infantry and artillery. French forces thus had to advance over ground that was both muddy and broken by their own shelling. In all, the September offensives, including Foch's failed second attempt at the Vimy Ridge, had been disastrous. Total casualties reached 100,000 French, 60,000 British, and 65,000 German.

The ramifications of these losses reached deep. The most senior casualty was Sir John French. Haig, one of his subordinates and a former friend, had long been intriguing to have him removed. Lady Haig had close connections to the royal family; and Haig himself had maintained, by royal invitation, a personal correspondence with King George V. In letters to the king, Prime Minister Asquith, and Kitchener, Haig had complained about French's conduct of the war. Sir John's public rantings about government failures to provide him with shells adequate in quality and quantity did not help his position. Nor did Joffre and the French government believe in him any longer. As a result, the government removed Sir John from the command of the BEF on December 17, naming him commander of forces in the United Kingdom. In May 1918 he received the unenviable assignment of Lord Lieutenant of Ireland in the wake of the civil war then raging there.

In his place, the government named Haig, the very person whose intrigue had partly prompted Sir John's dismissal. A former top graduate of Sandhurst and son of a wealthy Scottish distiller, Haig was a soldier in every sense of the word. He was then, and remains today, controversial. Few generals ever inspired such loyalty from those around them and such condemnation from journalists, politicians, and many historians. Haig was so tongue-tied around British politicians that Lloyd George thought him a dunce. Thoughtful and creative at times, Haig could also be cold, aloof, and arrogant. His most important attributes in December 1915 were his superior ability (compared with Sir John) to work with Joffre and his absolute faith in the eventuality of a British victory.

Joffre survived 1915, but not without some difficulty. The heavy losses and minimal gains of the year notwithstanding, Joffre remained popular with the men of the French Army. As was the case in all armies, of course, few soldiers ever saw their commander. Joffre spent most of his time in the sumptuous Château de Chantilly, enjoying the finest foods and entertainers from nearby Paris. Still, his men continued to refer to him as "Papa" and, insofar as they thought about him at all, generally believed that he was as good a commander as they could expect.

Joffre's biggest problem had to do with his poor relations with French politicians. Joffre believed that war was the exclusive province of soldiers, and he reacted angrily at the mere suggestion that the minister of war, the prime minister, the legislature, or even the president had the authority to question his judgment. During the French government's four-month exile from Paris to Bordeaux, Joffre had created a "Zone of the Armies" in northeastern France, which he ran like a dictator. He banned many powerful politicians from entering the zone and once threatened President Poincaré with imprisonment if he strayed from the agenda set for him by Joffre and his staff. He also attempted to remove General Maurice Sarrail, a favorite with most left-leaning French politicians. In revenge, in October 1915 Parliament forced the resignation of Alexandre Millerand, a firm Joffre supporter, as war minister, replacing him with Joffre's long-time rival Joseph Gallieni, the hero of the Marne. Joffre's battlefield defeats and his attempts to sit above the French government weakened his position, but his popularity with the soldiers and on the home front spared him from Sir John's fate for another year.

Nevertheless, Joffre's days, too, were numbered. During the winter of 1915–1916 evidence mounted of a major German concentration of forces near Verdun. Joffre dismissed the possibility of a German attack there and reacted angrily to accusations that he needed to pay more attention to Verdun. He was particularly sensitive to these charges because he had denuded Verdun's ring of powerful fortresses of their heavy guns in order to provide extra firepower for his failed Champagne offensive. Joffre's critics, however, were right: the Germans were planning an offensive at Verdun for 1916. It became the longest, bloodiest, and most important of the war.

[4]

ORDERED TO DIE

Gallipoli and the Eastern Fronts

What in the devil have we come here to do?

—A French soldier at Salonika, 1915

THE frustrations of the western front led the generals and politicians to look for other places to force a decision. The events of 1915 had made the 450-mile-long front in France and Belgium a line of virtually impregnable subterranean fortresses. Even careful planning, such as that for Neuve Chapelle, had produced no more than ephemeral success. Nevertheless, most western front generals continued to insist that the war would be won or lost only in France. Allied politicians, many of them increasingly frustrated with what they saw as the failures of their senior officers, disagreed and began to look elsewhere.

Not surprisingly, most French politicians and generals insisted that the western front continue to be the primary Allied focus. Still, even many Frenchmen came to recognize the value in looking for decisive action elsewhere. The less directly threatened British were generally more eager to experiment. Their army grew increasingly powerful as the New Armies trained and learned how to fight while their most important military asset, the dominant Royal Navy, sat relatively idle. Although Britain's navy blockaded Germany and protected shipping lanes, many of its senior leaders grew anxious for it to do much more.

Consequently, the great British plan for an eastern operation in 1915 came from the Admiralty, not the Army. First Lord of the Admiralty Winston Churchill believed that the Royal Navy could achieve a great success at limited cost against the Ottoman Em-

95

pire. He had high hopes for the plan, which involved rushing a Royal Navy squadron through the Straits of the Dardanelles and threatening Constantinople. Churchill hoped that the presence of the Royal Navy might produce a host of positive transformations: removing the Ottoman threats to the Suez Canal; opening a direct warm-water shipping lane to Russia; enticing Bulgaria, Rumania, and/or Greece to join the Allies; causing a revolt among the Ottoman Empire's Greek, Kurdish, Armenian, and Arab minorities; and pressuring a Turkish government that Churchill believed to be weak into surrendering.

Like many Allied senior leaders, Churchill vastly underestimated the determination of the Ottoman Empire. To be sure, from the perspective of 1914, the Ottoman Empire, known as the "sick man of Europe," looked to be no match for the British Empire. For the past half century, it had been on a precipitous decline. In 1878 a military defeat to Russia forced it to recognize the independence of Montenegro, Serbia, Rumania, and Bulgaria. Russia also acquired the strategic Caucasus regions of Ardahan, Kars, Batum, and Bayazid. The weakness of the Ottoman state made it powerless to prevent Austria-Hungary's annexation of Bosnia in 1908, Italy's annexations of Libya and the Dodecanese Islands in 1912, and Great Britain's increasing influence in Egypt and Persia, both of which remained under Ottoman suzerainty in name only.

Ottoman military defeats led to the rise of the Young Turks, a group of nationalist reformers who hoped to restore Turkey's lost glory. They took power in 1908, but their reforms did not stem the tide of Turkish frustration. In 1912 and 1913 the Ottoman Empire fought against Bulgaria, Serbia, Greece, and Montenegro, loosely gathered together as the "Balkan League." Turkey lost the First Balkan War, ceding all of its European territories except the Gallipoli peninsula and the area immediately surrounding the capital of Constantinople. Infighting among the members of the

Balkan League led to the Second Balkan War in 1913, in which Turkish forces regained the important city of Adrianople.[1]

The Balkan Wars cost all of the belligerents deeply, but the Ottoman Empire suffered the most. The Ottomans lost an estimated 100,000 men in the two wars, many to disease. The Ottoman army also lost enormous stores of military equipment. As a result, in 1914 they were short 280 heavy artillery pieces, 200 machine guns, and 200,000 rifles. Ottoman supply and administrative corps were far below western standards, and their internal lines of communication were so primitive that the rapid transportation of men and supplies across the vast empire became almost impossible.[2] Moreover, the exposed Ottoman Empire needed to protect several strategic areas, including its European frontier against a Bulgarian or Greek invasion; the Black Sea coast and Caucasus regions against the Russians; the Gallipoli peninsula that guarded the approaches to Constantinople; and Persia/Mesopotamia and the Arabia/Suez regions against the British.

Churchill might thus be forgiven for believing that the Ottoman Empire could not withstand a determined British attack. Despite its obvious shortcomings, however, the Ottoman Empire still had considerable strength. After the end of the Second Balkan War, the Young Turks began an aggressive plan of reform that included the replacement of 1,300 officers. Several men of talent, foremost among them Mustafa Kemal, rose to senior leadership positions. Most important, the army now had a core of combat-hardened men, many of whom had fought well in the Balkan Wars when given the opportunity to do so, especially when fighting close to home.

The Ottomans responded to their military shortcomings by growing increasingly close to Germany. Both nations shared a mistrust of the Russians and a desire to increase their influence in the Balkans. In the summer of 1914, a German military mission of seventy officers, enlisted men, and technical experts arrived

The Great War in the Balkans was often an extension of the region's traditional hatreds and scores left unsettled from the two Balkan Wars. These Bulgarians fought on the side of the Central Powers as irregulars. (© Hulton-Deutsch Collection/Corbis)

in Turkey to assist in the modernization of the Ottoman Army. German officers prepared the Ottoman Army's 1914 mobilization plan, and German colonels assumed command of three Ottoman infantry divisions. German General Otto Liman von Sanders commanded the mission and quickly assumed a key role in developing Ottoman strategy, operations, and tactics.

Ottoman ties to Germany led to a secret treaty signed on August 2, 1914, as German troops entered Belgium. The treaty (written in the European diplomatic language, French), pledged that each of the two signatories would come to the other's aid if Russia attacked either one. Turkey also agreed to remain neutral in the war between Austria-Hungary and Serbia. At the same time, ten-

sions with Britain rose as a result of Churchill's decision to im-
pound two ultramodern battleships then being completed in English dockyards that had been earmarked for sale to the Ottomans.
The Ottoman Navy had been depending on these ships to improve its position in relation to the Greek and Russian navies. The
ships, moreover, had been financed in part by public subscription,
making Churchill's decision appear as a slap in the face to the Ottoman people.

The Germans made considerable political gain out of this situation by dispatching two of their own warships to Constantinople
and transferring them to Ottoman control. Dodging the Royal
Navy ships assigned to track them, the *Goeben* and the *Breslau*
moved through the Straits of Messina after bombarding French
positions in Algeria. They arrived in Turkey on August 10, 1914,
and strongly influenced the Young Turks' desire to move away
from the Entente and toward Germany. The most direct step toward war between the Allies and the Ottoman Empire came on
October 1, when the Ottomans closed the Dardanelles to international shipping. The move cut the only warm-water link between
Russia and its western allies. Ottoman naval bombardment of
Russian Black Sea positions increased tensions. By November 5,
the Ottoman Empire was at war with Britain, France, and Russia.

Churchill's 1915 plan to rush the straits involved the greatest
concentration of naval power ever assembled in the Mediterranean Sea. The British and French armada boasted Britain's newest
dreadnought-class battleship plus a battle cruiser, 16 pre-Dreadnought battleships, 20 destroyers, and 35 minesweepers. To defend
the straits, the Turkish Army had 11 forts, 72 artillery pieces, 10
minefields incorporating 373 mines, and a heavy underwater net
to stop submarines. The older outer forts presented less of a challenge than the forts at The Narrows, a 1,600-yard-wide passage.
To complement these forts, the Germans sent 150mm howitzer
batteries, whose high-angle fire proved deadly to ships and whose

mobility made them difficult for the British to pinpoint and destroy, as well as 500 German coastal defense specialists. The Turks had placed its veteran III Corps in the Gallipoli region. It was the only Turkish Army unit to survive the Balkan Wars intact and the only one to make all of its mobilization goals on time in August 1914.[3]

The Allied fleet aimed to destroy the forts and then rush through the straits, thus avoiding prolonged combat with the veteran soldiers of the III Corps. The Allied admirals planned to destroy the Turkish forts with their modern naval guns, then cover the approach of the more vulnerable minesweepers as they entered The Narrows. The flotilla approached the Gallipoli peninsula on February 19, 1915. Within a week, the British had neutralized the forts that guarded the entrance to the Dardanelles, leading one British sailor to write confidently to his parents, "if you would like to come and see me I will have great pleasure meeting you in Constantinople."[4] The writer could not have known that he then stood at the high point of Britain's campaign in the Dardanelles. Just two weeks after dispatching this letter, the sailor watched as three older Allied battleships struck mines, and the Allies could not rule out the much more dangerous possibility (false as it turned out) that German submarines were in the area. Unwilling to risk even greater naval losses, the Allied fleets pulled back.

The Allies were thus in an unenviable bind. The battleships could not proceed because of the dangers of the mines, but they had not done sufficient damage to the forts and mobile howitzers to permit the minesweepers to advance safely. Moreover, the Allies believed that they had invested too much moral capital to abandon the operation at this early stage. First Sea Lord Admiral Sir John "Jackie" Fisher, who often said that moderation in war is imbecility, argued for deploying the army onto the Gallipoli peninsula in order to eliminate the forts by land. Kitchener initially opposed sending the army, but eventually relented. As commander of the operation he named Ian Hamilton, an old

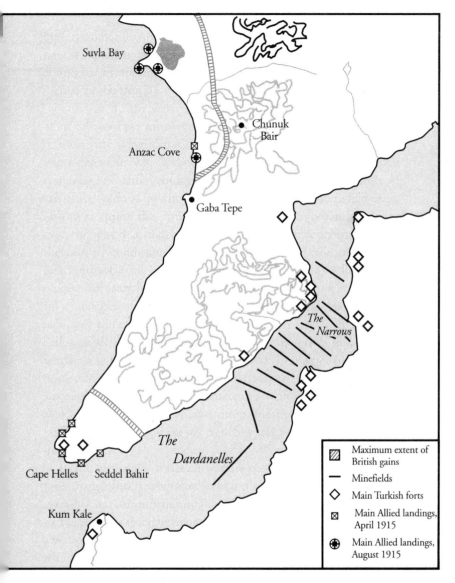

Suvla Bay

Chunuk
Bair

Anzac Cove

Gaba Tepe

*The
Narrows*

*The
Dardanelles*

Cape Helles   Seddel Bahir

Kum Kale

▨	Maximum extent of British gains
—	Minefields
◇	Main Turkish forts
⊠	Main Allied landings, April 1915
⊕	Main Allied landings, August 1915

The Gallipoli campaign, 1915

Kitchener protégé who knew the eastern Mediterranean well (he was born on the island of Corfu) and was a veteran of wars from such diverse areas as Afghanistan, South Africa, and Burma. Intelligent, charming, and eloquent, Hamilton seemed the perfect choice.

While the British and French assembled a 75,000-man army to send to Gallipoli, the Turks did not sit idle. They had planned to defend the peninsula against Greece in the Balkan Wars and in 1914 had named it one of four primary fortification zones (along with Adrianople, the Bosphorus, and Erzurum). Liman von Sanders took control of a reorganized Fifth Army with three German corps commanders under him, each based at the most likely Allied landing areas: Bulair, at the neck of the peninsula; Kum Kale, at the Asian side of the entrance; and Seddel Bahir, across the straits on the European side. The Ottomans received reinforcements along with construction crews to build roads, lay mines, and improve the peninsula's seaward defenses. Ottoman soldiers dug in on all of the important high ground. The Ottoman-German high command planned to defend the coastline lightly in order to avoid the withering fire of British warships, then counterattack with forces three to five kilometers behind the lines. In the wake of their turning back the mighty Royal Navy and defending their homeland, the Turks' morale was high.

British morale was high as well. Unwilling to deplete the western front, Kitchener relied on the volunteers of the Australia and New Zealand Army Corps (ANZAC) to shoulder the load. As they were then training in Egypt, where Ottoman agents carefully observed their every move, the choice seemed natural. Kitchener selected William Birdwood, another protégé, to command the ANZACs. Birdwood, a self-styled "soldier's general," did not insist on the letter of British discipline for his individualistic ANZACs. As a result, "Birdie" was popular with his men, most of whom took great pride in being nonprofessionals. Like their Turkish enemies, the ANZACs were tough, determined, and anxious to fight.

GALLIPOLI AND SALONIKA

The long-expected Allied landing came on April 25, 1915, in six different places to confuse the Ottomans and slow the dispatch of reinforcements. French troops landed on the Asian side to divert Turkish attention. The Ottoman-German high command had guessed that the main attack would fall at Bulair. The most powerful forces landed instead at the tip of the peninsula at Cape Helles and in the middle of the peninsula's western coast at a place soon to be renamed Anzac Cove. The operation began inauspiciously; instead of landing on level ground at Gaba Tepe, the ANZACs accidentally landed further north, opposite the critical high ground of Chunuk Bair. Still, Turkish forces offered only light resistance. The forces at Chunuk Bair, not expecting a major landing in their sector, had light supplies and soon ran out of ammunition.

The ANZACs would likely have captured the Chunuk Bair ridge if not for the actions of one of the most remarkable men the war produced, Lt. Col. Mustafa Kemal, who commanded the Turkish 19th Infantry Division. Kemal arrived at Chunuk Bair just as his men had begun to run away. Kemal seized the moment, telling his men that if they had no bullets, they would fight with bayonets. He sent a courier to tell Fifth Army headquarters of the situation before informing his men that they would stay and fight. When one of them protested that they lacked the strength to attack, he replied: "I do not order you to attack. I order you to die. By the time we are dead, other units and commanders will have come up to take our place."[5] The Ottoman line held at Chunuk Bair, as it did everywhere else. The Turkish Fifth Army had maintained its hold on all of the high ground and had contained the Allies to five small beachheads.

Two British offensives on April 28 and May 6 both failed, leaving the Gallipoli peninsula locked in the very trench stalemate that it was supposed to have alleviated. Supply problems mounted, with drinking water having to be transported from as

*Jewish, militia-trained, and an engineer by profession, John Monash was an
outsider who commanded the 4th Australian Infantry Brigade at Gallipoli.
He rose to become commander of the Australian Army Corps in 1918,
where his innovative ideas on warfare contributed to the Allies' victory.
(Australian War Memorial, negative no. A01241)*

far away as Egypt. The Ottoman Army tried offensives of its own
in May, June, and July, but found that it lacked the strength to
expel the British from their beachheads. Both sides fought on
through a blazing summer sun and the increasing burdens of disease and privation.

The heroism of Mustafa Kemal (shown here fourth from left) at Gallipoli launched him on a meteoric rise. After the war he became the first president of the modern state of Turkey and ordered the construction of a monument on the Gallipoli peninsula dedicated to the heroism of the Australians, his former enemies. (Australian War Memorial, negative no. P01141.001)

The British made an attempt to break the stalemate on August 6. They concentrated a landing at Suvla Bay, just north of Anzac Cove, and conducted two major diversionary efforts elsewhere. Confusion reigned, as the naval landing craft placed troops on the wrong beaches once again. Less than 1,500 Turks managed to hold off 20,000 disoriented British soldiers until reinforcements arrived. Another heroic charge by Kemal's men on the afternoon of August 10 drove the offensive back and recaptured all the high ground the Ottomans had lost that morning. The failure of the Suvla Bay landings effectively ended any hope of Allied success at Gallipoli, despite renewed attacks throughout the month.[6]

In September, Bulgaria joined the Central Powers, allowing the Ottomans to move forces in Thrace to Gallipoli, further solidifying their position on the peninsula and opening more direct lines

The Gallipoli campaign came to an end for these Turkish soldiers captured by British forces in 1915, but problems of strategy, supply, and tactics combined to doom British efforts to force the surrender of the "sick man" of Europe. (National Archives)

of communication to Germany. Allied generals grew frustrated at the lack of success, leading General Alexander Godley to remark that all of the Allies' efforts had gained them five acres of bad grazing ground. The British had not planned to supply the eight divisions then in Gallipoli through the winter; more than 10,000 men contracted frostbite when a November blizzard struck the peninsula. An Australian war correspondent, Keith Murdoch, presented strong criticisms of the British handling of the campaign to the British press as well as to Prime Ministers H. H. Asquith of Great Britain and William Hughes of Australia.

To resolve the controversy, the British government sent General Charles Monro to Gallipoli with orders to provide a fresh assessment. He was the first general to visit Suvla Bay, Anzac Cove, and Cape Helles all in the same day, despite the mere fifteen miles separating them, an indication of the problems within British leadership. Monro saw tired, demoralized men low on ammunition and without any gear for winter warfare. He listened to a plan by Admiral Roger Keyes to rush the straits one more time, but he advised Kitchener to close the entire Gallipoli operation before the end of the year. Churchill later belittled Monro with a famous allegation that the general "came, saw, and capitulated," but Monro had little choice.

In December 1915, the British evacuated almost 83,000 men without a single casualty, although it took the Turks nearly two years to move all the heavy equipment the British left behind. The 259-day campaign had cost the British 205,000 casualties, the French 47,000 casualties, and the Turks an estimated 251,000 casualties. At the insistence of the Conservative Party, Churchill had left the Admiralty in May and accepted a minor post. In November he left the government altogether to protest the decision to evacuate Gallipoli. He later served as commander of the 6th battalion of the Royal Scots Fusiliers on the western front. His Gallipoli adventure cost him many political allies and his post at the head of the Admiralty, but Churchill recovered from adversity to become minister of munitions in 1917. His career in government was not at an end after all.

French disaffection with Churchill's Dardanelles operation led to the government's decision to withdraw its troops from the theater in October. At the same time, Serbia faced a renewed Central Powers attack on three sides from Bulgaria, Germany, and Austria-Hungary. Bulgaria faced nearly insurmountable shortages of all of the implements of modern warfare, but its army was large, experienced, and anxious to avenge what its leaders saw as Serbian perfidy in the Second Balkan War. The Serbian Army faced annihilation if its allies could not find a way to help. The Allied governments decided to move one British and one French infantry di-

Australian soldiers at Gallipoli did not anticipate the blizzard that struck the peninsula late in the campaign. Their supply officers had not anticipated it either. The miseries of the campaign as reported by Australian journalists contributed to the British decision to abandon the operation. (Australian War Memorial, negative no. P00046.040)

vision to the Greek port city of Salonika. From there, the Allies hoped to supply the Serbians via a single rail line.

The first problem with the plan lay in the response of the Greek government. Prime Minister Eleutherios Venizelos saw the Allies as his best chance to further Greece's expansionist interests against Bulgaria and Turkey. He therefore invited an Allied landing at Salonika in the hope that, in exchange, Britain and France might help him acquire the Aegean Islands, Macedonia, and Smyrna. These ambitions later complicated Allied relations with Greece and led to a war between Greece and Turkey, but in 1915 Venizelos was giving the Allies a way around Greece's technical neutrality.

Venizelos, however, had failed to clear his decision with Greece's King Constantine. The king, who was a graduate of the Prussian War Academy and was married to the kaiser's sister, shared Venizelos's expansionism, but not the means by which he chose to pursue it. Constantine's wife influenced his own pronounced pro-German sympathies. Constantine hoped to keep Greece neutral and saw the Allied landings as an invasion that violated that neutrality. The Allies would thus be operating in a country whose head of government favored them, but whose head of state did not. Constantine relieved Venizelos of his duties as prime minister, whereupon Venizelos went to Salonika and formed a separate Greek government that was quickly recognized by the British and the French.

The second problem lay with the Salonika expedition's commander, French General Maurice Sarrail. He had led well in the war's early days when, as commander of the Third Army, he had held his positions in the Argonne Forest and Verdun. Sarrail was as competent as most other generals of the war and a good deal better than many. Sarrail's political intrigues, however, made him unpopular with his fellow generals. A vociferous republican and Freemason, his close links to socialist politicians led him to be promoted much more quickly than many of his peers. Most French generals saw him as little more than a politician in uniform; most of his soldiers thought that he was more interested in activities in the bedroom than the map room.

Sarrail's intrigues led Joffre to dismiss him as commander of the Third Army in the summer of 1915. Sarrail's political allies saw the firing as a nefarious move designed to eliminate one of Joffre's critics and rivals. French Prime Minister Aristide Briand decided to bring Sarrail, whom he saw as more politically reliable than Joffre, back into command. He sent Sarrail to Salonika in October at the head of the grandiloquently named Army of the Orient, 150,000 men strong by the end of the year. Briand complicated matters further by naming Joffre commander-in-chief of all French forces (not just those on the western front), making Joffre responsible for Sarrail's success. Thus Joffre had under him a man whom he had mistrusted so much that he had fired him, and Sarrail had a boss that he had intrigued to have removed from office. Even before the Salonika forces saw combat, the omens all pointed in the wrong direction.

The first winter demonstrated that the omens were not wrong. The Salonika force arrived too slowly to complete its initial mission of providing help to the Serbians. Harassed by three armies and Albanian guerrillas, the Serbian army marched 200 miles with little food or medicine to the Adriatic coastline. From there, Allied ships moved six divisions of Serbian soldiers to the safety of Corfu, then, in April 1916, to Salonika, where they joined four (soon augmented to nine) French divisions, five British divisions, an Italian division, and a Russian brigade. There they sat with no obvious mission and surrounded by Greek soldiers, many of whom supported their king and showed obvious sympathy for the Central Powers.

The Salonika force initially saw only infrequent combat as Sarrail's supply and alliance problems limited his possibilities. The multinational force opposing them preferred not to attack, content instead to allow the Allied garrison to become what the Germans called "the war's largest internment camp." The inactive men soon turned to alcohol and prostitutes, thereby adding venereal disease to typhus, cholera, and malaria as causes for the overflowing Salonika hospitals. Men soon began to speak wistfully of the western front, which was more dangerous, but had the higher purpose of defending France and at least permitted regular mail and occasional leave at home.[7] The Allied divisions finally saw combat in August 1916, when Bulgarian forces struck their positions to cover a German invasion of Rumania. They held their positions, but a counterattack by Sarrail ended in failure.

In 1917 the military side remained stalemated, but the political side witnessed dramatic events. The Allies threatened to march on Athens if Constantine did not cease his pro-German activities. In June, under such duress, he went into exile in Switzerland, where he remained until the end of the war. His departure paved the way for Greece to enter the war on the Allied side. Venizelos returned to Athens and ordered the full mobilization of the Greek army. Meanwhile, the military situation deteriorated further, leading French Prime Minister Georges Clemenceau to refer derisively to the Allied garrison as the "gardeners of Salonika."

In December 1917 Clemenceau replaced Sarrail, eventually settling on the closest general the French Army had to his polar opposite, Louis Felix Marie François Franchet d'Esperey, nicknamed "desparate Frankie." Catholic, royalist, and energetic, Franchet d'Esperey had revived the French Fifth Army after replacing General Charles Lanrezac in 1914. All evidence during the war notwithstanding, he remained a firm advocate of the offensive and had long supported renewing the attack at Salonika. Now he had his chance, albeit with a demoralized force that had not yet known anything but failure.

Franchet d'Esperey, undaunted by the conditions he found at Salonika, told his men that he expected "ferocious energy" from them and took the unusual step of placing two French infantry divisions under Serbian command.[8] Using flamethrowers and cavalry, Allied forces targeted the beleaguered Bulgarians, whose situation was so desperate that many of them lacked clothes and shoes. On September 18, 1918, the Allied assault tore a hole in the line and sent the Bulgarians into a headlong retreat. Within two weeks an armistice ended the fighting at Salonika. Although the campaign ended on a high note, the experience at Salonika had cost the Allies much more than it had gained them. Sarrail may have summed up the frustrations of Salonika best when he remarked to Clemenceau, "Since I have seen alliances at work, I have lost something of my admiration for Napoleon."

GORLICE-TARNÓW AND THE
GREAT RETREAT FROM POLAND

Coincident with the British and French adventure at Gallipoli, the German army planned its own eastern offensive. German senior leadership had grown as pessimistic as many of their British and French counterparts about the prospects of reaching a decision on the western front. By contrast, they had already won three major victories in the east at Tannenberg, the Masurian Lakes, and Lódz; and they had an established and confident leadership, headed by the dynamic team of Hindenburg and Ludendorff. Furthermore, the relatively open spaces of the east were much better suited to the doctrine and training of the German army than the stasis of the west.

An eastern offensive, moreover, promised to provide needed succor to Germany's faltering Austro-Hungarian ally. Holger Herwig estimates that the battles of 1914 had cost the Austro-Hungarian army 190,000 dead, 500,000 wounded, and 278,000 prisoners of war. These figures included 75 percent of the army's prewar captains and lieutenants.[9] The failures of the Austro-Hungarian army led to increased tensions with Germany, prompting the kaiser to remark that the Carpathian Mountains were not worth the bones of a single Pomeranian grenadier.

The imminence of Italian entry into the war on the Allied side made the Austro-Hungarian situation even more serious. German attempts to convince Austria-Hungary to mollify the Italians with territorial concessions further strained relations. Germany then offered Italy Austrian territory in Trentino and Gradisca, the west bank of the Isonzo River, a free hand in Albania, and the conversion of Trieste into a free port. The outrage felt by the Austrians at German offers of Austrian territory to a nation that had reneged on its alliance commitments in 1914 increased when Italy accepted even more generous terms from Britain and France. Italy quickly became the one enemy that all of the empire's minorities could agree to hate.

Despite the kaiser's dismissive evaluation of the Carpathians and the growing tensions between Germany and Austria-Hungary, the Germans could not afford to lose their most important ally. To provide immediate help, the Germans decided on an attack east of Cracow between the towns of Gorlice and Tarnów. If successful, the attack would rescue the Austro-Hungarian position in the Carpathians and end the Russian threat to Hungary and Silesia. A January offensive by the Germans toward Warsaw directed Russian attention north, as did a second battle in the Masurian Lakes region in February.

Falkenhayn came east to supervise preparations for the new offensive. He ordered Hindenburg's Eighth Army to maintain pressure on the Russians north of Warsaw and created a new Eleventh Army under Mackensen. The Eleventh Army contained large troop transfers from the west, a movement that the Second Battle of Ypres successfully masked. Lacking any confidence at all in the Austrians, Falkenhayn also transferred control of the Austro-Hungarian Fourth Army, positioned to Mackensen's left, to the Eleventh Army headquarters. Conrad had no choice but to acquiesce.

Opposite this buildup the Russians sat, largely unaware of the imminent attack and in pitiable shape. One in three Russian soldiers lacked working rifles, and those that they did have came from several sources and used several different calibers, immensely complicating the manufacture and supply of ammunition. The siege of Przemysl continued until March 22, occupying Russian attention and providing a deceptive morale boost when it finally fell. Shortly thereafter, the tsar made a state visit to Galicia, distracting the attention of staff officers.

On May 2, 1915, the Germans began the Gorlice-Tarnów offensive with a four-hour artillery barrage. For the first time in the war, they complemented their artillery with airplanes that flew strafing missions against Russian lines of communication. The Eleventh Army concentrated its attacks in a twenty-eight-mile-long region between the two towns and drove into the second-rate Russian X Corps. The X Corps's rapid collapse created the flanks that World War I commanders so eagerly sought. With German units surrounding them and no reserves available to plug the gaps, the X Corps' parent unit, the Third Army, decided on a massive retreat.

The building Russian defeat soon led to chaos, confusion, and poor decisions. The retreat, orderly in some areas, devolved into a rout in others. In two weeks, the Germans fired more than 2 million artillery shells, advanced 95 miles, captured 153,000 Russians, and seized 128 field guns. The large number of prisoners testified to the growing war weariness among Russian soldiers and their increasing separation from the regime and their own officers. In general, the Russian officer corps reacted poorly to the crisis, quickly losing control of the situation in their own units.

As a result of the Third Army's collapse, the entire southern face of the Polish salient fell to the Germans. Russian supply and reinforcement systems broke down entirely, leaving many units without food, ammunition, or medical supplies. German and Austro-Hungarian forces retook Przemysl on June 3 and Lvov (again renamed Lemberg) on June 22, and crossed the Dniester River on June 23. Behind these lines sat a succession of outdated Russian forts that could not resist the German tide. To complicate the situation even further, the Germans began a general offensive with eight armies across the entire 700-mile eastern front.

By the end of July, German forces had reached the western suburbs of Warsaw. More than 350,000 residents fled east as more German forces turned north to cut off the city's Russian defenders. The Russian lines contained many gaps easily exploitable by the advancing enemy forces, and critical shortages of artillery shells made an active defense of the city impossible. On August 5, the Russians withdrew to the east bank of the Vistula River and destroyed the bridges around the city to cover their retirement. Two days later, the last Russian soldiers voluntarily abandoned Warsaw. In doing so, they gave up an important symbol of Russian power in eastern Europe, but had saved the Russian army from encirclement.

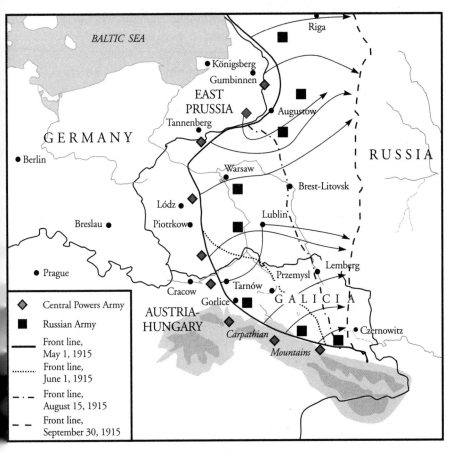

The eastern front, 1915

In response to the deteriorating situation all along their line, the Russian general staff reluctantly ordered the evacuation of the entire Polish salient. The retreat moved the lines in the east more than 300 miles in Germany's favor. Brest-Litovsk fell on August 25, and Vilna fell on September 19. The kaiser's timing finally served him well when he witnessed the fall of the Russian fortress of Novogeorgievsk northwest of Warsaw along with its 700 artillery pieces. The Russian armies, however, had survived, despite losses estimated at more than 2 million men, half of them prisoners. Russian units established a straight line (without exposed salients) that ran from Riga in the north to Czernowitz in the south. Gorlice-Tarnów had produced results beyond Falkenhayn's wildest imagination.

Despite his great success, however, Falkenhayn remained far from enthusiastic. He had not sought to repeat Napoleon's mistake of chasing the Russians deep into their own country. His two-front war dilemma had now become even more pronounced, with extended supply lines and winter approaching. He understood that the Russians would fight harder on Russian soil than they had in Poland and that the fragile Russian supply system would benefit from the shorter distances it now had to cover. He had dealt the Russians a terrific blow, but they had survived, meaning that Germany would be unable to dedicate as many resources to the western front in 1916 as he had hoped.

By late September, the Russians had indeed responded with an aggressive series of actions. They built a four-layer defensive belt around Riga, reorganized their remaining manpower reserves, called up new draftees, and built up the ice-free port of Murmansk, complete with new sled and rail links to connect it to Russian supply centers. A window to the west's supply convoys thus remained open. Poor commanders, like southwest front commander Nikolai Ivanov, were reassigned or removed, and competent ones, like Alexei Brusilov, were promoted in their place.

On September 1, the tsar announced, to the amazement of many, that he had reassigned his uncle, the Grand Duke Nicholas, to the Caucasus theater.[10] Thereafter, the tsar would command the Russian armies himself. Brusilov received the news as "most painful and even depressing." The Grand Duke, for all his faults, was well liked by the army; and, the Gorlice-Tarnów disaster notwithstanding, he deserved much of the credit for saving the Russian army from envelopment. The tsar, in Brusilov's words, "understood literally nothing about military matters."[11] He would therefore rely heavily on his competent, but controlling, chief of staff, Mikhail Alekseev. The tsar's assumption of command created a direct link between the success of the war and the regime's prestige. There would be no one else to blame if Russia's war fortunes did not quickly improve.

The Central Powers reformed their staff system as well. The great success at Gorlice-Tarnów had been the product of the German staff system, a fact that the Germans frequently reiterated to their Austro-Hungarian allies. Falkenhayn believed that the Gorlice-Tarnów triumph had occurred in spite of, not because of, the help of the Austro-Hungarians. He called the Austro-Hungarian general staff "childish military dreamers" and the Austrian people "wretched."[12] As a result, he worked to increase German dominance over the Austrians. In June, Mackensen and the German general staff assumed control of the Austrian Second Army.

By September, an independent Austro-Hungarian Army had virtually ceased to exist. German staff officers made most of the critical decisions and reorganized the Austrian system along German lines. Conrad remained in the dark about decisions reached by his German counterparts (Falkenhayn did not even bother to inform him of the great offensive he was then planning for Verdun), but he had to coordinate all of his own planning with German officers. Although Gorlice-Tarnów had been a tremendous success, it also spelled the end of Austria-Hungary as a great power. Few Austrians appreciated the irony that their steep decline had come despite the achievement of two of their most important goals from 1914: the end of an independent Serbia and the humiliation of Russia.

THE CAUCASUS CAMPAIGN

Turkey, too, had an eastern front. The Caucasus Mountains represented an ancient convergence point of Christian and Islamic peo-

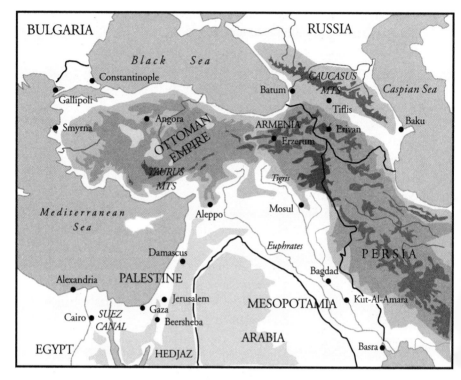

The Turkish front, 1915–1918

ples. As such, they had been fought over for centuries. In 1071 the
Ottoman Turks won a crucial victory over the Byzantines in this
region at the city of Manzikert. In 1878 the Ottoman Empire had
lost significant parts of the Caucasus to Russia. Their reconquest
quickly became a major aim for Ottoman forces, especially for
War Minister Enver Pasha, an ambitious leader of the Young Turk
movement and the most powerful politician in the country. Enver
hoped to create a great Pan-Turanic Empire in the east to compensate for Ottoman losses in the Balkans.

The Caucuses, however, do not lend themselves to successful
military campaigns. Temperatures can drop to as low as −50°C,

and winter snows are often best measured in feet or even meters. Road and rail links from western and central Turkey to the Caucasus were few and primitive. Nevertheless, Enver planned a great offensive to destroy the Russian units in the area and return the Caucasus to the Ottoman Empire. The Russians beat him to the punch, launching a successful offensive toward the Ottoman fortress of Erzurum. Enver, who had played a key role in recapturing Adrianople during the Second Balkan War, came east to lead Ottoman forces personally. He planned an attack on the town of Sarikamish reminiscent of Tannenberg. One corps would hold the Russians in place while two other corps would surround the Russians and cut off their retreat.

The ensuing battle set the pattern for the war in the Caucasus. By the time the Ottoman advance began on December 22, 1914, the temperature had fallen to −26°C and one foot of snow slowed the attack. The Russians counterattacked and drove the Ottomans back with losses of nearly one-third of the Ottoman force, many to frostbite. A typhus outbreak added to the misery on both sides. Anxiety among the Turkish forces grew, as they feared both a massive Russian counterattack and a rebellion among the local Armenian population. The Ottoman forces soon used the pretext of the discovery of Russian-built weapons in some Armenian homes to begin a policy of brutal repression.

In April 1915 Enver announced the arrest of important Armenian leaders and the forced relocation of the entire Armenian population from the Caucasus to Syria and Mesopotamia. Local leaders were supposed to assume responsibility for the welfare of the Armenians during the removal, but few bothered. The result was the destruction of the Turkish Armenian community. Denied food, water, medicine, and appropriate clothing, hundreds of thousands of men, women, and children died. Foreign journalists and observers recorded the entire tragic process, including the intentional mistreatment of Armenians by the same local officials charged with caring for them. The Allied govern-

*Armenian orphans leave Turkey on barges destined for Greece.
Hundreds of thousands of Armenians died when they were forcibly
moved from their homes with little thought given to their welfare by the
Ottoman officials charged with their care. (Library of Congress)*

ments, then fighting the Ottomans at Gallipoli, could do little; and the Germans chose not to pressure their allies. The extent to which the Turks planned to exterminate (rather than remove) the Armenians remains hotly debated, but whether due to intent or indifference, the end result was the same.

Throughout 1915 combat in the Caucasus continued, with the Russians gaining the upper hand. As the British threat to Gallipoli receded by the end of the year, the Turks were able to relocate forces and supplies, so that by mid-1916 almost half of all Turkish forces were in the Caucasus.[13] They were in relatively good spirits as a result of the Gallipoli victory, but Turkish forces were then also engaged in Mesopotamia, Sinai, Galicia, Romania, Macedonia, Persia, and Arabia. Only the British Empire sent men to fight in so many places so far apart.[14] The pressures on Turkey continued to mount, especially as the empire's fragile transportation network began to collapse under the weight of so many deployments across so much territory.

Even with half of the army stationed there, the Caucasus region was too big to defend foot by foot. The Ottoman Army therefore guarded the main roads and based its positions around the old fortress of Erzurum. The complex there included more than 40,000 men, 235 heavy artillery pieces, and 20 separate forts and outposts. Expecting Erzurum to hold out indefinitely, Enver did not hurry reinforcements to it. In February 1916 the Russians stunned the Turks with a five-axis approach on the fortress, capturing it in just five days. The Ottomans lost 15,000 men and virtually all of their artillery in the Caucasus region. The loss of Erzurum stunned Ottoman military leadership. Their inability to move men to the region quickly led to the loss of several more strategic positions. By the summer, Ottoman losses for 1916 exceeded 100,000 men. Enver responded by naming Mustafa Kemal Second Army Commander with responsibility for turning the momentum in the Caucasus.

Kemal's good fortunes continued as an unusually fierce winter slowed Russian activity until 1917. By the time the weather had improved, the Russian political situation had collapsed to the point that Russian forces no longer posed an immediate threat to Turkish forces. The Ottomans, meanwhile, continued to reform and reorganize. By January 1918 Enver believed that conditions favored a renewed Ottoman offensive in the region. The disintegration of the Russian navy, caused by the Bolshevik Revolution, allowed the Ottomans to move men and supplies across the Black Sea, thereby overcoming the poor Turkish rail and road systems. With only a small army of Russian Armenians in their way, the Ottomans moved quickly. By March the Turks had recaptured Erzurum, and in April they moved into northeastern Persia.

Ironically, the Germans looked upon the success of their Turkish allies with trepidation. They feared that a Turkish advance into Russia might lead the Russians to void the recently signed Brest-Litovsk agreement and reenter the war. Consequently, they brokered an unusual deal to create an independent Georgian state under German protection. The Ottomans were furious, but decided not to challenge the new arrangement. Instead they marched on the oil center of Baku on the Caspian Sea. The British dispatched a small force from Mesopotamia to hold the city, but wisely evacuated it in September.

Thus, even as the war was ending poorly for the Ottomans in Palestine it ended with the Ottoman Army in firm control of the Caucasus. As was the case with Austria, the Ottomans had lost the war despite achieving a key prewar aim. At the Paris Peace Conference, American President Woodrow Wilson rejected a British plan to have the United States assume mandate control of an enlarged Armenian state that would have included Erzurum at its center and one-third of the southern coast of the Black Sea. Without an international sponsor, the Armenian state had little chance of surviving. The new state of Turkey, behind its president, Gallipoli hero Mustafa Kemal, signed an agreement with the Soviet Union in 1922 that included Turkish recognition of Soviet incorporation of most of Trans-Caucasia. Turkey and the Soviet Union also agreed to divide Armenia between them.

Unsure of how to resolve the long-standing hatreds of the region, British diplomat Lord Curzon had facetiously suggested at the Paris Peace Conference that the best solution was to "let them cut each other's throats." Foreign Secretary Arthur Balfour shocked Curzon with his curt reply: "I am all in favor of that."[15] Armenia and the Caucasus were too far away and too impoverished to merit the sustained attention of the victorious powers.

5

GORDIAN KNOTS

American Neutrality and the Wars for Empire

[We] demand that the Germans shall no longer make war like savages drunk with blood; that they shall cease to seek the attainment of their ends by the assassination of non-combatants and neutrals.

—*New York Times* editorial after the German sinking of the *Lusitania*

Between 1900 and the outbreak of World War I, Great Britain's Royal Navy led a dramatic revolution in naval affairs. Already the unquestioned ruler of the seas, in 1906 the British launched HMS *Dreadnought*. Fast, agile, heavily armored, and boasting turret-rotating large guns, it could destroy any ship then in existence without even getting in range of the enemy's guns. *Dreadnought* made all existing battleships obsolete. The Royal Navy, which liked to claim that the enemy's coast was Britain's frontier, now had a weapon that had no equal anywhere in the world.

Dreadnought naturally inspired imitators. Germany enacted a massive naval building program that cost the Germans tremendously without ever even allowing that country to approach parity with the British Navy. The kaiser held a childish envy of his cousin King George V's naval power and unwisely devoted disproportionate funds to a "luxury fleet" whose power was always more deterrent than offensive and more symbolic than effective. The British Parliament more than met the German threat by subsidizing a "two-power standard" that pledged Britain to maintain more naval tonnage than the world's next two naval powers combined. First Lord of the Admiralty Winston Churchill noted the importance of Dreadnought-class battleships in British thinking in his

Germany's "luxury fleet," shown here at Kiel in 1914, required tremendous resources to build and maintain but never achieved parity with the British Royal Navy. The two navies fought just one large battle, the inconclusive engagement at Jutland in 1916. (National Archives)

own inimitable way: "The Admiralty asked for six, the Cabinet proposed four, and we compromised on eight."[1]

Geography has always served the Royal Navy, and in its naval rivalry with Germany it served the British exceptionally well. Germany possessed a narrow coastline with only two outlets toward Britain. The eastern approach involved a long course between Denmark and Sweden, entering the North Sea south of Norway. The western approach involved a few narrow lanes through the sandbanks of the Heligoland Bight. The Royal Navy could therefore monitor any large-scale German naval activity. To connect the two approaches, the Germans built the Kaiser Wilhelm Canal at Kiel. It was completed just before the outbreak of the war in order to allow the oversized German Dreadnoughts to pass through, but it did not solve Germany's essential strategic dilemma.

THE WAR AT SEA AND THE RIGHTS OF NEUTRALS

The British had enough warships to divide the Royal Navy into two fleets. The Home Waters Fleet, as it name implies, held the responsibility of guarding the long British coastlines. The Grand Fleet held the responsibility of containing the Germans and securing the sea lanes that fed and supplied the home islands. Altogether in 1914 the British outgunned the Germans by 24 Dreadnoughts to 13; 40 pre-Dreadnought battleships to 22; 102 cruisers to 41; 301 destroyers to 144; and 78 submarines to 30. The superiority of British shipbuilding meant that construction continued to outpace that of their German rivals as the war went on. The British also had the advantage of being allied with the French, Russian, and (after 1915) Italian navies.

Timing and circumstance also helped the British. The Royal Navy had been involved in a practice mobilization when the July crisis began. The mobilization aimed to test how long it took reservists to report to their duty stations and how well they performed. As a result, the Royal Navy was mobilized even before its service was required. Reservists were in place and many of the problems involved with getting the Royal Navy ready for war had been worked out. Churchill wisely decided not to end the test as scheduled at the end of July. Instead he kept the reservists with their ships and had them deployed into the North Sea by the time hostilities were declared, giving the British a critical first jump.

This dominance notwithstanding, the Royal Navy remained cautious and defensive. Almost two-thirds of the food needed to sustain the British people came from overseas, and the responsibilities of the Empire stretched to every corner of the globe. The Royal Navy also had to deploy and supply troops on four continents. The eastern coast of England and Scotland, moreover, was lightly defended and the bases there were not fully submarine-proof. A major British defeat at sea would leave the home islands dangerously vulnerable. As late as December 1917 British planners

were still unwilling to rule out the possibility of a German amphibious landing in the home islands.[2] For this reason, Churchill
described Grand Fleet commander Admiral Sir John Jellicoe as
the only man who could lose the war in a single afternoon. Jellicoe
had the responsibility for using the mighty Royal Navy to destroy
Germany's High Seas Fleet without taking losses that would place
Great Britain in peril. His was not an enviable position.

As a result of these constraints, Jellicoe and the admirals of the
Royal Navy decided on a strategy of offense by defense. The
navy's first priorities remained the defense of the home islands and
the continued British control of sea lanes. Simultaneously, the
Royal Navy imposed a surface blockade on Germany to deprive it
of foodstuffs and industrial goods from overseas. The Admiralty
would deploy the Grand Fleet in such a manner as to force the
German fleet to remain in port. The British would not fall for the
bait of attacking the Germans in their ports or close to their outer
defenses. Instead, the Royal Navy, as one historian wrote, would
"only seek battle when it commanded overwhelming force and
when the circumstances were exactly right."[3] A German fleet per-
petually confined to its home ports, the Admiralty reasoned, was
almost as good as a German fleet destroyed in battle.

Germany's one significant advantage lay in its submarines. Only
submarines could regularly escape from German ports without
being observed by the Royal Navy. Although the British had more
submarines than the Germans, the British saw them as best suited
for coastal defense. Consequently, 65 of the Royal Navy's 78 submarines were assigned to the Home Waters Fleet. The Royal
Navy, moreover, sought to fight the war by surface blockade,
which was recognized under international law and was a traditional element of British warfare. To be legal, a blockade had to be
effective, declared, visible, and respectful of the rights of neutral
vessels. Submarines, of course, could not follow these laws. The
use of submarines for blockade, therefore, was technically illegal.
The British, possessing a massive surface fleet and in firm control

*Admiral John Jellicoe became commander of the Grand Fleet upon
the outbreak of war. Accused by some of being overly cautious, he
received much of the credit for the minor British victory at Jutland
but was later dismissed for his inability to neutralize the German U-
boat threat. (Imperial War Museum, Q67791)*

of the North Sea, had the luxury of following the laws of blockade
and still remaining effective. In 1915 alone, the Royal Navy intercepted 3,098 ships headed for German ports and claimed, proba-
bly correctly, that not a single surface ship passed through the
Straits of Dover without British permission.[4]

Germany did not have the same advantages. Submarines therefore became the most logical way to strike at British lines of supply. Submarines could approach silently, strike swiftly, and escape
safely. They were, however, vulnerable to enemy fire if detected
and could not follow the laws of warfare regarding sinkings, cap-
tures, and crew treatment. Moreover, submarine commanders had
much less time to determine if the ship in their sights belonged to
an enemy belligerent or a neutral. Appearances could easily deceive. The British practice of flying an American flag on their

merchant vessels to deceive submarines became so commonplace that President Woodrow Wilson registered a formal complaint. The later British deployment of merchant ships with hidden guns and military personnel in civilian clothing (called Q Ships) further confused submarine commanders. The longer a submarine remained surfaced to gather all the evidence, the longer its period of liability.

At first, the Germans authorized submarines to attack only warships. In the early months of the war, they sank four cruisers and a pre-Dreadnought battleship, providing ample evidence of the potential of submarine warfare against unarmed merchantmen. Other early events suggested that, disadvantages notwithstanding, the Germans might be able to gain important maritime advantages. The daring rush of the *Goeben* and *Breslau* into Turkish waters had been a major morale boost for the Germans and a humiliation for the Royal Navy. German cruisers harassed British shipping in Sumatra, Zanzibar, Madras, and Brazil. Two more British cruisers fell to German action in November off the coast of Chile in the Battle of Coronel.

First Sea Lord Admiral John "Jackie" Fisher and the Royal Navy responded with the type of aggressive action that Britain expected of them. Fisher rushed a squadron of ships to South America, reaching the Falkland Islands from Portsmouth in just three weeks. There they hunted down the German cruisers, sinking four of them and effectively ending the German threat to British convoy lines in the South Atlantic and eastern Pacific Oceans. Unbeknownst to the Germans, the British also had a set of the German codes, provided to them by the Russians from a wrecked German ship in the Baltic Sea. The British established a top-secret project, known as Room 40, to crack the German codes and enable them to divine the activities of the German Navy.

In January 1915 Room 40 produced its first important victory. A German cruiser squadron headed into the North Sea to clear the area of British patrols and to mine British approach lanes.

The British depended on their dominance of the seas to win the economic war. A British film crew recorded the sinking of the cruiser Blücher *in 1915, with 950 German sailors drowned. This still from that film was engraved on the cigarette cases of many Royal Navy officers. (National Archives)*

Thanks to Room 40, the British tracked the squadron's movement from Whitehall and, using radio communications, were able to direct British warships toward the oncoming German ships. Using their Dreadnoughts, the British won the ensuing engagement, known as the Battle of the Dogger Bank. British Dreadnoughts were so devastating that the Germans nicknamed their pre-Dreadnought battle ships "five-minute ships" in reference to their expected survival time in battle. The Germans lost the cruiser *Blücher* (ironically named for the Prussian field marshal who fought with Britain against Napoleon at Waterloo) and 950 sailors. Britain lost no ships and just 15 dead. As a result, the German surface fleet confined itself behind its defenses for the remainder of the year.

Halfway around the world, in the western Pacific, the German navy suffered repeated defeats. Japan, allied to Great Britain via a naval agreement signed in 1902, declared war on Germany in August 1914. Before the year was out, the Japanese had obtained a promise from the British that they could annex any German colonies north of the equator that they seized by conquest. Japan soon defeated German naval and land forces in China's Shandong Peninsula and occupied the Marshall, Caroline, and Mariana Islands as well as Palau. Australian and New Zealand forces seized German New Guinea, the Bismarck Archipelago, the Solomon Islands, and German Samoa. Without these Pacific bases, the Germans could not hope to interdict British Pacific sea lanes or Britain's critical links with India and Australia.

Therefore, if Germany were to use its navy to interfere with British commerce, it would have to rely on its submarines. On February 4, 1915, Germany announced unrestricted submarine warfare (USW) by declaring the waters around Great Britain to be a war zone. The Germans argued that USW had to be "most brutal" and that it would target shipping of all kinds, including those from neutral nations.[5] The navy therefore told its submarine commanders that they would not be held accountable for any neutral vessels sunk. The United States quickly protested, stating that it had the right to trade with any nation it pleased and that its citizens had the right to travel on any vessel of any nationality. President Wilson warned Germany that the United States would hold it responsible for any loss of American life or property.

USW and the British surface blockade therefore raised delicate questions of neutrality and legality. Neutrality admitted more than one definition. It could mean equal impact on the war for all belligerents, no impact on the war at all, or freedom to trade with any and all belligerents. The Americans firmly insisted on the last definition. In practice, American firms traded much more frequently with Britain and France than they did with the Central Powers, leading the Germans to argue that the United States was not a true neutral since its policies financially benefited the Allies.

The British responded to German attempts to order American goods by forcing American ships into British ports for inspection. If they discovered any contraband items destined for Germany, they seized the items and cancelled all future contracts between the British government and the items' manufacturer. Such a policy irritated American manufacturers, but was legal according to international law. The Americans and British also disagreed on the definition of contraband goods. The Americans insisted that cotton and food did not qualify as contraband, but the British took a more restricted view, seizing both. The British also seized ships headed to Holland, a neutral nation through which Germany expected to receive much of its goods. The Americans thus had complaints with both sides in the ongoing economic warfare on the high seas.

As the Germans saw the situation, American "neutrality" benefited the Allies to such an extent that the Americans became a virtual belligerent. Isolationism notwithstanding, many Germans were angry at what they perceived as a soft American foreign policy toward Britain. A German propaganda cartoon from this period lampooning American behavior showed two British thugs robbing Uncle Sam on a street corner. The British crooks say "Stop! Uncle Sam, you are carrying on your person contraband goods. Therefore we have no choice but to seize from you whatever we need." After the two thieves have run away, Uncle Sam says "Fortunately, they have left me my pen. I will be able to write an energetic protest!"[6]

Because the Americans insisted on maximum flexibility in their definition of neutrality, greater conflict with Germany was all but

OUR MUTUAL FRIEND

This political cartoon depicts American frustration with both British and German naval policies. The sinking of the Lusitania, *however, led many Americans to see the German policy as targeting people, not just commerce. (Library of Congress)*

inevitable. Distinctions between submarines and surface ships also proved to be critical. Submarines did not permit escort, and they had no room in which to store contraband goods or safeguard a ship's crew. They could only either sink a ship or let it pass. On May 7, 1915, the Germans sank the liner *Lusitania* off the coast of Ireland, killing 1,198 people, including 128 Americans. Wilson knew that the ship had been carrying contraband goods, but the loss of life led him to overlook the ship's cargo. Germany's callous reaction, striking a commemorative medal and continuing USW even as bodies continued to wash up on the Irish coast, only fanned American anger further. Neither did Americans accept the German argument that they were not responsible for the fate of the passengers on the *Lusitania* because the German government had taken out newspaper ads warning of the danger of traveling across the Atlantic.

The United States did not intervene in the war as a result of the *Lusitania*. The incident did, however, place sufficient diplomatic and economic pressure on Germany to force it to reconsider its use of USW. On August 19, German submarines torpedoed the British liner *Arabic*, with three more Americans losing their lives. American rhetoric became more bellicose. President Wilson's strongest critic and rival, former President Theodore Roosevelt, began to argue forcefully for American preparedness. "What befell Antwerp and Brussels," he wrote, "will surely someday befall New York, San Francisco, and may happen to many an inland city also."[7] Roosevelt soon became one of the leaders of a Preparedness movement that had little support from the Wilson administration, but plenty of economic support from the nation's elite. Reminiscent of his Rough Rider days of 1898, Roosevelt called for the creation of at least one division of American volunteers to be ready to fight in Europe if and when the need arose.

Wilson, while arguing that the United States was "too proud to fight," nevertheless protested the sinkings to the German ambassador with enough force to convince him that the United States might indeed declare war if USW continued. The ambassador, Count Johann von Bernstorff, had been in his post since 1908 and was married to an American. He knew from firsthand experience that the United States had isolationist sentiments, but that it also had enormous economic and military potential if it chose to use them. Himself a political moderate and an opponent of USW, Bernstorff advised the German government to change course. On September 1, 1915, the Germans issued a pledge to follow the laws of warfare, meaning that a ship would receive notice before a sinking and would be permitted to remove its passengers to lifeboats. In practice, the Germans ended USW altogether and even offered the American government an indemnity for the lives lost. For the time being at least, USW was over.

The *Lusitania* incident did not incline Americans to seek war in order to support the cause of the Allies, but it did make it impossible for the United States to sympathize with Germany. The Americans continued to protest British policy; but, as Wilson himself said, British policies merely inconvenienced people—German policies killed them. Wilson continued to insist that the United States remain neutral, even forbidding the army's general staff from preparing war plans. Wilson proudly campaigned for reelection in 1916 under the slogan that he had "kept us out of war." His narrow victory over Republican Charles Evans Hughes that fall returned him to the White House after a campaign in which the Democrats often accused the Republicans of being linked to "militaristic extremists" like Roosevelt.[8] The close election revealed the growing difference of opinion among Americans regarding the war in Europe.

JUTLAND AND THE RESUMPTION OF USW

German naval frustrations led to reconsiderations and new personnel at the top. Admiral Reinhard Scheer replaced the terminally ill Hugo von Pohl as commander of the High Seas Fleet in

January 1916. Scheer proposed a renewed surface war against the Royal Navy and advocated the immediate resumption of USW. German Army commander Erich von Falkenhayn agreed. In March, however, the kaiser decided against resuming USW after the accidental sinking of the *Sussex,* a ferry ship that a submarine commander had mistaken for a troop transport. Three Americans were among the fifty people who died, prompting another demand from President Wilson for the Germans to renounce submarines. The German Reichstag responded with an immediate call for USW to be resumed. Just two days later, a German submarine sank a hospital ship, killing 115 patients, nurses, and crew. The international outrage was enough to lead the German government to issue a new pledge in May that it would obey the laws of warfare.

Scheer and the German admirals disagreed with the decision to abandon USW and believed that politicians had shackled Germany's best naval asset, its submarines. Scheer understood that the German surface fleet's qualitative and quantitative inferiorities placed it at a tremendous disadvantage. Still, he did not want the High Seas Fleet to remain idle. The longer Germany waited to seek action, he argued, the larger the gap between British and German naval power would become. He therefore hatched an aggressive and ambitious plan to defeat the Royal Navy by separating its constituent parts. He did not believe that he could destroy the Royal Navy, but he did believe that he could inflict enough damage to begin to turn the naval tide toward Germany's advantage.

On May 31, 1916, elements of the German fleet left its bases in two groups. The first, commanded by Admiral Franz von Hipper, was designated as the bait. Hipper was to steam north to lure the British battle cruisers in the North Sea towards him, then turn south, leading the pursuing British directly into the teeth of the second German group, commanded by Scheer himself. Hipper's group contained 40 fast surface ships and 16 submarines. The lat-

German submariners were spared the horrors of the western front,
but, as this photograph shows, they did not have a comfortable war.
The Germans lost 178 U-boats and their crews during the war.
(National Archives)

ter would deploy ahead of the surface squadron and interdict any
attempt by the capital ships of the Grand Seas Fleet to come to
the rescue of the battle cruisers. The physical and psychological
damage to the Royal Navy, Scheer hoped, would offer Germany a
chance for another victory at a time and place of its choosing.

Room 40's cryptologists gave the British advance warning of
Scheer's plan. On May 16 they discovered the departure of the
German submarines and identified their approximate locations.
The British battle cruisers therefore appeared to fall for the bait,
but they carefully eluded the submarine net, as did the battleships
that followed. A key component of Scheer's plan therefore failed
from the outset. The British also knew that Hipper had command
of the bait squadron. His bombardment of the British coastline in
1914 had resulted in what were then considered heavy civilian ca-

sualties and earned him the nickname "the baby killer" in the British press. Now the Royal Navy had a chance at revenge.

Commanding the British battle cruisers was Admiral David Beatty, a veritable prototype of the British naval officer. Handsome, dashing, and bold, Beatty enjoyed the absolute confidence of Jellicoe, Fisher, and Churchill. Thanks to rapid responses to Room 40's intelligence, the British held a large numerical advantage. Beatty's scout force possessed 52 ships, including 4 brand-new Dreadnoughts. Jellicoe followed with the main strike force of 99 ships, including 24 Dreadnoughts. Hipper's bait squadron led the British into Scheer's main force, which held 59 ships, including all 16 German Dreadnoughts. Britain thus held a 28 to 16 advantage in Dreadnoughts and a 26 to 11 advantage in cruisers. Thanks to Room 40, Germany's 45 submarines never saw action.

The battle plans for each side were thus mirror images. Hipper was planning to ambush the British, who, having learned his intentions, had set a trap for him. The British would likely have won a crushing victory if not for a design failure that proved to be deadly. British cruisers went to battle vulnerable to fire that moved down from the gun turrets to the magazines below. The highly explosive ammunition storage areas sat dangerously exposed. Accurate German fire opened up at 3:30 on the afternoon of May 31, destroying three British cruisers and nearly sinking Beatty's own flagship. "There seems to be something wrong with our bloody ships today," Beatty famously remarked.

Sensing his disadvantage, Beatty turned north to lure the Germans into Jellicoe's powerful Dreadnought force. Hipper, and Scheer behind him, both followed, unaware of the presence of Jellicoe to the north. Once in range, Jellicoe's ships twice performed the elegant naval maneuver of "crossing the enemy's T," meaning that his ships could unleash their full fury. His Dreadnoughts, moreover, did not suffer from the design flaw that had crippled Beatty's cruisers. During the second crossing of the T,

Jellicoe scored twenty-seven hits to Scheer's two. The British fleet then began to position itself between Scheer and his home ports, hoping to cut the German ships off from protection and destroy them. The onset of darkness allowed Scheer to escape the noose and get back to German bases.

On the tactical level, Jutland could be counted a German victory. Britain lost 3 battle cruisers, 3 light cruisers, 8 destroyers, and 6,784 sailors. Germany lost 1 pre-Dreadnought battleship, 1 battle cruiser, 4 light cruisers, 5 destroyers, and 3,039 sailors. The kaiser viewed Jutland as a great German success, handing out medals and declaring that "the magic of Trafalgar has been broken."[9] The German fleet, hopeful that the kaiser had been right, sortied out again in August, but again British cryptographers detected the move. This time, German zeppelins observed the movement of Jellicoe's battleships south, and Scheer abandoned the plan.

The August encounter demonstrates that, numbers notwithstanding, the battle of Jutland was in fact a British triumph, albeit not on the Trafalgar model. After Jutland, the German High Seas fleet rarely left the security of its bases, leaving the surface of the North Sea to the Royal Navy. The British, moreover, could more easily absorb the numerical losses in both men and ships, meaning that Jutland did nothing to reduce Britain's relative advantage. In the end, the war's largest naval battle had little strategic impact on the war. It certainly did not change the fortunes of the armies on the western front, nor did it enable Germany to break Britain's surface blockade, which was coming to have a deeper and deeper impact on the lives of German civilians.

As a result of Jutland, the kaiser promoted Scheer and gave him Germany's highest award, the French-inspired *Pour le Mérite.* Scheer nevertheless understood that a surface victory against Britain was increasingly unlikely. He therefore resumed his arguments for the reintroduction of USW. Scheer dismissed the likelihood that USW would bring the United States into the war, but Chancellor Theobald von Bethmann Hollweg did not. In late August he succeeded in keeping the kaiser from resuming USW. The arguments for USW were, however, winning over more and more converts. With the ground war deadlocked and the surface war seemingly unwinnable, USW grew more and more appealing.

In December 1916 the German navy prepared and presented the Holtzendorff Memorandum. Its principal author, Admiral Henning von Holtzendorff, had come out of retirement in 1915 to head the German Navy. The kaiser held him in much greater respect than did his fellow admirals. Holtzendorff did, however, agree with the consensus opinion in the German navy that USW had to be resumed. On January 9, 1917, he told the kaiser that USW could force Britain out of the war in six months or less, long before the Americans could have an impact even if they did declare war. Bethmann Hollweg reiterated his concerns about the impact of USW on American popular opinion and warned the kaiser that the resumption of USW might lead the Americans to enter the war, with tragic consequences for Germany. Holtzendorff argued that American belligerence would only provide more targets for German submarines, including American troop transports. In one of the biggest misjudgments of the war, he told the kaiser, "I will give Your Majesty my word as an officer that not one American will land on the continent."[10]

On February 1, 1917, Germany announced its resumption of USW. In April, German submarines sank 881,000 tons of shipping, compared to 386,000 in January. Holtzendorff had been correct in arguing that the heavy shipping losses would affect Great Britain. But Bethmann Hollweg, who had by then joined the kaiser, Hindenburg, and Ludendorff in supporting USW, had also been right. On April 6, the United States declared war against Germany. The race was now on. Germany would need to win the war before the Americans could translate their massive resources into military assets.

THE WAR IN THE MIDDLE EAST AND THE ARAB REVOLT

The waters around the home islands remained the Royal Navy's most pressing concern, but the security of the Suez Canal was almost as important, for several reasons. Obviously, the loss of the canal would greatly lengthen British sea communications with Persia, India, Australia, and other points east. The British also feared that the loss of the canal might lead to the loss of all of Egypt. Although Egypt was far less important to the British Empire than India, British leaders understood that the Ottoman reconquest of Egypt would serve as a major propaganda victory in Ottoman attempts to define the war as a pan-Islamic struggle against the Christian allies. The possibility of an Islamic revolt in India haunted British planners and gave the kaiser another motivation for supporting the Ottoman Empire. In one of his less coherent tirades, the kaiser had ranted, "Our consuls in Turkey and India, our agents, etc., must rouse the whole Moslem world into wild rebellion . . . ; if we are going to shed our blood, then England must at least lose India."[11]

The link between India and Egypt grew even closer when the British decided to use Indian soldiers to guard the Suez Canal region. Although occupied by Great Britain, by law Egypt remained an Ottoman province under the religious guidance of the Turkish sultan. The Egyptian Khedive, Abbas Himli II, had openly pro-Ottoman sympathies and had been in Constantinople when the war began. The British forced his deposition in favor of his more pliant uncle and declared martial law in November 1914. Henry McMahon, who replaced Kitchener as High Commissioner for Egypt when the latter became Secretary of State for War, decided against using Egyptians for the defense of Suez because of their presumed pro-Ottoman sentiments. Two Indian infantry divisions thus formed the backbone of Britain's Egyptian strategy, which established the canal itself as the main line of defense, surrendering Sinai to the Ottomans.

In February 1915 the Ottomans attacked the canal, hoping to seize Suez and inspire a revolt of Egyptians against the British. To avoid gunfire from Royal Navy warships, the Ottomans aimed their assault at the center of the canal. Two companies of Ottoman soldiers crossed the canal but could not hold their positions. Significantly, no uprising occurred inside Egypt. The offensive, which the British read as little more than a raid, had failed. Despite the ease with which they had defended the canal, the British soon increased the force defending it to 150,000 men, who were lavishly supplied in contrast to their Ottoman foes.

Throughout 1915, frustrations at Gallipoli led the British to a renewed respect for their Ottoman foes and a determination not only to hold Suez, but also to protect it by advancing into the Sinai. The British improved rail lines in the region and dug more water wells to support an offensive. They also moved gunboats into the canal itself. To organize this force, which had grown to twelve divisions by January 1916, Kitchener sent General Sir Archibald Murray, a veteran of British colonial operations worldwide and the former chief of staff to Sir John French. Murray quickly set to work organizing the Egyptian theater for both the defense of the canal and an offensive as far as Palestine and Gaza.

Simultaneously, Ottoman successes at Gallipoli led to Turkish confidence that their soldiers could take the canal with a fresh effort. Throughout the year, the Ottomans improved their own rail and road links from the front line to the Ottoman Fourth Army headquarters at Beersheba. In April 1916 the Ottomans stopped a British advance on the oasis of Qatiya, east of the canal. In August, they advanced close enough to the canal to damage it with artillery fire, but Murray drove them back at the cost of 16,000 Ottoman casualties. The British, who had suffered only 1,500 casualties, decided not to pursue because of a lack of drinking water, a major factor during the hot Sinai summer.

To the east, the Ottomans formed a new Sixth Army to hold off a British advance from Basra in Mesopotamia. Its commander

Australian soldiers on camels as they train in Libya for the Palestine campaign. Australian Light Horse regiments played a critical role in the fighting in the Middle East. (Australian War Memorial, negative no. H12853)

was a seventy-two-year-old Prussian field marshal, Colmar von der Goltz. Formerly the military governor of occupied Belgium, von der Goltz had been reassigned to Constantinople after having fallen from favor with the German political leaders, who had grown frustrated at what they saw as his soft treatment of the Belgians. As commander of the Sixth Army, he dreamed of leading an Ottoman invasion from Mesopotamia into Persia and perhaps even into the crown jewel of the British empire, India.

First, however, von der Goltz had to deal with a combined British and Indian force led by Sir Charles Townshend that by July 1915 had entered the Mesopotamian cities of Nasiriya on the Euphrates and Amara on the Tigris. From Amara, Townshend moved north 150 miles to Kut, which he planned to use as his main base for an offensive on Baghdad, just 80 miles further up the Tigris River. Ottoman General Nurettin Pasha set up his defense 20 miles south of Baghdad, at Ctesiphon. Protecting his right flank by anchoring it on the river, Nurettin established two solid defensive lines with 20,000 troops, many of them from first-rate Ottoman units.[12] Outnumbered, in hostile territory, and without hope of reinforcement, Townshend nevertheless attacked, counting on Ottoman morale to break as it had at Nasiriya. By the end of November, the British and Indian force had succeeded in seizing the Ottoman first line, but could not break through the second line. Ottoman morale held despite suffering twice the number of casualties that the British had taken.

Unable to take Baghdad, Townshend decided to withdraw to his base at Kut, which he reached on December 3. With his back to the Tigris River, Townshend had a garrison of 11,600 British and Indian soldiers, 3,300 noncombatants, and 7,000 locals under his care. He estimated that his ammunition and food could last sixty days. His forces easily defeated a Christmas Eve attack by Nurettin's forces, leaving Townshend confident in his ability to withstand the Ottomans until relief arrived. The Ottomans, however, rapidly surrounded the city and starved the garrison out while additional forces stopped three British efforts to relieve the garrison. In one case, the Ottomans stopped a ship carrying 270,000 tons of food by stretching a metal chain across the Tigris River. Two Ottoman divisions wore out the Kut defenders by constantly forcing them to respond to feigned attacks.

Townshend's two-month food supply quickly dwindled. The men held on into April, eating their horses and any other unfortunate animals living in Kut. Disease soon ravaged the camp, with cholera (which also affected the besiegers, killing von der Goltz in April) weakening the men even further. The British government, desperate to avoid the humiliation of a mass surrender, offered the Ottomans £2 million in gold in exchange for the garrison's safe release. The British also promised that, if released, none of the men from Kut would be returned to military service against Turkey. The Ottomans refused.

Finally, on April 29, 1916, Townshend surrendered along with 2,591 British and 6,988 Indian soldiers. Of that group, more than half died either en route to prisoner of war camps or in Ottoman captivity. Townshend was one of the survivors. Instead of sending him to a prison camp, the Ottomans established him in a villa on the island of Prinkipo near Constantinople. They afforded him excellent treatment and even allowed him to go hunting. The contrast between his comfortable existence and the wretched experience of those under his command forever haunted Townshend, who had signed what was then the largest capitulation in British history.

Unable to achieve rapid military decisions and faced with unexpected Ottoman resolve, the British turned to diplomacy and intrigue. As the Germans were attempting to instigate an Islamic revolt in India and Egypt, the British were attempting to spark an Islamic revolt in Arabia. While neither produced results that quite matched their authors' expectations, the British variant proved to be significantly more effective. For Britain, an Arab revolt in the land of the Islamic holy cities would undermine the Ottoman caliph's calls for jihad, thereby splitting the Islamic world. It might also offer a chance to create a British-influenced Arab empire to complement the one Britain already had in India. To Kitchener, an old Egypt and Sudan veteran, the plan had particular appeal.

Even before the war, Kitchener had been engaged in conversations with Emir Abdullah ibn-Hussein, second son of the Sharif of Mecca, who held the title of King of the Hejaz (roughly corresponding to western Arabia). The Hussein family boasted lineage to the prophet Mohammed and therefore had the figurative power to offer a rival Islamic voice to the Ottomans.[13] The family also resented Young Turk attempts to suppress Arab culture and further Turkish control of Arab territories, the latter symbolized by the construction of the Hejaz railroad (largely financed with German money), which enabled the Ottomans to move soldiers into Arab lands more rapidly. Accordingly, the Husseins did not support the Ottoman call for jihad in November 1914, although they stopped well short of declaring support for the Allies.

Throughout the war's early months, Sharif Hussein learned of the pro-independence sentiments of many Arab officers inside the Ottoman army. In July 1915, he sent McMahon a letter indicating his willingness to initiate an Arab revolt if the British agreed to support the independence of an Arab state under the Husseins at the end of the war. McMahon agreed, although he was careful to leave the exact borders of future Arab lands vague. Sufficient to secure Hussein's support, McMahon's letter later caused great confusion when British and Arab understandings of the borders conflicted. The Hussein-McMahon agreement also contradicted the 1917 Balfour Declaration, in which the British government promised to support a Jewish homeland in Palestine. To complicate matters even further, the British recognized Hussein's rival, Ibn Saud, as ruler of eastern Arabia, and signed the Sykes-Picot Agreement, a secret pact with France that would divide most of the Ottoman Empire's Arab lands between France and Britain.

Unsure of Britain's trustworthiness, Hussein hesitated to call for an Arab revolt until the June 1916 Ottoman dispatch of troops to the garrison in the Arabian city of Medina. Hussein and his eldest son, Emir Faisal, reacted by leading an attack on the Hejaz railway and isolating Medina. The Arab revolt had begun. A mercurial British officer who spoke fluent Arabic and had, according to his British colleagues, "gone native," arrived as a liaison officer to the Arabs in October 1916. T. E. Lawrence ("Lawrence of Arabia") quickly identified Faisal as the most promising of the Arab leaders. It was the start of a relationship that eventually took Lawrence to the Paris Peace Conference as Faisal's advisor.

The Medina garrison held out despite the revolt, but Arab forces, 50,000 strong, seized the holy city of Mecca and three

Red Sea ports within a month. The British provided arms and Royal Navy transports across the Red Sea to facilitate Arab efforts. Faisal, with Lawrence by his side, provided inspired leadership and proved to have an aptitude for guerrilla warfare. The Arabs cut rail lines, distracted thousands of Ottoman soldiers, and made a British offensive into Sinai possible. In August 1917, 2,000 Arabs entered Aqaba, a key Red Sea port, marking a dramatic turning point in the Arab revolt.

Lawrence then rode across the Sinai, arriving in Cairo to report on the capture of Aqaba and the larger success of the Arab revolt. There he learned of the secret Sykes-Picot Agreement, which threatened to deny Arab independence after the war. Meeting up with Faisal again, Lawrence urged Arab forces to push further and harder, hoping that Britain and France would not be able to deny the Arabs the independence of lands already in their possession. Damascus, under the French zone according to Sykes-Picot, quickly became the Arab goal. In October 1918, just before the end of the war, Arab forces entered the city, adding more confusion to an already complicated postwar picture in the Middle East.

The British made many contradictory and confusing promises in order to win the war, and those promises later proved to have many unforeseen complications; but at the time that the Arab revolt began, the British moves seemed to be paying enormous dividends. The British had been preparing for a general offensive into Sinai, building 140 miles of railroads and 15 miles of water lines per month.[14] In March 1917, as a renewed British offensive in Mesopotamia finally seized Baghdad, the British attacked into Gaza. The British enjoyed initial success, but failed to follow it up. A second attack in April involved tanks, gas, and naval gunfire support, but it too failed, with 6,400 British casualties.

The First and Second Battles of Gaza led to important changes on both sides. The British replaced Murray with General Edmund Allenby, whose failures on the western front had led to what he considered a demotion to a backwater front. British Prime Minister David Lloyd George, who had grown frustrated with the stalemate on the western front, told the temperamental Allenby that he did not see Palestine as a minor theater. The prime minister informed Allenby that he would support a large-scale offensive in Palestine, but he expected Jerusalem to be in British hands by Christmas. Lloyd George made good his promise by sending tanks, airplanes, and reinforcements.

British goals in Palestine went beyond merely delivering a battlefield defeat to the Ottoman Empire. Secret negotiations between the British and French had already placed Palestine into an "international" area to be administered by the British. In reality, the scheme promised to add Palestine, Trans-Jordan, and Iraq into the British Empire in everything but name. Allenby told a colleague before leaving England that he would ensure that "the 1,335 years of Mohammedan rule [in Palestine] would end in 1917."[15] Just weeks after his arrival in the Middle East, Allenby learned of the death of his only son in battle on the western front. He folded the telegram and placed it in his pocket without saying a word. He threw himself body and soul into capturing Jerusalem. Allenby moved his headquarters from the hotel room in Cairo that Murray had used to the front lines and became as visible as any British commander during the entire war.

The Central Powers did not remain passive. In May 1917, the Ottomans accepted the arrival of German General Erich von Falkenhayn, who created the Yildrim (lightning) Army Group. Falkenhayn placed sixty-five German officers (as opposed to just nine Ottoman officers) in staff positions. This German dominance led Mustafa Kemal to resign his position as commander of one of the Yildrim armies and return to Constantinople, complaining that Falkenhayn had turned Turkey into a "German colony."[16] Falkenhayn placed the Yildrim Army Group along a line from Gaza to Beersheba, where it faced a British force that had a 2 to 1 advantage in infantry and an 8 to 1 advantage in cavalry.

Allenby boldly attacked Beersheba on the night of October 31, with a full moon illuminating the way. A daring cavalry charge by the Australian Light Horse allowed the British to capture the city and its critical water wells intact. The next day, British artillery prepared an attack on Gaza with 15,000 shells. Falkenhayn had little choice but to stage a fighting withdrawal, allowing British forces to enter Palestine and capture Jaffa, Jerusalem's chief port, on November 16.

Allenby planned to take Jerusalem itself via a rapid encirclement, both to spare the city damage and to fulfill his pledge to Lloyd George. The first British attempt failed on November 25, but it became clear that Ottoman morale was cracking. On December 8, Ottoman forces began their withdrawal from the holy city, allowing Allenby to enter it on December 11, two weeks ahead of schedule. Four centuries of Ottoman rule in Mecca, Baghdad, and Jerusalem were over.

Anticipating a German attack in France in 1918, the British sent many elements of Allenby's force back to the western front. Still, in the spring, Allenby resumed the offensive, taking Jericho in February and raiding Amman in March, causing Falkenhayn to be demoted to Lithuania. By the end of the summer, Arab and British forces were working in tandem, with the former harassing Ottoman lines of communication and latter bringing air and artillery assets to bear. At the Battle of Meggido in September the British annihilated the Turkish Eighth Army, opening the roads to Nazareth, Haifa, Acre, and Damascus. In the war's final weeks, the Ottomans lost Beirut, Aleppo, and Mosul as well.

The Palestine and Arabian campaigns thus marked significant military victories for Great Britain. Their many promises to many groups, however, soon created an untenable situation. The British reneged on the implied guarantees in the Hussein-McMahon letters and also reneged on a promise to the 5,000 volunteers of the Jewish Legion that they could settle in Palestine after the war. They also delayed implementing the Balfour Declaration. Instead,

Britain stayed true to the Sykes-Picot Agreement, which gave the British control of Palestine, Trans-Jordan, and Mesopotamia while France took control of Lebanon and Syria. The result was a series of anti-Jewish Arab riots in 1920 and 1921 and a Gordian knot that the British could not possibly cut. The Middle East's tortured twentieth century had been born.

6

BLEEDING FRANCE WHITE

The Agony of Verdun

> My friends, we must take Verdun. Before the end of February, the conquest must be complete. The Emperor will then arrive and hold a grand review on the Place d'Arms in Verdun and there we will sign the peace treaty.
>
> —Crown Prince Wilhelm to his troops, February 1916

"We have made Italy," said Giuseppe Garibaldi shortly after Italian unification in the 1860s; "now we must make Italians." A half century later, that process remained woefully incomplete. Localism remained powerful, and regional distinctions often overrode nationalist impulses. The concept of an Italian nation was still embryonic in 1914, and serious obstacles stood in the way of efforts to form a unified state. As in other multiethnic European states, the Italian elite envisioned using the army as a unifying force, to teach local men what it meant to be Italian and, more pragmatically, how to speak and read the national language instead of local dialect. In some regiments, this aim far superseded that of efficiency, leading to a gross imbalance in the quality of Italian units. In 1914, the social and cultural unification of Italy through a common military experience had yet to come to fruition. Most Italians, especially those in the south, continued look upon the new state with more suspicion than affection.

These internal divisions combined with budget problems to impair the modernization of the Italian military. Officers and men were poorly paid and were used mostly to break strikes and quell domestic unrest, a role that did little to increase either unit morale or national sentiment. Materially, the army was short of almost everything, possessing just 595 motor vehicles and 8 aircraft squadrons in 1914. Italian industry stood in no position to rectify these shortcomings. As late as May 1915 Italian factories produced 27,000 fewer artillery shells per month than the minimum number the army deemed necessary. Civil-military relations were among the worst in Europe, and the army suffered the unexpected blow of the death of its chief of staff on July 1, 1914, just as the continental crisis began to brew.

With the developing crisis in Europe, the Italian government decided to fill the void at the top of the army by naming Luigi Cadorna to be its commander. Cadorna was the son of the legendary Raffaele Cadorna, the general who occupied the Vatican States in 1870. Luigi was ready to retire when the unexpected vacancy at the top emerged. His father's name, his royal connections, and his Piedmontese pedigree seemed to offer stability and predictability. He was, however, a poor choice. He had never heard a shot fired in anger and had been severely criticized for simplistic tactics at the 1911 Italian war maneuvers. His writings reflected outdated and mediocre strategic thinking that stressed frontal charges and underplayed the role of firepower. Worse still, he believed that only the harshest discipline could make soldiers out of southern Italians, whom he considered little better than mules. Arrogant and paranoid, Cadorna proved to be one of the worst senior commanders of the twentieth century.

ITALY AND THE ISONZO

Italy had few compelling state interests affected by the July crisis, and it was not directly threatened by any of the Great Powers. It had been a signatory to the Triple Alliance, binding it by treaty to Germany and Austria-Hungary. Few European diplomats believed that Italy would honor those obligations. Since the 1882 signing of the alliance, which had been conceived as protection against France, tensions between Italy and Austria-Hungary had steadily risen. Italian nationalists stirred up public ire against Austrian oc-cupation of areas with significant Italian populations, most nota-bly the strategic Tyrol area, the Isonzo River valley, and the port cities of Fiume and Trieste. Predictably, as the July crisis grew, It-aly argued that because Austria-Hungary had been the aggressor against Serbia and the Triple Alliance was a defensive arrange-ment, Italy was not bound to enter the war. In public, Austrian and German officials expressed outrage at what they called Italian perfidy, but in private few of them expressed any great surprise or even any great disappointment.

Neutrality would have served the Italians best, but Cadorna and others saw the war as a chance to annex "Italian" territory and increase their influence in Albania. A victory of arms, they hoped, would propel their young nation into the ranks of Europe's great powers and unite the Italian people. Because most of the territory they sought lay inside the Austro-Hungarian Empire, an alliance with Britain and France made the most sense. Italy's long, exposed coastlines, moreover, made a war with Britain a particularly un-pleasant option. Russia's initial successes in the Carpathians weak-ened the Austrians, who, facing several fronts, appeared to be an easy target.

In March 1915 the Italians approached Britain with an offer to enter the war if the Allies would recognize Italian annexation of southern Tyrol, the Trentino, Gorizia, Gradisca, Trieste, Istria, Dalmatia, and the Albanian port of Valona. These conditions rep-resented a considerable reach and undermined Italy's own nation-alist logic, but they cost the Allies nothing at all. Britain, anxious to see the Italian navy as an ally and not a threat to Mediterranean lines of communication, convinced Russia and France to accept the Italian conditions. In the resulting Treaty of London, signed in April, the Allies also agreed to protect the Italian coast and shipping lanes, continue Russian offensives against Austria-Hun-gary to prevent the latter from threatening Italy, increase Italy's Af-rican empire by adding Eritrea and Ethiopia, and loan Italy £50

Not all soldiers spent the war in trenches. These elite Italian ski troops on the Isonzo front were trained to infiltrate enemy lines and destroy communications and supplies. (United States Air Force Academy McDermott Library Special Collections)

million for military modernization. In the diplomatic realm, Italy had done quite well for itself.

In order to claim all of these promises, however, Italy would have to win on the battlefield. On paper, it held many advantages. The Italians could focus their 900,000-man army on a single enemy, Austria-Hungary, while the Austro-Hungarians were already engaged against Serbia and Russia. Conversely, the Italian front would of necessity have to be a secondary one for Austria, giving Italy numerical superiority. Enormous Austrian losses in the Carpathians in 1914, moreover, had destroyed much of its army's professional core. Cadorna confidently predicted an easy victory, claiming that he and his men would walk to Vienna.

The road to Vienna, however, went through the Isonzo River valley and the heights of the Julian Alps. It was ideal terrain for the defender and anything but a walk for the attackers. Austro-

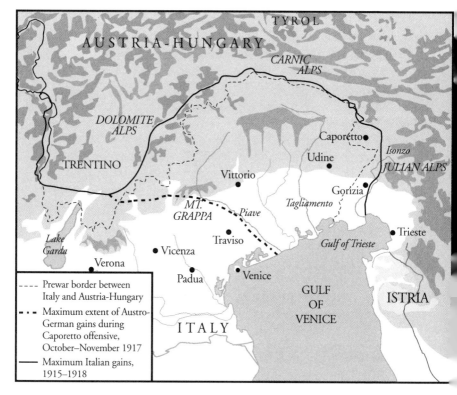

The Italian front, 1915–1918

Hungarian troops, moreover, were outraged by Italy's entry into the war. They were reminded that Italy had used Austria's preoccupation with Prussia in the 1866 war to seize Venice and its surrounding areas. Italy soon became the enemy that all of the empire's many ethnic groups could rally to fight. Thus war against Italy became the one part of the war that Austro-Hungarians saw as "necessary and just." Such unity of purpose did not exist on the Serbian and Russian fronts.[1]

To command the defense of the Isonzo, the Austrians assigned Svetozar Boroević, a talented Croatian general. He had been one of the few Austro-Hungarian generals to lead well in the Carpathians in 1914, preventing a much larger Russian force from crossing the mountains and later turning back a Russian push toward Cracow. Conrad, with whom he had fallen out of favor, believed that Boroević's experiences in mountain warfare in 1914 would serve him well against the Italians at the Isonzo. He therefore decided to give Boroević another chance as commander of a new Fifth Army.

Low on manpower and ammunition, Boroević set out to make maximum use of the terrain. Cadorna decided to attack before Italian forces had fully mobilized. He hoped to rush through the Austro-Hungarian positions before Boroević could establish them. Still, the Austrians had more than 114,000 men and 230 heavy artillery pieces along the Italian front by late May. Cadorna's inexperienced and ill-equipped army had a large numerical superiority (there were 400,000 Italians in the region by June), but lacked wire cutters, heavy artillery, ammunition, reconnaissance aircraft, even steel helmets. The First Battle of the Isonzo lasted from June 23 to July 7. The Italians established some strategic positions, but lost 15,000 men and failed to break through. Cadorna's easy walk to Vienna had begun poorly.

Nevertheless, Cadorna tried again almost immediately. Italy's agreement with the Allies had stipulated that Russia would assist Italy by mounting continuous pressure against the Austrians. Instead, Russian setbacks at Gorlice-Tarnów forced the Italians to attack before they wanted to in order to relieve the beleaguered Russians. In the Second Battle of the Isonzo, the Italians succeeded in forcing Austria to transfer eight more divisions to the region by the end of the year, but this battle yielded nothing more than temporary gains. In October, Cadorna launched his third Isonzo offensive, again without adequate artillery. It, too, failed.

Cadorna tried one more attack before the year ended. In November, amid snow, food shortages, and an outbreak of cholera, the Italians pushed the Austrians back, but failed to take the key

*The terrain on the Isonzo front presented tremendous problems.
This remote outpost in the Julian Alps offered little protection from
harsh mountain winters. (United States Air Force Academy
McDermott Library Special Collections)*

town of Gorizia. The first four battles on the Isonzo had cost Italy
almost 230,000 dead and wounded. Cadorna had not been the
only general to suffer enormous losses in 1915, but he was the only
one who persisted in fighting on the same ground with essentially
the same tactics four times. His offensives had bled Italy of its best
prewar officers and soldiers as well as its enthusiastic early volunteers. In exchange, Cadorna had seized no important piece of
ground and had made himself look foolish for his earlier promises
of an easy war.

Cadorna reacted by blaming everyone around him, from journalists to junior officers to the "lazy" southern Italians who formed
the bulk of the army. He instituted a brutal disciplinary system
that convicted 170,000 men of various offenses, handed down
4,028 death sentences, and executed more men than were exe-

cuted in any other army. In some cases, the Italians resorted to the Roman Empire's practice of decimation, introduced into the Italian army by Cadorna in January 1916. Men were executed at random, either as a means of punishing a whole unit for substandard performance or for an individual crime when the perpetrator could not be found. As the war ground on and as men became increasingly dissatisfied with the performance of their generals, acts of indiscipline increased, leading to more and harsher punishment by military authorities.

The very randomness of the Italian disciplinary system worked against itself. In theory, random punishments were meant to scare men into behaving and fighting as Cadorna wished. Instead, men grew to hate their own officers so deeply that combat effectiveness broke down. Cadorna refused to consider any other method of improving morale, such as increased leave or the provision of better food. Even if one accepts the strategic necessity of his continuing the offensive, his unwillingness to listen to his soldiers' legitimate complaints reveals a man who did not want to learn. Harsh and unpredictable discipline remained his manner of dealing with his men.[2]

Cadorna was less apt to use decimation on his officers, but he turned his wrath on them as well. Men who challenged his judgment received demotions and transfers to other theaters and, in some extreme cases, were jailed for insubordination. Cadorna's headquarters remained a place where one did not question his outlook or strategy. He and his staff often quoted an old Piedmontese dictum that the "Superior is always right, especially when he is wrong."[3] He replaced so many officers that units lost continuity in their leadership. Programs to commission new officers had to be shortened to replace both the men who had died and the men Cadorna had removed from command. As a result, the Italian Army suffered from a terrible shortage of qualified leaders.

By the beginning of 1916, then, Italy was no closer to realizing any of its dreams then it had been when it had joined the Allies. Their own offensives had stalled and failed, with terrible human cost. Their British ally had failed in the Dardanelles and on the western front. Russia, from whom the Italians had expected help in occupying the Austria, had retreated from Poland and was in no shape to provide any meaningful assistance. As for France, it had survived the bloodletting of 1915, but in 1916 it was about to endure a trial of fire that no one could have imagined.

THE PLACE OF EXECUTION: VERDUN

General Erich von Falkenhayn spent the closing days of 1915 reassessing Germany's strategic position. On Christmas Day, he composed a memorandum for the kaiser in which he stated that the entry of Italy and the German failure to force Russia out of the war had given the Allies greater resources, which sooner or later they would bring to bear. By January 1916 the Allies would have 139 divisions in France and Belgium (including the divisions of the British New Armies) as opposed to 117 German divisions. Falkenhayn remained optimistic, however, because he believed that one of those Allies, namely France, was at the "limits of endurance." France, he believed, could be defeated in 1916 and, once France was defeated, Britain would have little choice but to sue for peace. "To achieve that object," he wrote, "the uncertain method of a mass breakthrough, in any case beyond our means, is unnecessary."[4] Falkenhayn had other ideas.

His plan amounted to "bite and hold" on a theater level. He planned to attack the French Army at a place so critical to France that Joffre would have no choice but to fight to the last man to take it back. The Germans would then be in a position to take advantage of their more tactically powerful defensive position and destroy the French as they attacked. In this way, Falkenhayn wrote, the Germans could "bleed France white" and, in the process, knock "England's best sword" out of her hands. Falkenhayn thus proposed to introduce attrition warfare on an enormous scale to the western front. He did not care about breaking enemy lines, capturing territory, or advancing on communication nodes. He sought instead to kill Frenchmen faster and more efficiently than they could kill Germans.[5]

Falkenhayn had a reputation for ruthlessness. He had introduced poison gas at Ypres, argued vehemently for unrestricted submarine warfare, and had sponsored a plan for random aerial bombardment of Allied cities. Casualties, including German casualties, bothered him even less than they did most of his colleagues. He held almost all of the German generals in contempt and admitted few of them into his confidence. This furtiveness later had important consequences. Falkenhayn flattered the kaiser (thereby improving the chances of his plan's being approved) by proposing to place the main attack under the kaiser's son, Crown Prince Wilhelm. Unwilling to tell the crown prince that the battle plan involved attrition and the spilling of blood on an entirely new scale, Falkenhayn instead led the crown prince to believe that his task would be nothing less than the honor of attaining the main objective. Thus the crown prince held a dangerously mistaken concept of Falkenhayn's plan. "Seldom in the history of war," wrote the battle's most famous historian, "can the commander of a great army have been so cynically deceived as was the German Crown Prince by Falkenhayn."[6]

The main objective, the crown prince believed, was to capture the city of Verdun. A fortified region since the time of the Romans, the very word Verdun meant "powerful fortress" in a pre-Roman Gallic dialect. The city was bisected by the Meuse River and guarded all communications from Metz to Reims and, 160 miles to the west, Paris. The great engineer and architect Vauban had built the city's first modern defenses for Louis XIV. After the Franco-Prussian War, France had reinvested in Verdun, building or improving 60 individual forts and outposts, along with miles of underground passageways and shelters. The largest single fortification, Fort Douaumont, covered almost eight acres of land and could protect a garrison of 500 to 800 soldiers.

Verdun's true significance for Falkenhayn's purposes lay not in its strategic value, but in its symbolic value. At Verdun in 843 Charlemagne had divided his empire into three parts: two of those portions formed the core of the future states of France and Germany, while the third developed into the middle battleground that included Alsace and Lorraine. In 1792 and 1870 Verdun had heroically withstood German sieges before eventually falling. According to French national legend, the fort's commander in 1792 had committed suicide rather than surrender Verdun to France's hereditary enemy. Painted on the door of Douaumont's main entrance were the words "Better to be buried under the ruins of the fort than to surrender it."

In the early days of the war, Verdun had held its position once again. Verdun had been the easternmost French position during the Battle of the Marne. Without Maurice Sarrail's staunch defense there, the rest of the French Army's effort at the Marne might well have been for naught. His successful defense left Verdun at the center of a salient that bulged deeply into German lines. Vigorous combat occurred near Verdun in the first half of 1915 as both sides sought unsuccessfully to move the lines in their favor. By the end of that year, however, Verdun was not as strong as it appeared. In fact, it was more susceptible to enemy attack than anyone on the German side knew. Had Falkenhayn actually wanted it and planned for its capture, Verdun might have been his for the asking.

Verdun's vulnerability resulted from the intentional neglect of the fortresses from the very people charged with its defense. The rapid German destruction of the forts of Belgium in 1914 convinced many French generals that fortifications had outlived their utility in modern warfare. Other French generals saw how well Verdun had held the Germans in 1914 and 1915 and concluded that the pride of French fortresses was impregnable. Both arguments implied that Verdun should not merit primary attention from French headquarters. The Germans had seemingly learned their lesson, moving their center of gravity north to Flanders in 1915. Verdun, French headquarters concluded, no longer figured into German plans.

Having decided that Verdun would remain a calm sector for the foreseeable future, Joffre removed many of the fortress's heavy artillery pieces. By doing so, he believed that he could compensate for the general lack of French heavy artillery and thereby give his 1915 Champagne offensive a better chance of succeeding. He also denuded the Verdun garrison of men, leaving just enough troops to form a single thin trench line to the north and east of the main fortifications. No true second line existed, just a series of poorly connected outposts and individual strongpoints. The French also had too few men to occupy the thick woods immediately opposite their position, thereby allowing the Germans to move and reinforce virtually undetected.

The vulnerability of the Verdun sector worried many of the officers charged with defending it, especially as evidence mounted of a German concentration there in late 1915. The commander of the Fortified Region of Verdun, an elderly artillery officer with the distinctly un-Gallic last name of Herr, had warned Joffre's staff about the weakness of his position. Fort Douaumont, once one of the most powerful forts in the world, had been reduced to just one gun larger than 75mm in caliber. Its 500-man garrison stood at just 60 reservists, most of whom were deemed too old for service in the trenches.[7] When Joffre's staff rebuked him for his criticisms, Herr informed War Minister Joseph Gallieni of Joffre's unwillingness to see the urgency in the situation at Verdun. "At every demand I addressed them [Joffre's staff] for reinforcement in artillery, they replied with the withdrawal of two [artillery] batteries or two and a half batteries; 'you will not be attacked. Verdun is not the point of attack. The Germans do not know that Verdun has been disarmed.'"[8]

Joffre and his staff ignored the mounting danger at Verdun in part because of their obsession with plans for their own offensive in 1916 along the Somme River. Joffre seems to have assumed that the Germans would remain inactive through the first half of the year. He therefore made the critical mistake of guessing that his enemies would do what he wanted them to do. Joffre and his staff dismissed Herr's worries and hoped for relative quiet on the western front until the time when they could themselves take the offensive, planned for midsummer.

Herr's was not the only voice warning of impending disaster. Another challenge came from Lt. Col. Emil Driant, a battalion commander in the woods outside Verdun and a member of the French Chamber of Deputies. Driant wrote to his colleagues to warn them of the danger that France faced if, as he predicted, a German attack on Verdun materialized. He particularly criticized Joffre for not establishing a solid second line of defense and frankly told the Deputies that France lacked the strength to defeat a determined German assault on this sacred national shrine. Joffre exploded with anger at what he considered an insubordinate act by an officer under his command. He also refused to take the advice of Gallieni, telling him that the Minister of War had no right to question operational decisions made by the commander-in-chief.

"I ask only one thing," Joffre blithely told a committee of concerned Parliamentarians: "that the Germans should attack and should do so at Verdun. Tell the government so."[9] Attack they did, in the opening phase of what Falkenhayn called Operation *Gericht* (Judgment). The assault opened on February 21, 1916, with the heaviest artillery concentration to date, employing over 1,600 artillery pieces. By one estimate, German guns fired 100,000 shells per hour along a narrow eight-mile front. The German heavy guns fired shells and gas at French artillery positions, rendering them ineffective in a process known as counter-battery fire. High-angle trench mortars struck the thin French first line, and howit-

One of the war's most terrifying innovations, the flamethrower, was often as dangerous to use as it was to face. Most flamethrower crews were, ironically, made up of men who had been firefighters in their civilian lives. (National Archives)

zers hit the few outposts on the French second line. The near-total tactical surprise of the assault left the French positions vulnerable to this immense weight of shells.

Artillery, however, was only part of the plan. Special Assault Detachment soldiers, more commonly known as storm troops, formed an integral element as well. All the armies had been working on the idea of forming small groups of fast-moving elite troops that could operate independently without waiting for orders from a higher unit. In October 1915 the Germans had experienced success with these formations in limited roles in the Vosges Mountains. At Verdun, the Special Assault Detachment worked with pioneer units to infiltrate French lines. Their mission was to cut French barbed wire and use a new invention, the flamethrower, to eliminate resistance from concrete machine gun outposts.[10] More conventional infantry followed the pioneers and storm troops to hold the ground thus gained, while reinforcements brought up supplies and entrenching materials.

The plan worked too well. By the second day of the assault, the Germans had captured virtually all of their objectives. The French position had crumbled so quickly that General Herr ordered the forts still in French hands to be rigged for demolition. This success placed Falkenhayn in an unexpected position. If the Germans actually seized Verdun, the French might decide that it could not be retaken and therefore not fall for the bait in his attempt to draw the enemy into a struggle of attrition. Paradoxically, the Germans might well hold a victory march through Verdun, but leave Falkenhayn without the bloody triumph he had sought.

Fortunately for Falkenhayn, and tragically for hundreds of thousands of men on both sides, Joffre did take up the challenge. Verdun had already become a symbol in yet another war. On day one of the attack, Driant and his two battalions of men had been in the Bois de Caures, directly in the path of the oncoming German assault. They fought, badly outnumbered, and when their ammunition ran out, they fought with bayonets. Driant held his position, tending to his wounded men and burning his papers before he was struck by a shell and killed. His heroism had slowed the German assault and set the model for French service at Verdun. In the words of French historian Pierre Miquel, "the infantry now knew that it had just one responsibility: to die as Driant and his soldiers had. . . . The mechanism of sacrifice was in place."[11]

French prisoners escorted away from Verdun. The tremendous blood-letting of the ten-month-long battle affected all of the subsequent events of the war and left scars that lasted well beyond 1918.
(Library of Congress)

A second major blow to French pride and prestige came on February 25, when a small but audacious group of German soldiers entered Fort Douaumont via an unguarded passageway. The stunned garrison of 57 second-line territorials surrendered the fort without firing a shot in its defense. Reputed to be the strongest fort in the world, Douaumont had fallen into German hands with stunning ease. Its loss immediately placed the entire French line in jeopardy. It also became an important symbol in Germany, where church bells rang and children were dismissed from school to celebrate a victory that might open the road to Paris and end the war within a matter of weeks.

Joffre, so slow to see the danger at Verdun, now reacted quickly. On February 25, he sent his second-in-command, Edouard Noël de Castelnau, to Verdun to assess the situation and recommend a course of action. General Herr advocated abandoning the right (east) bank of the Meuse and focusing French defenses on the left bank. Castelnau disagreed and ordered that both sides of the Meuse would be defended inch by inch at whatever the cost. Sensing the urgency, he issued the appropriate orders without clearing them with Joffre. He also decided that General Herr should be removed from command at Verdun.

In Herr's place, Castelnau gave authority for both banks of the river to a perceptive but gloomy general named Henri-Philippe Pétain. Pétain began the war as a colonel out of favor with the French military hierarchy because he had been a firm advocate of defensive warfare. "Firepower kills" was his oft-quoted maxim. In the days prior to the war, his thinking ran against accepted French orthodoxy and as a result his career stagnated. His defensive mind-set, however, was much better suited to the actual war of 1914 and 1915 than Joffre's doctrine of *offensive à outrance* (offensive to the utmost). As such, Castelnau thought Pétain the perfect general to command the defense of Verdun. While Castelnau was reaching this conclusion, Pétain was in a Paris hotel with the woman whose father had forbidden her to marry him because he did not want an army officer in the family. One of Pétain's staff officers found him there at three o'clock in the morning and told of him of his promotion to commander of the Second Army.

Pétain understood the dire nature of Verdun's situation as well as anyone. He saw the need to rush reinforcements, food, and ammunition to the region as quickly as possible. For the moment his pessimism receded. His famous exhortation "They shall not pass" became the watchwords of Verdun. Because of its position in the salient, however, Verdun could only be resupplied from one direction, the southwest. The only secure railroad in the sector stopped at Bar-le-Duc, almost fifty miles away. From there, one seven-yard-wide road led into Verdun. If Verdun were to hold out, that road, soon named *La Voie Sacrée* (Sacred Way), would have to carry sufficient supplies into the sector.

The French abandoned their reliance on the light 75mm field artillery piece. In its place came larger guns, such as this Schneider 155mm, which was introduced in the middle of the war. (United States Air Force Academy McDermott Library Special Collections)

To ensure a constant flow of men and materiel along *La Voie Sacrée*, Pétain enlisted the same *Service Automobile* that had rushed men to the front via taxicabs to the Battle of the Marne. Almost 9,000 men worked on the road day and night, adding stones to permit transport over winter and spring mud, building repair stations, and even operating hydraulic presses along the roadside to repair tires. In two weeks, *La Voie Sacrée* transported 190,000 men, 22,500 tons of munitions, and 2,500 tons of food and other supplies. By May 1, it had allowed Pétain to rotate 40 infantry divisions in and out of the Verdun sector. It was an amazing logistical feat, permitting the French to fire more than 5 million artillery shells in the battle's first seven weeks.[12]

This massive weight of shell and the dispatch of so many French soldiers turned Verdun into a gory slugging match between roughly equal armies. In May, the French began the bloody process of taking back all of the ground they had lost. Instead of attacking with rifles and bayonets as they had in 1914, however, they attacked with enormous quantities of artillery. Although they did not always achieve their immediate goals, the millions of shells the French fired caused casualties on the German side that Falkenhayn had never imagined. The German commander had counted on killing French soldiers at a 5 to 2 ratio. By late June, the French had indeed suffered terribly, with 275,000 casualties. But the Germans had suffered almost as badly, taking 240,000 casualties.

The "sausage grinder" of Verdun wore down both armies. The intense fighting continued day after day with little respite. Reinforcements from both sides could see, hear, and smell the battle from miles away as they approached Verdun. Pétain's policy of rotating men in and out of the sector kept men sane, but the knowledge that they would soon have to return contributed to a psychological malady that doctors soon termed "shell shock." Men with no physical wounds grew senseless and numb from fatigue and the constant presence of death. "It was often better to speak of those men as the condemned to die," recalled one French officer, "so many of their wits were shot and their faces yellowed. Thirst devoured them, they no longer had the strength to speak. I told them that tonight we would undoubtedly be relieved. The news left them indifferent, their only desire was for a liter of water."[13]

In an attempt to retake Fort Douaumont, the French fired 14 million pounds of shells in one week over an area barely 150 acres in size. It amounted to at least 120,000 individual artillery shells. Still the fort held, its subterranean passages offering its defenders shelter. Robert Bruce points out the "tragic irony" that Douaumont's powerful defenses, designed to protect the French, now sheltered the German army from French guns.[14] Douaumont remained in German hands throughout the summer. It had become as much a symbol of German resistance as it had once been of French power.

Control of Douaumont notwithstanding, Falkenhayn's grand plan had manifestly failed. The German army did not capture

Verdun, nor did it inflict the kinds of cheap casualties on the French that Falkenhayn had envisioned. As early as March, the crown prince had informed his father of his growing pessimism about the Verdun campaign, fueled, no doubt, by the realization that it was to be a battle of gory attrition, not glorious conquest. The crown prince grew increasingly frustrated and distant, spending more and more of his time chasing French women behind the lines while his men died by the thousands.

Frustrated with the course of the campaign, the kaiser relieved Falkenhayn in August, sending him east to fight the Romanians. In his place, the kaiser turned to the Hindenburg-Ludendorff team, now placed in charge of all German army operations. Hindenburg's head told him that the best course of action was the abandonment of German positions at Verdun and an end to the campaign. His heart told him that too many Germans had died there to withdraw voluntarily. The honor of Germany, he felt, was at stake even if the campaign had lost all strategic value. The killing at Verdun thus continued.

Pétain's ability to save Verdun in February led to his promotion to commander of Army Group Center in May. In his place at the head of Second Army (which was a part of Army Group Center) came the aggressive Robert Nivelle. Like Pétain, Nivelle had begun the war as a colonel. His deft use of artillery had contributed to the Allied victory at the Marne, leading to his rapid promotion. At Verdun, Nivelle perfected two complex artillery tactics that made him popular with his superiors and with Prime Minister Aristide Briand. The first, called a "deception" bombardment, halted shelling long enough to allow the Germans to return fire and thus reveal their positions, which Nivelle's heavy guns then silenced. The second, a "creeping barrage," involved laying down a curtain of fire that preceded the infantry by measured steps. If done correctly, a creeping barrage silenced the enemy's machine guns, allowing the infantry to advance to their targets.

Throughout the summer, Nivelle worked closely with Charles

"The Butcher" Mangin to develop a plan for the reconquest of Douaumont. Mangin's nickname was well earned. Wounded three times before the war during colonial service in Africa, he was notoriously reckless with the lives of his men. His time in Africa had somehow convinced him that Africans had a higher threshold for pain than Europeans and, wherever possible, he used African soldiers in the first wave of an attack. It was said that after the war he was the only French general who could stand on a Paris street corner in full dress uniform and not be approached by a single veteran wanting to shake his hand. To his credit, Mangin did not ask anything of his men that he would not do himself. He led charges personally at the age of fifty and rarely attacked until he had meticulously prepared every detail.

By October, Mangin had the massive artillery support he needed to make another charge at Douaumont. France then had 300 artillery pieces heavier than 155mm and had introduced gigantic new 400mm guns. On October 24, Nivelle laid his best deception bombardment yet, destroying German artillery pieces opposite Mangin's division. His creeping barrage protected Mangin's troops as they advanced toward Douaumont. The months of artillery bombardment had converted the fort's exterior works from one of the world's strongest buildings to a pile of broken concrete and uprooted earth. Still, it remained an effective underground shelter and a tremendous symbol to both sides.

At approximately 4:30 that afternoon, French soldiers in the nearby fort of Souville watched as three soldiers in French uniforms rose to the top of the rubble that had been Douaumont and waved their arms in the air. The fort was French once again. Supporting troops moved the line almost two miles in France's favor. One week later, they retook Fort Vaux, effectively reclaiming all of Germany's gains since the summer.[15] By the time the two armies finally wore themselves out in December, the lines sat almost exactly where they had been in February. An estimated 162,000 Frenchmen and 142,000 Germans were listed as dead or

The peaceful village of Vaux sat along the front lines during several major offensives, including Verdun. The American Second Division finally captured the town for the Allies in July 1918. (United States Air Force Academy McDermott Library Special Collections)

missing. Most of the latter were victims of artillery so powerful that it became impossible to identify a man precisely enough to give him his own grave. The anonymous remains of an estimated 130,000 victims of Verdun now sit in a massive ossuary near Douaumont.

Verdun thus became the battle of attrition that Falkenhayn had envisioned. Contrary to his plan, however, the battle wore down both sides. The mammoth struggle shaped the destinies of the German and French armies through 1917 and 1918 and well beyond. It also led to the removal of Joffre, who was blamed for his inattention to Verdun in 1915 and held responsible for the massive casualties of 1916. To soothe the transition, the government resurrected the rank of marshal, which had been out of use since 1871, and named Joffre the Third Republic's first man to hold the rank. In his place came Robert Nivelle, who promised French and British politicians that he could repeat his successful Verdun formula across the western front.

The bloodletting at Verdun reached far beyond the two armies directly involved. Verdun had an important effect on the British, Russian, Italian, Austro-Hungarian, and Romanian armies as well. Verdun became synonymous with sacrifice, death, and battles that defied the traditional definitions of winning and losing. One French veteran's recollection of the battle accurately sums up the state of the French and German armies at the start of 1917: "We waited for the fatal moment in a sort of stupor . . . in the middle of a demented uproar. The entire French army had passed through this trial."[16] Whether that army could survive 1917 remained an open question in the minds of many on both sides.

WAR IN THE THIRD DIMENSION

Among its other notable characteristics, Verdun gave birth to the modern notion of air warfare. At the outbreak of the war, several generals belittled airplanes as little more than playthings for Europe's upper classes. The many lucrative speed and endurance contests in the years before the war contributed to such an impression. Nevertheless, as cavalry lost its traditional reconnaissance role on the battlefield, airplanes became the logical replacement. Their contribution in locating Kluck's turn to the south before the Battle of the Marne helped supporters make the case that airplanes might prove to be a deciding factor in the war. In the open spaces of the eastern front they quickly became critical tools.

Ludendorff and Joffre became two of the most important early converts.

The importance of aviation led to massive increases in spending to improve both the quantity and quality of aircraft. The war's belligerents had fewer than 800 airplanes among them in 1914. During the war, however, they built nearly 150,000 airplanes. Engines grew more powerful, and air frames became larger and more durable. To service these planes the great powers trained thousands of pilots, mechanics, spotters, and other support personnel. Enormous growth in aviation occurred in all of the belligerent nations. Britain's Royal Flying Corps grew from 2,000 personnel in 1914 to 291,000 in 1918, by which time it had become the world's first independent air force.

Aviation soon became sufficiently complex to merit specialization into three areas: observation, pursuit, and bombardment. Observers not only spotted and reported on enemy movements, but also helped to target artillery fire. By developing communication systems with gunners, aviators could correct inaccuracies. They thus enabled more systematic use of "indirect fire," wherein gunners did not actually see their targets. By using airborne observers as their eyes, gunners could conceal themselves and therefore protect their batteries from the enemy's own artillery.

Such a system depended on mastery of the skies. Pursuit (or fighter) aircraft were soon developed, with the specialized mission of ridding the skies of enemy observation planes and clearing the way for one's own observers. Dutch aircraft designer Anthony Fokker's invention of an interrupter gear for the Germans allowed for synchronization between an airplane's engine and its machine guns. For the first time, a pilot could fire "through" his propeller blade, allowing him to fly and keep his guns targeted at the same time. Until the Allies perfected a similar system, the "Fokker scourge" gave the Germans a critical advantage in the air.

By 1915, airplanes had grown strong enough to enable a third

Aviation was used at the beginning of the war as a means to spot artillery and observe enemy movements. By 1916 modern fighter tactics had evolved. By 1918 airmen had envisioned or practiced all of the roles of modern air forces except in-flight refueling. (Courtesy of Andrew and Herbert William Rolfe)

mission: aerial bombardment. In May, British planes targeted a German poison gas factory, dropping 87 bombs on it, with mixed results. By the end of the war, aerial bombardments of both military and civilian targets had become commonplace. Germany's Gotha bombers had the range to reach London and the capacity to carry 1,000 pounds of bombs. Raids by bombers and airships (zeppelins) killed 1,400 British civilians during the war. Although introduced too late to see action, Great Britain's Handley Page V/1500 had a range of 600 miles and a bomb load of 7,500 pounds. Had the war continued into 1919, Britain would have had 36 V/1500s ready for combat, with more on the way.

Verdun witnessed the first concerted efforts to link the success of air forces to the fate of ground troops. German aerial reconnaissance planes, protected by pursuit planes, photographed every foot of the Verdun salient before the attack. Once the battle began, German bombers supplemented the artillery by striking bridges, marshalling areas, and enemy gun batteries. Notably, they did not target *La Voie Sacrée* because Falkenhayn did not want to destroy the means by which France could continue to feed men into his slaughterhouse. The French responded to the German aerial threat by creating pursuit squadrons that worked in tandem, concentrating firepower and forcing German airplanes away from the battlefront. These squadrons included an American volunteer unit, the Lafayette Escadrille, whose impressive combat record added to the publicity value of Americans fighting alongside the French.[17]

By March 1916, France had won the air war over Verdun. The introduction of the Nieuport 11 aircraft, an agile plane with a top speed of nearly 100 miles per hour, gave French pilots a significant technological edge until the German introduction of the Albatross III in early 1917. Technological advances notwithstanding, aviation remained a branch for only the most daring. A pilot's life expectancy was even shorter than a machine gunner's. France lost 2,000 pilots in training accidents alone. Those who could master the new technology became folk heroes. Men like France's Georges Guynemer (54 kills), Germany's Oswald Boelcke (40 kills) and Baron von Richthofen (16 kills), and Britain's Albert Ball (44 kills) all innovated the art of air warfare; all four died in combat before the war's end.

By 1917 air power had become critical to the triumph of any operation. At the beginning of that year, Pétain told new War Minister Paul Painlevé, "Aviation has assumed a critical importance; it has become one of the indispensable factors of success. . . . It is necessary to be master of the air."[18] The general did not need to convince Painlevé. A gifted mathematician and scientist, Painlevé had already become one of the world's great experts on aviation. As Wilbur Wright's first European passenger, he had set an endurance record of one hour, ten minutes. He then went on to teach France's first course in aeronautical engineering. Under his direction, France sat at the forefront of military aviation, a critical component to eventual Allied triumph.

7

A WAR AGAINST CIVILIZATION

The Chantilly Offensives and the Somme

They were singing some music-hall tune, with a lilt in it, as they marched towards the lights of all the shells up there in the places of death. I watched them pass—all these tall boys of a North Country regiment, and something of their spirit seemed to come out of the dark mass of their moving bodies and thrill the air. They were going up to those places without faltering, without a backward look and singing—dear, splendid men.

—Philip Gibbs, "The Historic First of July"

L IKE Falkenhayn, Joffre and the other Allied generals reflected on the meaning of the events of 1915. Joffre concluded that Germany's success had been due in large part to two factors. First, Germany had taken advantage of interior lines, which meant that the Germans could move forces between fronts across the excellent German rail network in a way that the Allies obviously could not. In this manner, the Germans had been able to concentrate forces for offensives such as Gorlice-Tarnów. Second, the Central Powers had never faced a concerted effort by all of the Allied armies at the same time; they had had the luxury of dealing with just one enemy at a time.

THE MEETING AT CHANTILLY

Joffre could do little about the geography of Europe, but he could attempt to coordinate Allied offensives. Accordingly, he hosted a high-level meeting at his Chantilly headquarters in December 1915 attended by senior members of the British, Russian, Italian, and

Serbian armies and governments. Joffre argued that by midsummer 1916 the Allies would be ready to conduct simultaneous offensives on multiple fronts, thereby impeding Germany's ability to transfer forces and placing pressure on the Central Powers from all sides. By the summer, he predicted, three conditions not only would make such a strategy possible, but also would guarantee its success. First, the British New Armies would at last be ready for large-scale combat. Second, French industry should have delivered sufficient quantities of the heavy artillery pieces that Joffre thought were vital to success. Third, Russia should have recovered from the disasters of 1915 sufficiently to resume the offensive. Secondarily, the abandonment of sideshows such as Gallipoli and Salonika could provide more men for the offensives Joffre envisioned.

Chantilly in theory represented a major step toward the Allies fighting the war as a single entity. It fell far short, however, of creating a unified command structure, or even a permanent mechanism for discussing strategy. Like all alliance efforts, the Chantilly agreement amounted to a series of compromises. Russia agreed to undertake an offensive in 1916 in tandem with its allies only if Joffre agreed to keep the Salonika front open. Joffre reluctantly conceded, meaning that the forces in Greece would stay there instead of moving to theaters he envisioned as primary combat areas for 1916. The British, too, forced Joffre to agree that some of the troops evacuated from Gallipoli would be sent to Egypt instead of France.

Joffre and the generals at Chantilly hoped to wait until midsummer to launch their grand offensives, meaning that the Germans would have to oblige them by remaining on the defensive themselves. As we have already seen, they did not. Verdun threw into question all of the conclusions reached at Chantilly. The French army, rather than leading the summer offensives, was now in a desparate position. The Chantilly offensives thereafter needed to draw German resources away from Verdun, thereby giving the French a chance to survive.

Falkenhayn had counted on the British launching an offensive to assist the French at Verdun. He hoped that by striking at Verdun early in 1916, he could compel the British into attacking prematurely, before their New Armies and artillery support were in place. His forces could then destroy the inexperienced British as they advanced. The Germans would have the advantage of high ground and well-prepared defensive positions wherever the British attacked. Haig did not fall for the bait, insisting to an increasingly ardent Joffre that he had to wait until midsummer to launch his offensive. When he finally did, on July 1, the first days generally matched Falkenhayn's prediction.

The first Chantilly offensive came in March 1916 from Luigi Cadorna and the Italians. In order to help his French ally, Cadorna launched the Fifth Battle of the Isonzo weeks ahead of schedule, before the spring thaw had melted the Alpine snows. Cadorna was far less concerned about the fate of the French than the fate of the Italians if the Germans attained victory on the western front and could thereafter focus additional strength against Italy. Despite the terrible weather conditions and the decreasing morale of his army, Cadorna was unusually confident. He held a 350 to 100 advantage in infantry battalions and a 1,400 to 467 advantage in artillery pieces.[1] He therefore did not worry about the deep snow or the complications involved in speeding up an offensive by a matter of weeks.

Cadorna also remained blithely unconcerned about the strength of Austro-Hungarian positions all along the high ground. From these positions, Boroević and his staff had been able to monitor the Italian massing of men and materiel for the offensive. They therefore moved their men away from their front-line positions at the start of the Italian preparatory bombardment. For forty-eight hours Italian shells struck the Austro-Hungarian first line, damaging trenches and positions; most soldiers, however, had moved back, away from the front line. Enveloped by fog and snow, and lacking any real objectives beyond moving toward the town of Gorizia, the Italian army moved slowly and uncertainly. After five days, Cadorna decided that he had done enough to comply with the spirit of the Chantilly agreement and called the battle off. The battle cost each side thousands of pointless casualties and had no impact on the fighting at Verdun.

On March 19, Boroević counterattacked, taking back some of the high ground the Italians had won. The Austro-Hungarians were careful to limit their goals and the resources they committed, and the operation was a complete success. Suffering just 259 casualties, the Austro-Hungarians took 600 Italian prisoners and inflicted an equal number of killed and wounded. The latest Isonzo failures lowered Cadorna's stock in the eyes of the Italian politicians, but the general continued to insist that he answered only to the nominal Italian commander-in-chief, King Victor Emmanuel III. The king was a shy, but personally brave, man who often visited the front and occasionally came under fire. He saw the problems at Cadorna's headquarters, but retained an unwarranted faith that the general would learn from his mistakes and set the problems right.

Contrary to what one might expect, Conrad and the Austrian general staff had grown as frustrated with the Isonzo stalemate as Cadorna had. Conrad, under pressure to prove his worth as an ally to the Germans, had long planned an offensive of his own. He hoped to take advantage of Italian concentration in the Isonzo valley to attack out of the South Tyrol region onto the Asiago plain. If successful, the Austro-Hungarian army might threaten Verona, Padua, and Vicenza, and maybe even cut northern Italy into two indefensible zones. Conrad argued that by creating a second front for the Italians, he could at the very least relieve the pressure from the Isonzo and stretch Italy so thin that a decisive breakthrough on one of the fronts would become possible. Falkenhayn dis-

Wounded soldiers await transportation to a field hospital on the Isonzo front. Untold thousands of soldiers in all the armies died needlessly of minor wounds because of a lack of proper sanitation and medical care. (United States Air Force Academy McDermott Library Special Collections)

agreed, but allowed Conrad to go ahead as long as he used only Austro-Hungarian soldiers. Germany, occupied at Verdun, would not contribute.

The massive Austrian offensive on the Asiago plain began on May 15, 1916, and caught Cadorna completely unprepared. Two Austro-Hungarian armies overran the Italian First Army, capturing thousands of prisoners and seizing important high ground. Cadorna at first saw the offensive as a feint. A spring snowstorm at the end of the month stalled the offensive and provided the Italian general staff a respite, giving Cadorna time to see the severity of the situation and reinforce the sector with eight divisions, constituted as a new Fifth Army. The Italians had taken 148,000 casualties and lost several key strategic positions, but they had held their secondary positions and had inflicted 100,000 casualties on the Austrians, who were close to the end of their manpower reserves. Fortunately for Italy, in early June the strategic situation changed again when the Russians launched their Chantilly offensive under the command of their most impressive general, Alexei Brusilov.

THE BRUSILOV OFFENSIVES

The Austro-Hungarians' focus on the Asiago offensive led them to misread several important indications of an impending attack from the Russian southwest front, commanded since March 1916 by Alexei Brusilov. An aristocrat and cavalryman from a military family, Brusilov had the rare gift of being able to understand that the tactics of the nineteenth century were ill suited to the twentieth. Like Ferdinand Foch, Brusilov soon set out to unlearn everything he had once believed. Before most Russians made the transition, Brusilov had determined that machine guns, artillery, and careful staff work had replaced individual heroism, the horse, and the bayonet. As commander of the Eighth Army he had experienced moderate success and enjoyed a reputation as the finest commander in the Russian army.

From intelligence reports that included aerial reconnaissance, Brusilov developed a reasonably accurate picture of the Austrians' intentions. He correctly divined that Italy had become an obsession to Conrad and his staff, a notion that the Asiago offensive served to underscore. Six Austro-Hungarian infantry divisions had been transferred to the Asiago front, leaving the Galician front undermanned. Brusilov also knew that the Austrian lines opposite his southwest front amounted to a strong forward crust with little in the way of elastic defenses behind it. If he could crack the line, he might be able to impose a defeat on the Austrians similar to the one Germany had imposed on Russia at Gorlice-Tarnów.

Brusilov also had the rare Russian military gift of subtlety. He did not intend to fight the ensuing battle by pushing forward with massive weights of shells and men. Russian munitions shortages forbade such an approach in any case. Instead, Brusilov carefully trained his men to infiltrate enemy lines and encircle the Austrian defenders, capturing them alive and hopefully reducing his own casualties. He built carefully designed training centers behind the lines and, most importantly, concealed key elements of his plan from the hangers-on at the tsar's court, among whom he suspected were many pro-German sympathizers.

Alekseev and the tsar originally opposed Brusilov's plan. They argued that Russia lacked the strength for a major offensive plus the several large-scale feints that Brusilov had planned. They preferred a maximum concentration of Russian effort in one small area. Brusilov insisted, even threatening to resign if Alekseev made major modifications to his plan. The Asiago offensive's threat to Italy and the German threat to France at Verdun forced a decision. The tsar approved Brusilov's offensive. The Russians believed that they did not have much time to waste. As a result, the offensive was scheduled for June 4.

Brusilov planned the main attack to occur near the towns of Lutsk and Kowel. Control of the latter would cut the north-south railroad that supplied Lemberg. If successful, the offensive might even permit a renewed drive on Cracow and Warsaw. His former unit, the Eighth Army, would lead the assault under the command of a Brusilov protégé, Alexei Kaledin. Opposite Kaledin sat the Austro-Hungarian Fourth Army, led by the Archduke Josef Ferdinand, godson to Kaiser Wilhelm. Like many aristocrats, he owed his position exclusively to his noble birth. Unlike most aristocrats, he refused to compensate for his ignorance by listening to the advice of the professionals around him. He preferred hunting and the company of the women at his headquarters to the daily operations of his army, leaving his men without even nominal leadership. The archduke held the Russians in utter contempt and judged them incapable of breaking his defenses.

The archduke received a rude present on June 4, his forty-

fourth birthday. Russian gunners made a virtue out of their ammunition shortages by firing intense, accurate, and brief "hurricane" bombardments. The heavy pieces targeted the Austro-Hungarian artillery batteries, which Russian aircraft had spotted and
marked. Lighter guns struck the enemy wire. As Brusilov had predicted, the Austro-Hungarian soldiers in the front line sought
shelter from the guns in their deep dugouts, leaving them unable
to fire on the advancing Russians. Thousands became prisoners
when the Russians overtook their positions and surrounded them.
Ethnic Czechs, Ruthenes, and Serbs, unhappy with the war and
fed up with Austro-Hungarian leadership, surrendered the fastest,
although all groups felt the weight of the Russian steamroller.

By the end of day one, Brusilov had achieved a breakthrough
that most World War I commanders had only dreamed about.
The gap in the Austrian lines was twenty miles wide and five miles
deep. Conrad refused to believe the reports coming into his headquarters because he did not believe the Russians were capable of
such a success. Even if there had been losses, he proclaimed, counterattacks would soon recover them. "At most," he told a staff officer, "we will lose a few hundred yards [of] land." Neither he nor
Josef Ferdinand thought the crisis serious enough to warrant leaving the birthday dinner being held in the archduke's honor.[2]

Within a few days, however, Conrad realized his error. With no
substantial defenses behind the first line of trenches, Brusilov's
men moved quickly, capturing more than 200,000 demoralized
Austrian troops in just three days. The Austrian Fourth Army had
virtually ceased to exist, with its 110,000 men having been reduced
to just 18,000 effectives. On June 8, Conrad went to Berlin to ask
for help. Rather ungracefully, he demanded that Falkenhayn move
German forces to Asiago under Austrian command because, he
told Falkenhayn, the Asiago offensive was succeeding whereas
Verdun was not. Falkenhayn lectured Conrad on his failure to
prepare for the Russian attack so intently that Conrad later told

his staff that he would rather have "ten slaps in the face" than turn to the Germans again.[3]

Despite his annoyance with Conrad, Falkenhayn could see the realities of the situation in the Carpathians. Accordingly, he transferred four German infantry divisions from France and five more from the general reserve. He also told Conrad to abandon his Asiago offensive and move four divisions from that sector to the Carpathians. The new German and Austrian forces came under the command of German General Hans von Seeckt, sent by Falkenhayn to assume control of all Central Powers forces in the east. Conrad was deeply humiliated by Falkenhayn's rebukes, but the German reinforcements prevented Brusilov from crossing the Carpathians and likely saved the Austro-Hungarian Empire from a complete collapse.

The first phase of Brusilov's offensive had yielded spectacular results, even if they came against the demoralized and wholly unprepared Austrians. The second phase depended on the actions of Russian western army front commander Alexei Evert. Brusilov's advance had been so dramatic that his forces had outrun their supply lines and created an exposed salient. Although they had inflicted heavy casualties, the Russians had taken casualties as well and were worn out. Brusilov ordered his army to halt and rest on June 9. Evert was to occupy Austrian forces and cover Brusilov's northern flank by advancing with fresh troops and supplies. He was well supplied for the attack, possessing two-thirds of the Russian army's artillery pieces and more than a million men.

Evert was to have begun his attack on the same day that Brusilov halted. In some variants of the Brusilov plan, the Russian general staff had envisioned Evert's attack as the main one and Brusilov as an early diversion. Evert had to attack if the offensive were to retain its momentum. But he claimed that his forces were not ready and spuriously complained that his army was insufficiently supplied with shells. Evert's natural caution had grown after the beating his soldiers took during Gorlice-Tarnów when, separated from all the other Russian armies, they had fought a retreating action for 300 miles. Evert wanted no part of another offensive in 1916 and continued to invent excuses for his inaction.

Brusilov railed at Evert, telling Alekseev that Evert's failure to follow the plan would "turn a won battle into a lost one." Brusilov's men began referring to Evert as a traitor and disparaged his German-sounding last name.[4] Without a supporting attack to the north and short on supplies and reinforcements, Brusilov could not go forward. His northernmost army, the Eighth, could not resume the offensive because of the risk of exposing a flank. Kaledin therefore ordered it to halt and prepare for an enemy counterattack. Brusilov was furious, but had to acquiesce.[5]

By June 20, the Germans had completed an impressive feat of logistics. They had added ten infantry divisions to the front opposite Brusilov. Under German supervision, the Austrians had built solid lines of defense, reestablished discipline, and prepared for the next Russian move. Alekseev unwisely ordered Brusilov to resume the offensive against these new forces on July 28. The new Central Powers divisions, with Germans often in charge down to company level, repulsed the attack, with considerable Russian losses. Brusilov tried once again in a bloody offensive from August 7 to September 20. Russian forces approached the Carpathian foothills, but wore themselves out. The offensive petered out in October as Brusilov's army group ran out of supplies and reinforcements. Evert's western army group never attacked in force sufficient to draw German and Austrian forces away.

Brusilov's offensive struck a tremendous blow against an incompetent Austro-Hungarian general staff that led a demoralized army. It had, however, failed to achieve its principal objective, the elimination of the Austro-Hungarian Empire from the war. The German transfers meant that Russia could not hope to have a numerical superiority on the eastern front sufficient to resume the offensive in the near future. Even Brusilov understood that "to advance a few miles more or less was of no particular importance to the common cause."[6] Alekseev and the tsar looked upon Brusilov's offensive as a failure, although they might have more accurately turned their blame on Evert.

Austria-Hungary remained in the war, but the Brusilov offensives had destroyed it as an instrument capable of attacking. Estimates vary, but as many as 1.5 million men of Austria-Hungary's 2.2-million-man army may have been killed, wounded, or captured in the course of the campaign. Russia, too, suffered badly, losing nearly a million men. The painful losses caused a major spike in the desertion and indiscipline levels on both sides. Brusilov, like many others, blamed the hopelessly antiquated tsarist system for the failure to exploit the early gains of the campaign. He began to believe that only a revolution could remove the tsar and give Russia a chance to modernize its war effort before it was too late.

The disaster of 1916 also spelled the end for Conrad's command. Emperor Franz Joseph continued to hold him in high esteem, but Franz Joseph died in December 1916, at age eighty-six. When his successor, Emperor Karl, assumed the throne, one of his first military acts was to demote Conrad, sending him to command the weakened Austrian armies in the south Tyrol, where he played only a minor role in the war's final years. For the Germans, Brusilov's offensive had pushed them into assuming even more responsibility for the eastern front, although it did not seriously affect their effort at Verdun.

Germany was becoming stretched further and further. The British blockade continued to cut into both the economic health of the German state and, more importantly, the food supply of the German people. A study completed in 1928 calculated that from spring 1915 to February 1917 the caloric value of German daily rations fell from 3,000 to just 800. Hunger and privation "became the overwhelming fact of life on the home front" in both Germany and in Austria-Hungary.[7] The miserably cold winter of

1916–1917 became so difficult that it was dubbed the "turnip winter" because turnips were the only food source in ready supply.

The kaiser and his family grew increasingly out of touch, symbolized by the crown prince's playboy activities at Verdun. The kaiser himself barely understood the new way of war, spending part of a visit to the eastern front in 1916 ranting on about a pet project to supply arms to Japan if it would declare war on the United States.[8] His unrealistic pronouncements on the war increasingly embarrassed those around him who knew better. The German system was unraveling.

TWO YEARS IN THE MAKING, TEN MINUTES IN THE DESTROYING: THE NEW ARMIES ON THE SOMME

Even as they contained the Brusilov offensives, the Germans had to deal with yet another crisis. On July 1, Britain began its largest battlefield effort to date in concert with the French from both banks of the Somme River in the south to the Ancre River in the north. Joffre had originally conceived the attack on the Somme as the major western front attack resulting from the Chantilly conference. As the Somme River represented the rough meeting point of the British and French armies, both forces would take part. From its first conception Allied generals designed the Somme as the "coalition battle *par excellence.*"[9] Joffre initially envisioned using 40 veteran French divisions to assume the main weight of the attack, with the inexperienced New Armies advancing to their north.

The dire situation at Verdun changed the calculus for the Somme dramatically. Joffre met the challenge at Verdun by moving increasing numbers of French units into the sector. Although he was still willing for France to play a role at the Somme, Verdun forced the French portion of the offensive to decline from 40 divisions to 16. Accordingly, the amount of the front that sat in the French sector also fell, from twenty-five miles to just eight. The campaign

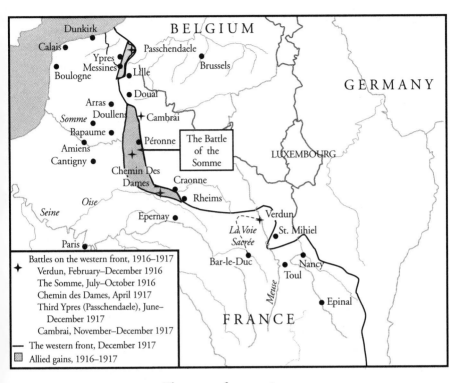

The western front, 1916–1917

therefore became increasingly dominated by the eager, but untested, British New Armies. Sir Douglas Haig accepted the new role, understanding all too well that Britain had to relieve some of the pressure from Verdun if the French army were to remain a viable fighting force.

German Second Army commander Fritz von Below expected an attack to come in his sector. Like most German generals, he guessed that the British and French would try an operation somewhere on the western front to relieve Verdun. His instincts told him that the British had his sector in mind. Aerial reconnaissance soon confirmed his belief. Falkenhayn, however, thought an operation near Arras or in Alsace more likely. He therefore did not send the Second Army the reinforcements or supplies Below demanded. Falkenhayn complicated Below's position even further by telling him that the Second Army must hold all of its ground if attacked and that any territory lost had to be reconquered as rapidly as possible.

The terrain of the Somme did not invite an easy Allied attack. From the Ancre to the Somme, the Germans had held high ground since 1914. The Germans converted the villages and farmhouses of the region into strong redoubts and had placed numerous machine guns in the region's most thickly wooded areas. The region's chalky soil permitted the digging of deep dugouts and the subterranean emplacement of powerful machine gun positions. Some of these dugouts went as far as 30 feet underground, often reinforced by strong wooden timbers and concrete. A British journalist who witnessed the campaign saw German dugouts with paneled walls, electricity, wine cellars, furniture, and, in one case, a piano.[10] The Germans had held these positions for two years and felt possessive about them. They did not intend to surrender them without a fight.

Below strengthened his position by creating as many as seven layers of defensive lines. Individual dugouts and redoubts were connected by subterranean passageways, and some were linked to headquarters by buried telephone lines. New coils of barbed wire, several feet thick in places, guarded many strongpoints. German defenses stretched back as far as five miles from the front. Below placed six infantry divisions in the forward defenses to prevent an Allied breakthrough and held five more divisions in reserve. These forces could either plug holes in the line or, in the event the Allies did capture some positions, they could counterattack.

The British and French understood full well the strength of the German position. Winston Churchill later called the Somme region "undoubtedly the strongest and most perfectly defended position in the world."[11] Haig would have to attack these formidable

The armies of the war used artillery shells at astonishing rates.
This munitions factory is stockpiling shells to feed the insatiable
appetite of British artillery pieces. (National Archives)

positions with green troops untested in modern warfare and short
on leaders. Just 150 officers remained from the old BEF, which
by July 1916 was just "an heroic memory."[12] The French, too, understood the challenge in front of them. Ferdinand Foch, overall commander of French forces in this battle, called his task "impossible"; but, seeing the crisis at Verdun, he believed that his
men must try the impossible, at whatever cost. "We have done
everything and completely succeeded in preventing disaster [at
Verdun]," he said in May, "but we have done nothing to achieve
victory."[13]

The solution, Haig believed, lay in the massive artillery batteries that the British and French had been constructing and assem-

bling for more than a year. Seemingly limitless stocks of artillery ammunition were stacked everywhere. The shell crisis had apparently ended. Now artillery fire could properly prepare the ground for the infantry. The British planned to clear the way for their infantry by annihilating the German positions with seven days of artillery fire. The untrained men of the New Armies should then be able literally to walk across No Man's Land and occupy the German positions.

The troops would then hold surviving German positions or dig new ones and repulse the inevitable German counterattacks. In order to do so, they carried a heavy load of supplies with them, including ample ammunition, food, entrenching tools, barbed wire, and grenades. This heavy pack, weighing in excess of sixty pounds, would slow the British troops when they made their assault, but British generals believed that to send their untrained men into the front lines without adequate supplies would leave them too vulnerable to subsequent German attacks.

The artillery bombardment that began on June 24 impressed (or terrified) all who saw it. More than 1,500 heavy guns fired 1,627,824 rounds over a front barely ten miles long. On the morning of July 1, the barrage increased in intensity, leading one man who saw it to remark, "The enemy was being blasted by a hurricane of fire. I found it in my heart to pity the poor devils who were there, and yet was filled by a strange and awful exhilaration because this was the work of our guns and because it was England's day."[14] British forces also hit the Germans from below, detonating seven mines that they had tunneled through the Somme's chalky soil underneath enemy positions. The two largest mines contained 24 tons of explosives each, creating craters 100 yards wide.

After the detonation of the mines, the British guns changed targets to the German second line, and the infantry advanced. Many British soldiers quite logically concluded that nothing could have survived a week's artillery bombardment of that magnitude.

Seventy thousand soldiers climbed out of their trenches and began a slow advance on the presumably empty German lines. On one part of the front Captain Wilfred Nevill gave each of his four platoons a soccer ball with the words "The Great European Cup. The Final. East Surreys vs. Bavarians. Kick off at Zero." He offered a cash prize for the platoon that advanced its ball the furthest.[15]

Nevill and his men did not imagine the horror that awaited them. Unbeknownst to the infantry, one in four of the Allied shells were duds and two-thirds of them still contained shrapnel.[16] Had the Germans been in trenches, the shrapnel might have been more effective. Their deep dugouts and redoubts, however, could only be destroyed by a direct hit from high explosives, of which the British still had an inadequate supply. The Allied focus on heavy guns also led to insufficient production of gas shells, which, if available on the Somme, could have delivered poison down into the dugouts and caused tremendous casualties.[17] Haig compounded the problem by ordering that the shelling be spread to a depth of 2,500 yards, the extent of the German position that he hoped to capture on the first day. As a result, Gary Sheffield wrote, "artillery support was spread fatally thin."[18] The shrapnel shelling did prevent the Germans from moving food and water up to many of their men. Some went without both for a week. Many of these men, some of them dazed from the noise and driven half-mad by a week living underground, surrendered to the first British troops who found them.

Enough Germans, however, survived the bombardment to make the British advance anything but a walk. The surviving Germans quickly resighted their machine guns and began firing at the rows of slow-moving soldiers in front of them. In most places, the heavily laden British soldiers had to advance over a shell-marked No Man's Land that in most places stretched uphill for 200 to 400 yards. British casualties were horrendous. Philip Gibbs, who watched it happen, continually described the effect of the machine guns as being like a scythe. The heavy British shelling demolished many of the fortified villages and farmhouses, but had left piles of rubble, which the Germans used to conceal more machine guns. Some British units that managed to advance left their flanks open to enfilading fire from Germans to the right and left. Others were shot down from the rear after passing over redoubts from which hidden Germans emerged.

There were some successes on the first day, with an Ulster division capturing an important redoubt and other troops taking the appropriately named Crucifix Trench. British troops in that trench fired a red rocket to indicate that it was now in British hands and to signal that the British gunners should move their shells forward. Unfortunately, a German battery saw the signal as well, guessed its meaning, and fired mercilessly into the position. As in many places on July 1, British success proved to be short-lived.

In the first hour alone, the British had taken an astonishing 30,000 casualties—500 men killed, wounded, or captured per second. Fourth Army commander Sir Henry Rawlinson, who had been a corps commander at Neuve Chapelle and Loos, did not fully understand what was happening across the large front. He had initially disagreed with Haig's plan for the offensive, arguing for more limited objectives and believing that British forces could not hope for the breakthrough that Haig thought was possible. Now, in the first hours of the campaign, he continued to send men into the battle, and the scythe continued its deadly work. The British took portions of the German first line, but this accomplishment paled in light of the human cost.

July 1, 1916, remains the single bloodiest day in the history of the British army. Of the more than 100,000 men sent into combat that day, 57,470 became casualties; of these, 19,240, including Captain Nevill, were dead. Over the next few days combat continued as the British slowly pieced together the magnitude of the first

*Joseph Joffre (left), Douglas Haig (center), and Ferdinand Foch (right)
meet during the Somme campaign. Haig and Foch were veterans of
some of the western front's most important battles. Haig supported
Foch's 1918 appointment as generalissimo of the Allied forces. The two
men learned to work together, although their personal relationship was
never warm. (Australian War Memorial, negative no. H08416)*

day's losses. On July 5, the Germans counterattacked, with heavy
losses. A relative pause followed, allowing both sides to retrench
and regroup.

To the south, French attacks proceeded with more success,
leaving Joffre "beaming."[19] Foch's Northern Army Group, made
up of western front veterans, fought with different tactics from
those of their British counterparts. From Verdun the French had
learned the value of advancing in small groups instead of in line,
shoulder to shoulder. They also benefited from weaker German
positions and stronger, heavier, and more accurate French artillery
fire. On day one, the French seized all of their objectives, took

4,000 German prisoners, and did not even need to call in re-serves.[20] Unfortunately, the French attack was only a sideshow to the larger British offensive to the north.

Throughout July, both the British and the Germans reinforced the Somme sector. Facing limited infantry reserves and dwindling artillery stocks, Haig reduced the size of the offensive zone at the Somme front from 27 kilometers to the southernmost 10 kilometers. The northernmost 17 kilometers became part of the reserve, with a purely defensive mission. This pause in the British attack allowed the Germans time to reinforce and create new defensive lines. By July 9, new German artillery batteries were offering greater resistance to both French and British attacks. On July 10, the French concluded that the German line was stronger than it had been at the start of the campaign.

To break this deadlock, the British called on all stretches of the empire. Every nationality and region soon came to know places on the Somme battlefield where its men fought and died. Today many of these areas are held in perpetuity by these nationalities, where they have erected monuments and, in virtually every corner of this part of France, built cemeteries. Thus Delville Wood will forever be associated with South Africa, Thiépval with Ulster, Beaumont Hamel with Newfoundland and Scotland, and Pozières with Australia. Although Australian forces are often associated with Gallipoli, they lost more men in six weeks on the Somme than they did in eight months in the Dardanelles.[21]

On July 14, Bastille Day, the men of the British Empire attacked again. Rawlinson prepared and oversaw a daring and imaginative night attack. Instead of attacking along the entire front, the British concentrated on a 6,000-yard front. Each position on this part of the German second line received five times the number of shells that it had on July 1. The artillery support amounted to 660 pounds of shell per yard of German line. British forces succeeded in capturing large portions of the German second line at relatively light cost. A German prisoner of war told Gibbs that although the Germans had prevented a breakthrough by British forces, the latter's "amateur army" had inflicted a terrible blow on the Germans. "The English," he told Gibbs, "are stronger than we believed."[22] Nevertheless, the British had captured only a few hundred yards of the first two German lines. At least two more lines lay beyond, with German reinforcements strengthening their positions every day.

The summer heat slowed, but did not halt, operations, principally due to the difficulty of getting sufficient supplies of drinking water to men in forward positions. The relative calm gave Haig a chance to reassess the fighting. He resisted French requests to resume the battle as a coordinated Franco-British offensive, preferring to continue local attacks where British forces had temporary advantages. In mid-August he wrote to Joffre that "the forces at my disposition are not sufficient to allow me to launch an attack along a large front."[23] The French, accordingly, cancelled plans for a coordinated offensive and limited themselves to operations in support of the British.

By this point, Haig had invented a new rationale for his battle. If he could not achieve a spectacular rupture in German lines, he could at least wear the Germans down sufficiently to make a future breakthrough possible. The logistical problems in the battle thus far had proven the impossibility of sustaining a breakthrough in any case. His new strategy of attrition might take longer to show results, but Allied failures to create a breakthrough had left him with little choice. A British officer came to the same conclusion in a September comment to Gibbs: "It was the [German] shell fire which made our position untenable. But in any case we put a large number of Boches out of action, and that is always worth doing, and brings the end of the war a little closer."[24]

For attrition to work, however, enemy casualties either need to be significantly greater than one's own or the enemy must have a greatly reduced capability to replace losses. Otherwise, as Dennis Showalter memorably put it, attrition becomes little more than the "mindless mutual commitment of forces until at some unspecified time the last three surviving French and British soldiers would totter on aged legs across No Man's Land and bayonet the two remaining Germans, then toast their success in prune juice."[25] By midsummer 1916 both Verdun and the Somme had surely become battles of attrition, yet it remained far from clear which side would break first. All of the armies engaged had suffered enormous casualties and had few reserves upon which to call. In Britain, the situation grew severe enough to prompt the unprecedented step of introducing conscription. In short, the war of attrition that Falkenhayn, Haig, and, to a lesser extent, Joffre were fighting showed few signs of benefiting one side exclusively.

The generals' policies of regaining lost ground wore their own armies down as effectively as any enemy offensives. The 330 separate counterattacks launched by the Germans at the Somme accounted for most of their casualties after July 1. The French desire to regain every inch of their soil at Verdun similarly proved to be tremendously costly, but is more understandable than Falkenhayn's obsession with holding every inch of "German" ground at the Somme. Falkenhayn warned Below that "the first tenet of trench warfare must be not to surrender a foot of territory, and, should that foot nevertheless be lost, to commit every last man to an immediate counterattack."[26] The Germans, like the French and British, often vacillated between the importance of holding ground and the importance of killing the enemy.

In an effort to win this war to kill men, the British turned to a new machine. In September, as part of a third major effort on the Somme, the British used their first tanks. A year earlier, war correspondent Ernest Swinton had developed the idea of building an armored vehicle with caterpillar tracks capable of climbing five-foot ledges and spanning a trench. The army received the idea with caution, but Churchill saw great promise in the idea, secretly (and illegally) diverting £75,000 from Admiralty funds to sponsor initial work.[27] The machines were shipped to France in

First introduced during the Somme campaign in 1916, tanks eventually became important tools in breaking the stasis of trench warfare. This British tank is shown crushing barbed wire to ease the advance of the infantry. (Imperial War Museum, Crown Copyright, P. 396)

crates marked "tank" to deceive onlookers as to their contents; this rather unusual name soon gained favor over the not-coincidentally naval-sounding name "landship."

By September 15, when the new vehicles first came into use, they still suffered from significant design flaws. Problems included a vulnerable fuel tank, a faulty steering system, and limited visibility. Still, the British rushed them into service in an attempt to turn the tide on the Somme. The Mark I tank, introduced at the Somme, came in two variants, both weighing almost 30 tons and requiring a crew of eight. The "male" version carried two six-pound guns and four machine guns. The "female" version carried six machine guns. They moved at approximately two miles per hour, and if they fell into a ditch they had to be abandoned. The first sight of these tanks often elicited peals of laughter, noted Gibbs, "for they were monstrously comical, like toads of vast size emerging from the primeval slime in the twilight of the world's dawn."[28]

Of the 49 tanks brought into action on September 15, only 18 saw action. Most of the rest fell victim either to mechanical problems or the accurate artillery fire of German guns. Those that did enter the fray and survived had an enormous impact on the morale of the men who saw them. German soldiers fled, terrified, and British soldiers ran behind, laughing and screaming. A British pilot signaled back to headquarters that "A Tank is walking up the High Street of Flers with the British Army cheering behind." The pilot then hung a sign from his plane reminiscent of London newspaper stands, reading "GREAT HUN DEFEAT. SPECIAL."[29] Tanks helped the British break the German third line, but their overall impact lay more in the potential that Haig and others saw. Haig soon reported back to London demanding 1,000 more.

Soon after the introduction of the tanks, the Germans countered with their own machines, a new generation of airplanes. The new Halberstadt DII and Albatross models DI and DII took back the skies from British pilots. British mastery of the air had proved to be decisive in spotting artillery and observing German movements. The new German planes took that mastery away, effectively blinding the officers at Haig's headquarters. The new airplanes were the first to be designed based on experiences from the actual combat of the war. Moreover, the Germans now organized their aircraft into "hunting squadrons" dominated by veteran pilots. Manfred von Richthofen, "the Red Baron," scored his first kills as part of legendary ace Oswald Boelcke's squadron.

A successful attack in late September proved that the British army had begun to learn from its errors. The target was a powerful German position on the Thiépval ridge, site today of a massive memorial on which are engraved the names of 73,367 British fatalities at the Somme who have no known grave. Instead of charging

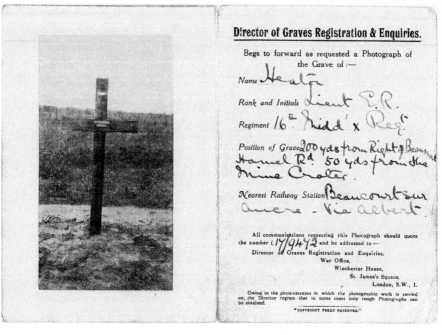

*The parents of E. R. Heaton, the volunteer from 1914 shown on
page 31, waited nine months to learn the location of his grave.
This graves registration booklet provided information as to the
grave's location and the nearest railway station.
(Imperial War Museum, Crown Copyright, E. R. Heaton)*

the ridge with a frontal assault, the British approached it from the
east, capturing the ruins of Mouquet Farm first. With careful artillery preparation and men specifically trained to seize this one
particular objective, British forces captured the ridge, which had
been a goal of theirs since day one of the Somme campaign.

Haig had hoped that the seizure of Thiépval (on the anniversary of Trafalgar, no less) signaled a new phase in the battle. He
sought a breakthrough once again, although it quickly became obvious that there was nowhere to break through to. The Germans
had constructed several more lines of defense in front of the town

of Bapaume, meaning that any "breakthrough" would only involve a new series of attacks on a new series of defenses. Heavy October rains turned the torn-up fields around the Somme into a quagmire, further complicating any attempted move. In November, another bloody attack, this one by Scots at Beaumont Hamel, seized a part of the line that had resisted British offensives since July 1. Its capture, however, did not change the fact that no strategic objectives remained that were worth the likely cost in men.

Of Britain's 56 infantry divisions, 53 fought at the Somme. More than 419,000 of the men in those divisions were killed, wounded, or captured as a result of the battle. French casualties amounted to more than 200,000. Estimates of German casualties range as high 600,000, on top of the 370,000 German casualties suffered at Verdun. In all, the lines moved no more than seven miles. About the only major strategic achievement the Allies could claim was their cutting of the road from Bapaume to Péronne, but both of these cities could be supplied from roads going east, so even this accomplishment amounted to little. The Germans did transfer several divisions away from Verdun, but their absence did not materially affect either side's fortunes there.

Claims that the Somme had been worth the sacrifice because the Allies had attrited the Germans hold merit, but as the Allies suffered almost equal casualties themselves, it is hard to take much comfort from that idea. As 1916 turned into 1917 nothing was certain except that the war continued, with no clear winner in sight. The astonishing bloodletting of 1916 had brought neither side any closer to victory. A German prisoner at the Somme spoke for thousands of soldiers when he told Philip Gibbs, "Europe is being bled to death, and will be impoverished for long years. It is a war against religion, and against civilization, and I see no end to it."[30]

8

DRIVING OUT THE DEVIL

Collapse in the East

The disintegration of our armies continues to develop. I have received word that in some units the officers are being slaughtered by their own men. Today I received a report that, in one division, the chief of staff was murdered in this fashion.

—Diary of Russian army chief of staff Mikhail Alekseev, June 10, 1917

THE tremendous manpower losses encountered by all sides prompted a search to find new allies. Romania was among the neutral nations coveted by both sides, and until the summer of 1916 had sat out the war. Bordering Russia, Bulgaria, Austria-Hungary, and Serbia, its geographic position offered many enticing possibilities. If it joined the Central Powers, a new southern offensive into Russia, possibly with Bulgarian support, became a viable possibility. If it joined the Allies, an invasion into the eastern ends of Austria-Hungary could place even more pressure on the withering empire, especially as Austria-Hungary was already heavily engaged in Italy and in Galicia.

As Italy had done, Romania played a waiting game. In such a stalemated conflict as the one that had developed by 1915, neutrals like Romania, Bulgaria, and Italy seemed to hold out a chance of changing the war's fortunes by the possibility of opening new fronts. Consequently, neutrals held bargaining positions considerably out of proportion to their military prowess. Of the neutral nations in 1915, only the United States held the economic and military potential to determine the course of the war. The neutral nations of Europe became a focus of diplomatic efforts, with each side hoping that the military stalemate could be broken by political means.

Because Romania faced no immediate threats to its interests, the Romanian government had the luxury of waiting for its suitors to assemble the most lucrative dowry before making a decision. Diplomatically, Romania was bound to the Central Powers through a defensive treaty with Austria-Hungary that dated to 1883. This treaty was so secret that only a few members of the Romanian elite knew of the specific terms. The Romanian government, fearful of Ottoman and Russian expansionism, had been careful to renew the pact as late as 1913. By the start of the war in 1914, the Ottomans had become less of a threat due to their defeats in the Balkan Wars. Age-old suspicions between the Romanians and the Russians, however, remained and had led to increased diplomatic, military, and economic links between Romania and Germany.

The Romanian ruling family was a branch of the German Hohenzollern family, providing strong links in the days when such connections might still matter. The kaiser frequently spoke of his confidence that his Romanian cousins would eventually join the Central Powers. Romanian Prime Minister Ion Bratianu received his job in part because of his avowed pro-German feelings, but like most Romanians he remained unenthusiastic about assisting the Austro-Hungarians. Nevertheless, all signs pointed to Romania's eventually joining the war on the side of the Central Powers.

These links to the Central Powers notwithstanding, Romania, like Italy, had territorial goals that could only be met by taking land away from Austria-Hungary. Romania sought Austro-Hungarian territory in Transylvania, Bukovina, and the Banat. Transylvania, which contained a large number of ethnic Romanians, remained the most important prize. In 1914, before the outbreak of war, Romania patched up some of its old disagreements with Russia, exchanging state visits and convincing Russian

Foreign Minister Sergei Sazonov to meet with disgruntled ethnic Romanians living under Austro-Hungarian rule. This move infuriated the Austrians, convincing them of Russia's intent to inflame nationalist passions inside the empire.

When war broke out, the Romanian government could find no reason to meet its treaty obligations and join the belligerents. Although most members of the Romanian elite still had pro-German sentiments, the thought of fighting alongside the Austro-Hungarians and their former Ottoman enemies remained an unpleasant one. German promises of giving Romania Russian Bessarabia in return for Romania's joining the Central Powers fell short of Romanian territorial desires. Transylvania remained the key. As a result, Romania remained on the sidelines throughout 1914 and 1915. Germany and Austria-Hungary contented themselves with Romanian neutrality. It seems never to have occurred to them that the Romanians might one day turn to the Allies. Consequently, they left the Austro-Hungarian frontier with Romania almost entirely unguarded.

Romania's first steps toward entering the war came at the end of 1914, when King Carol died. His nephew and successor, King Ferdinand, had more pronounced Allied sympathies, but a weaker presence and an unwillingness to make important decisions. Although he proved unable to sway Bratianu from his pro-German sentiments, the king came increasingly under the influence of his pro-Allied wife, who was the granddaughter of both Britain's Queen Victoria and Russia's Alexander II. His family situation did little to make the king more decisive. Meanwhile, two of his brothers were serving in the German army under the command of their cousin, Kaiser Wilhelm II.

In early 1915, the British made a secret commitment to give Transylvania to Romania if the latter country entered the war. The offer impressed both the king and Bratianu, who finally saw a chance to annex this coveted region. Yet the Romanians continued to vacillate, wanting even more and anxious to ensure that they would fight on the winning side. Bratianu's insistence on adding Bukovina and the Banat stalled negotiations until later in the year. By that time, the Russians had been driven from Poland and the British sat stalemated at Gallipoli. Bratianu decided that the time was not yet ripe for Romania to declare its intentions. The Romanians increased their trade with the Central Powers and waited for more favorable circumstances.

THE ROMANIAN CAMPAIGN

The events of 1916 changed Romania's situation dramatically. Russian success in the Brusilov offensives both wore down the Austro-Hungarian army and placed Russia in an advantageous position to claim the lands that Romania sought, most importantly Transylvania and Bukovina. Neutrality no longer seemed the best option. Accordingly, the Romanians concluded a secret treaty with the Allies in August 1916 by which the latter promised Romania the three provinces it most wanted and pledged to continue pressuring Austria-Hungary from the Russian and Salonika fronts. Romania declared war on Austria-Hungary, but not Germany, on August 27.

The 700,000-man Romanian army had fought inconsistently in the Balkan Wars. Facing no immediate threat and short of money, the state had invested lightly in the modernization of its army in the months before the outbreak of World War I. As a result, it lacked adequate artillery and had an officer corps that was woefully ill prepared for fighting in 1916. Primitive road and rail networks complicated movement and supply. Russia, meanwhile, quickly grew suspicious of the Romanians, criticizing them for entering the war only after Russia had done the dirty work. They saw the Romanians as little better than vultures, anxious to gain territory as a result of the blood spilled by Russian soldiers. "If His Majesty ordered me to send fifteen wounded soldiers to Romania," Alekseev said, "I would on no account send a sixteenth."[1]

His sentiment accurately reflected the mood of the Russian elite, most of whom continued to see Romania as a poor ally, and one with strong pro-German sentiments.

These problems notwithstanding, the Romanian army advanced quickly across the lightly defended Austro-Hungarian frontier. By mid-September they were fifty miles into enemy territory and controlled large parts of Transylvania. Germany, Bulgaria, and Turkey responded by declaring war on Romania. The Germans then sent Erich von Falkenhayn, recently removed as German chief of staff, to crush the Romanians with a new German Ninth Army. The ruthless Falkenhayn took the lessons he had learned at murderous places like Ypres and Verdun and unleashed his veteran forces against the terribly outmatched Romanians. A second Central Powers army, led by Gorlice-Tarnów veteran August von Mackensen and containing Germans, Bulgarians, and Ottomans, crossed into Romania from the south.

Invaded from two sides by experienced and well-led soldiers, Romania soon collapsed. Within just six weeks of declaring war, the Central Powers' double pincer movement had negated all Romanian gains. Russia chose not to reinforce the Romanians, leaving them helpless in the face of the overwhelming strength of the Central Powers advance. On October 23, Mackensen's men seized the key Black Sea port of Constanza, and less than two weeks later Falkenhayn broke through the last Romanian defenses in Transylvania. On December 6, less than four months after entering the war, the Romanians lost their capital, Bucharest. Their armies had not been defeated; they had been destroyed and humiliated. Romania lost more than 300,000 men in total casualties. The only help the Allies provided amounted to sabotage teams sent to demolish the Ploesti oil wells lest they should fall into German hands.

The ease with which the Central Powers devastated the Romanian armies meant that the Romanian campaign did not have a significant impact on the larger war. German treatment of the conquered nation, however, did have an important legacy. After agreeing to an armistice, the Romanians soon found themselves a virtual colony of the Central Powers. Angered by the betrayal of his relatives, the kaiser turned vengeful. Hindenburg and Ludendorff argued for outright annexation of Romania to the German Reich, but diplomats convinced them to leave a veneer of Romanian independence and divide the spoils with Austria-Hungary and Bulgaria in order to provide Germany's allies with needed succor.

The Central Powers immediately began the process of removing hundreds of thousands of tons of grain from Romania, leaving the civilian population near starvation. They also repaired the damaged oil wells and seized the oil thus produced, depriving Romania of its chief source of income. The Treaty of Bucharest, signed in April 1918, codified the harsh terms of occupation. It gave Germany a ninety-year lease on Romanian oil fields, minerals, and other natural resources. In the span of eighteen months, the Germans had managed to seize one million tons of oil and two million tons of grain. These resources helped to sustain the German war economy in the face of the British blockade. In effect, the Germans hoped to use eastern Europe to compensate for losses caused by the blockade.

The territorial adjustments forced onto Romania were no less harsh. Romania ceded passes in the Carpathian Mountains to Austria-Hungary, as well as much of the Black Sea coastline to Bulgaria, leaving Romania's borders virtually indefensible. The half of the Dobruja region north of the city of Constanza was to be ruled as a shared German-Austrian-Bulgarian mandate. As a result, Romania lost the entire Danube River delta. Bulgaria annexed the southern half of the Dobruja region (lost to Romania after the Second Balkan War) outright. In the final weeks of the war, with the Central Powers collapsing everywhere, Romania reentered the war on the Allied side, giving itself some leverage at the postwar Paris Peace Conference, where it recouped the losses

A German, a Bulgarian, and a Turkish soldier patrol together in Romania. Invasions by several armies on three fronts doomed the ill-prepared and ill-equipped Romanians. (© Hulton-Deutsch Collection/Corbis) (HU040549)

of 1916 and even succeeded in annexing Transylvania from the now-defunct Austro-Hungarian Empire.

Germany's brutal treatment of Romania sent a grave warning signal to the Allies. Romania was a relatively small and poor nation, and although it had reneged on treaty obligations, by 1917 it posed no obvious threat to any of the Central Powers. The Germans had treated it with unusual cruelty and had converted it into a virtual vassal state. The treatment of Romania, however, fit in with Germany's prosecution of the war more generally. The Germans had forcibly relocated 120,000 Frenchmen and 100,000 Belgians to German factories and had begun the process of removing Slavs and Jews from Poland to clear land for resettlement by Germans.[2]

German treatment of Romania underscored the possibility that if the Central Powers won the war, their treatment of the Allies would likely be even more harsh. No Frenchman had to be reminded of the immense costs and intentional humiliations that had accompanied Germany's victory in 1871. Britain, France, and Russia soon learned of German plans to annex Belgium, Luxembourg, Lithuania, Courland, and Poland, impose "the most ruthless humiliation of England," and take over control of the rich Longwy-Briey iron basin in France.[3] Only the most unrealistic optimists still held out any hope for a compromise peace. It was now a war of survival. As bad as fighting the war was for the Allies, losing it would be even worse.

THE FIRST RUSSIAN REVOLUTION

For the Russians the possibility of losing the war drew ever closer. The territorial gains of the Brusilov offensive had done little to convince the Russian people of the value of continued sacrifice. Even a victory, many concluded, would only serve to keep the hated Romanov family in power. In November 1916 Brusilov had publicly boasted that "if it were possible to take a vote of the entire population, ninety-nine out of every one hundred Russians today would demand the continuation of the war to a definite and final victory regardless of the price."[4] Privately, however, he had already concluded that his men would not fight for the tsar unless the regime could explain its goals and how they related to the average Russian. Brusilov had no confidence that it could do so. The tsarina and two former premiers were of German descent, and rumors quickly spread that the tsarina's mysterious adviser, Rasputin, was in the pay of German agents. His death at the hands of Russian conservatives in December 1916 did little to quell the suspicions of pro-German activity at the court.

The military leadership of the tsar did little to quell such rumors. Even casual observers could see how incompetent the tsar

Alexei Brusilov led Russia's last great offensive of the war. An aristocratic cavalryman, he developed innovative infantry and artillery tactics, but he later grew disillusioned with the tsar's poor conduct of the war. (Library of Congress)

was in military matters. A joke that circulated in Russia about two Jews living in the war zone in Poland reflects the contemporary attitude toward the tsar and his military acumen. One of the Jews, who is pro-German, boasts about the kaiser, telling his Russian friend (inaccurately) that the German leader runs from army to army, always leading from the front. The Russian Jew then turns to his friend and exclaims, "Your [kaiser] has no dignity; he runs around like a chicken. Our tsar sits at Headquarters and the front comes to him!"[5]

In the words of a November speech given by Duma member Pavel Miliukov, the question was whether the failures of the Russian government were the result of "stupidity or treason." Either way, Russia was approaching consensus on the need for change.

The inability of the government to respond to the miseries of the unusually cold winter of 1916–1917 led to open talk of revolution at all levels of society. The 1916 harvest had provided enough food, but the overtaxed Russian transport system could not efficiently deliver that food from the countryside to the cities. In addition, Russian economic policies produced inflation that removed what food did reach the cities from the average Russian's plate. Eggs, meat, sugar, milk, and fruit all but disappeared from the workers' diet. "A revolution, if it takes place," prophesized one far-sighted Russian official, "will be spontaneous, quite likely a hunger riot."[6]

The condition of the average Russian, never luxurious, declined into outright destitution. In response to these deteriorating conditions, strikes became common, leading to a nearly 50 percent decrease in industrial production at a time when the army desperately needed artillery shells and small-arms ammunition.[7] One strike in January 1917 attracted 150,000 workers in Petrograd. Urban unrest increased, and in the countryside draft evasion became an ever more serious problem. Inside the army, desertion and disobedience rose sharply. Among those soldiers who remained loyal, malnutrition led to high disease rates, further depriving the Russian army of men.

More strikes hit Petrograd in February, timed to coincide with the reconvening of the Duma. Finally, in March, the dam broke. From March 8 to 10, a wave of strikes paralyzed Petrograd. In an important and ominous sign for the tsar, Russian security forces were reluctant to fire on the protesters. Calls for the tsar's abdication became ubiquitous, from revolutionaries who wanted to destroy the old order entirely to conservatives who sought a more effective way of prosecuting the war. On March 9, the Duma formed a provisional government and arrested several of the tsar's ministers.

Nicholas had left for his military headquarters the day before the March strikes began. Ill-informed about the realities of life in Petrograd, he was slow to react. On March 11 he received the news about the creation of the provisional government and responded by ordering that the Duma be dissolved. When the Duma disobeyed his order, Nicholas headed back to Petrograd. At the city of Pskov, workers stopped his train and detained him. Alekseev and northern front commander Nikolai Ruzsky convinced Nicholas that he had no choice but to abdicate. He did so the next day, also abdicating in the name of his sickly young son. Nicholas then urged his younger brother, Grand Duke Michael, to assume the throne. Uninterested in power or its trappings, Michael feared for his safety, believing that the public would no longer accept the Romanov family as its divinely chosen rulers. The mythic bond that had united leaders and led, Michael concluded, had permanently broken. Thus the Grand Duke, whom Nicholas had banned from Russia for several years for marrying a twice-divorced commoner, refused his brother's request. Power then devolved to the provisional government.

Prince Georgi Lvov, who had been a vocal critic of the tsar's handling of the war, became the premier of the new government. Thirty-six-year-old Alexander Kerensky, who had only been in the Duma since 1912, soon came to be one of the government's most forceful officials. A centrist politician and brilliant orator, Kerensky had spent part of the war in Finland recuperating from illness. He returned to find a system that had entirely broken down as a result of the pressures of the war, leading him to call for the end of what he termed a "medieval" tsarist system. After assuming the office of war minister in May, he assured the Allies that Russia would continue to fight and would fulfill all of its obligations. He then went to the front, asking the men to show the world that "there is strength and not weakness in liberty." Now, he told Russia's soldiers, they would fight not for the tsar, but for their own freedom and the future of their homeland. His words drove thousands of soldiers to "hysterical patriotism" and seemed to open a new era for Russia.[8] Kerensky also persuaded important military and civilian figures to remain with the government. He

Tsar Nicholas II's limited understanding of military affairs placed his government in an awkward position after his assumption of the role of commander-in-chief in 1915. His inability to turn the tide of Russian fortunes cost him his throne and his life. (© Bettmann/Corbis)

convinced Brusilov, who had considered retirement, to accept command of all Russian forces.

Russian determination to continue fighting came in part from Germany's unwillingness to negotiate a lenient peace. Instead, the Central Powers decided on what became known as the Kreuznach program. Developed during an April meeting in Kreuznach, Germany, presided over by the kaiser and attended by key figures Chancellor Bethmann Hollweg and army commanders Hindenburg and Ludendorff, the program outlined German war aims in light of the developments in Russia. At Kreuznach, the Germans decided upon the complete annexation of Lithuania, Courland, and much of Poland. The remainder of Poland would form a satellite state linked politically and economically to Germany. The participants also outlined their goals for control of parts of Belgium, France, Africa, and the Balkans. Bethmann Hollweg initially objected, noting that only a complete military victory could bring about such results. He worried that Germany would have to fight unnecessarily long to achieve the ambitious goals laid out at Kreuznach. Nevertheless, the attendees signed the protocol, making it official German policy and committing the German leadership to fighting on in the east at a time when Kerensky might have negotiated.

The Germans also began an active program to destroy the Russian system from within. In April 1917 they transported three dozen exiled Russian revolutionaries to Petrograd in a sealed train. Among these men was Vladimir Ilyich Ulianov, better known as Lenin. Although Lenin came from a wealthy background, his family had a history of revolutionary agitation. His older brother had been hanged for attempting to assassinate Tsar Alexander III in 1887. Lenin had been living in Zurich when he learned of Tsar Nicholas's abdication. The Germans arranged for Lenin's transportation to Russia in the hopes that this "Beelzebub" could help them drive out the "devil," Nicholas II.[9] Lenin's passionate disagreement with Kerensky's calls to continue the war gave him an important common thread with the Germans, who now placed him in a position to take over the leadership of the Bolshevik party.

Lenin advocated an immediate end to the war, pledging to bring "bread, land, and peace" to the Russian people. The day after his arrival in Russia he published an editorial in the Bolshevik

Pledging "Peace, Bread, and Land," the Bolshevik Red Guards contributed to the pressure on the tsar to abdicate. Their promise to pull Russia out of the war was tremendously appealing to workers and peasants alike. (© Corbis)

newspaper *Pravda* in which he announced the party's intention not to cooperate with the provisional government and to seize power from it by force if necessary. From the front lines, Brusilov noted the growing influence among his soldiers of Lenin's ideas and rhetoric. Kerensky's calls to continue the war had rallied his men temporarily, but were "not at all what the soldiers had in mind" for the long run. Instead, they came increasingly to see the value in a more radical revolution behind the Bolsheviks, whose program even the aristocratic Brusilov could see as "beautifully plain and straightforward."[10]

With the Bolsheviks gaining power and influence every day, Kerensky decided upon an offensive. He believed that he had rallied the Russian soldiers and given them new reason to fight. A battlefield victory over the Central Powers, he reasoned, would restore Russian fortunes and, as important, give him some leverage against the more radical elements inside Russia. If successful, the offensive would also legitimate the provisional government in the eyes of the British and French and might even lead them to supply Russia with more weapons.

Achieving a victory would not be easy. The Central Powers had 80 divisions on the eastern front against just 45 under-strength Russian divisions. The Kerensky government could not identify its exact operational objectives, but it knew the man in whose trust they wished to place Russia's fortunes. Kerensky asked Alexei Brusilov to plan the offensive, hoping that he could repeat some of his success from the previous year. Brusilov himself was less than optimistic. "To tell the truth," he remarked, "the government itself did not know for certain what it wanted."[11]

Aware of his gross inferiority in men and weapons, Brusilov chose to focus his efforts opposite the worn-out Austrians. As he had done in 1916, he hoped to win a battle against second-rate troops, in this case the Austrian Second and Third Armies. Attacking these armies also held out the hope of capturing the Drohobycz oil fields and, behind them, the city of Lemberg, filled with symbolic significance. Brusilov had already routed the commander of this sector, the Italian-born Austrian Field Marshal Eduard Böhm-Ermolli, in 1916. Once the hero of the 1915 recapture of Lemberg, Böhm-Ermolli's career had taken a precipitous decline the following year. After the Brusilov offensives of that year had smashed through his ill-prepared lines, Böhm-Ermolli had been relieved of command at the Germans' insistence. Once the immediate crisis had passed, the Austro-Hungarian royal family convinced the Germans to reconsider. Not only was Böhm-Ermolli allowed to return to his Second Army, but his headquarters was one of the few in the Austro-Hungarian army that remained relatively free of German oversight.

The unfortunate field marshal might have been better advised to remain in retirement, for he was to be Brusilov's target once again. On July 1, 1917, two Russian armies attacked Austro-Hungarian forces in Galicia. Russian forces were tired and so short of equipment that many men advanced without rifles. Their commanders doubted whether the men would even fight. Bolshevik political agitators had circulated among the men, preaching revolution and mutiny. Officers greeted the sight of Russians moving toward the enemy line with an immense sigh of relief.

The Russians not only advanced, they experienced tremendous success. They broke open the Austrian lines along a forty-five-mile front, driving the enemy back twenty miles in some places. Their success came in part from Brusilov's concentration of men and artillery pieces along the main axis of attack. By denuding other fronts of resources, the Russians enjoyed numerical advantages in both the number of men and the amount of shells they could fire in the immediate area of the attack. The Russians also introduced the so-called Hussite Legion, composed of men recruited from Austro-Hungarian prisoners of war of Czech and Slovak descent. These men, believing that they were fighting to create an independent Czechoslovak state after the war, had high morale. The Russians placed them immediately opposite the Austro-Hungarian 19th Infantry Division, which was also heavily Czech. Rather than fight their countrymen, the men of the 19th fled or surrendered in large numbers.[12]

Nevertheless, as happened so often in this war, a temporary breakthrough did not lead to larger gains. Once again, supply difficulties and the lack of any decisive objective limited the attacker's success. The Russians' advance placed them in areas without field defenses, far from their supplies, and exposed to strong enemy counterattacks. These attacks came on July 19, led by General Max Hoffmann, the same man who had been so instrumental in routing the Russians at Tannenberg in 1914. His counterstrike force was heavily supported by artillery and contained nine German and two Austro-Hungarian divisions. Brusilov had no choice but to begin a retreat back to his original lines.

The failure of this offensive led to the end of Brusilov's command. Physically and emotionally exhausted, he stepped down as commander of Russian forces in favor of the monarchist General Lavr Kornilov. As commander of the army, Kornilov made extensive use of the death penalty on soldiers thought to have deserted or disobeyed orders. His bombastic political speeches calling for the return of the tsar made him appear a threat to the very government he was supposed to have been serving. Under Kornilov, the fighting power of the Russian army declined even further as the political situation in Petrograd grew ever more tenuous. Kerensky understood that his frail compromise government might not have the strength to survive another crisis.

The crisis that Kerensky feared came in September at the Baltic Sea port city of Riga, about 200 miles southwest of Petrograd. The Germans spearheaded their attack at Riga with newly organized Assault Detachments. The success of the storm troops at Verdun led to the creation of fifteen Assault Battalions by February 1917. The men were all volunteers; in exchange for their more dangerous work they received double rations and extra leave time, and were excused from fatigue and sentry duties. The introduction of light machine guns, flamethrowers, and light mortars gave these troops the mobile firepower necessary to cross No Man's Land and break into the rear areas of the enemy lines.[13] Several armies developed these tactics, but they were particularly effective in the eastern front's more open spaces. Given the low morale of Russian troops and their pitiable material state, a concerted attack by elite soldiers might produce enormous results.

The two men most commonly associated with the new tactics were General Oskar von Hutier and Colonel Georg Bruchmüller. Hutier perfected the idea of developing small groups of elite soldiers who would infiltrate enemy lines and destroy their communications and supply systems. Hutier built on French, British, and

Alexander Kerensky (right) tried to find a middle ground between tsarist autocracy and Bolshevism. His enthusiasm temporarily bolstered Russian morale, but the failure of his 1917 offensive doomed his government. (© Hulton-Deutsch Collection/Corbis)

Italian innovations and convinced the German general staff to devote critical resources to the project. Bruchmüller, who came out of retirement on the outbreak of the war, proved to be an important innovator in the use of artillery. He perfected the use of smoke, gas, and conventional shells to neutralize the enemy's command posts, assembly areas, communication nodes, and road crossings. The developments spearheaded by both men aimed to win battles by isolating and surrounding the enemy rather than fighting man for man. In this way, they believed, Germany could win a war on multiple fronts against a combination of enemies that together held superior numbers of men and material.

At Riga on September 1, 1917, Bruchmüller's artillery used a variety of methods to support Hutier's Thirteenth Army. The artil-

lery began by firing more than 20,000 gas shells to terrify or eliminate Russian opposition. Gas had the additional advantage of
leaving the terrain intact for the storm troops to cross. The specially trained men of Hutier's vanguard then crossed the Dvina
River in boats and captured its north bank. Once there, they fired
rockets to indicate their success and began to assemble pontoon
boats to permit the crossing of the regular infantry behind them.
Upon seeing the rockets, Bruchmüller's gunners began a rolling
barrage to cover the German advance.

As Hutier and Bruchmüller had predicted, the plan achieved
astonishing success at limited cost. Six German infantry divisions
crossed the river on day one, with three more divisions following
on day two. By day three of the operation, German forces had entered Riga. At the cost of just 4,200 German casualties, the Thirteenth Army had inflicted 25,000 Russian casualties and captured
more than 250 artillery pieces, the equivalent of five entire divisions' worth. While the success had come against a tired and demoralized army, the victory at Riga represented one of the most
decisive and dramatic in the entire war. In celebration, the German government declared the first national holiday since the defeat of Romania.

Hutier and Bruchmüller seemed to have perfected a new way
of warfare. While none of the individual elements used at Riga
was particularly novel, the integration of the system represented a
major change in battlefield tactics. For the first time on such
a grand scale, artillery, storm troops, and conventional infantry
had all fought together in one integrated system. Riga portended
great successes if the formula could be repeated. After Riga,
Hindenburg ordered that Hutier and Bruchmüller be reassigned
to the western front, where they began to prepare German armies
in France to repeat the magic of that victory. Four divisions of the
Thirteenth Army followed them, with another three German divisions going to Italy.[14]

Still, even the capture of Riga did not promise a quick German victory. The dreaded Russian winter was fast approaching, and few German generals were confident enough to predict an easy capture of either Petrograd or Moscow. Images of Napoleon's Russian campaign a century earlier still haunted the imagination of German officers. The two-front dilemma thus remained. The Germans did feel confident enough to rescind their halfhearted offer to create an independent kingdom of Poland. The failure of ethnic Poles to respond to the offer by joining the German army sealed its fate. Germany divided Poland between itself (which occupied 90 percent of Polish territory) and Austria-Hungary (which occupied the remaining 10 percent) and transferred the king of Poland's crown to the Austro-Hungarian royal family.

THE SECOND RUSSIAN REVOLUTION

To the Russians, the meaning of Riga was clear. The fall of the city, long believed to be a hotbed of German agitation, had only minor military importance. Nevertheless, it held dramatic consequences for Kerensky and his government. The failure of the 1917 offensive and the loss of Riga demonstrated that his plan to reverse Russian fortunes by remaining in the war had failed. "If the instability of our army makes it impossible for us to hold our defenses on the Riga Gulf," exclaimed Kornilov, "then the road to Petrograd will lie open. We cannot afford to waste time. Not even a single moment can be wasted."[15] But Russians did not agree on how to solve the crisis caused by the fall of Riga. Many soldiers, especially ethnic Finns, Poles, and Ukrainians, gave up altogether and deserted.

Kornilov was among those Russians who believed that the best course of action lay in the return of the monarchy. His dispatch of cavalry to Petrograd in September, ostensibly to protect it from a German raid, frightened revolutionary leaders, who believed that Kornilov's true goal was the destruction of the revolution itself. Bolshevik leader Leon Trotsky responded by organizing sympathetic soldiers, sailors, and urban workers into a Red Guard defense force. Kornilov thereupon ordered more men into Petrograd; but most of them, tired, hungry, and demoralized, simply went home.

The Kornilov "rebellion" led to the collapse of the provisional government and created the power vacuum the Bolsheviks needed. In mid-October, the Bolshevik leadership decided to seize power in Petrograd by force. "The time for words has passed," Trotsky told a huge audience in Petrograd. "The hour has come for a duel to the death between the revolution and the counterrevolution."[16] On November 7, Red Guards took up positions in the city and arrested key members of the provisional government, although Kerensky managed to escape, protected by an American flag flying from an America diplomat's car. By the end of the day, the Bolsheviks had control of the government.

Lenin's new government soon announced its intentions to end Russia's participation in the war and cancel its war debts to the Allies. It then published the terms of the many secret treaties it found in Russia's foreign ministry, including those pledging Allied support for Russian control over Constantinople. The Bolsheviks soon became a major political problem for the Allies. The secret treaties proved to be an embarrassment for British and French diplomats who tried to retain the moral high ground, especially with their new partner, the United States. As a result, the Allies soon began an active program of support for Lenin's most powerful foe, the antirevolutionary "White" forces led by many former tsarist officers, including Kornilov.

The Bolshevik takeover offered both opportunities and challenges for Germany. Their insertion of Lenin into the Russian maelstrom did lead, as the Germans had hoped, to the collapse of the pro-Allied provisional government. The Bolsheviks' call for global revolution, however, promised to have a serious backlash in Germany, where a small, but determined, Spartacist movement with pro-Bolshevik sympathies already existed. This movement opposed Germany's continued participation in the war and began to recruit followers from Germany's urban working classes. Many Germans soon had reason to rue their connection to the Russian Beelzebub.

The opportunity lay in Lenin's obvious willingness to end the war. In December, the two sides began the first discussions toward an armistice on the eastern front, meeting at the German-held city of Brest-Litovsk. Had the Germans been willing to offer Lenin reasonable terms, he might well have quickly accepted. The Germans, however, now saw a chance not only to accomplish their Kreuznach goals, but perhaps even to gain more. German Foreign Minister Richard von Kühlmann told Trotsky that Russia, as a beaten nation, could not expect to negotiate on equal terms. The kaiser put it rather less elegantly, thundering that Germany would "batter in with the iron fist and shining sword the doors of those who will not have peace."[17] German armies continued their advance, coming within seventy miles of Petrograd by February 1918 and capturing the Black Sea port of Odessa as a preliminary step toward a German offensive against British forces in Persia.

At a February meeting at Bad Homburger, the Germans were already planning for more. Hindenburg demanded annexation and occupation of the Baltic States "for the maneuvering of my left wing in the next war." Ludendorff announced that he had promises from wealthy German industrialists to fund even more German expansion. These men, he announced, would provide two billion marks for the conquest and exploitation of Armenia, Georgia, and the oil of the Caspian Sea region. The kaiser suggested a war against the Bolsheviks to chase and kill them in a manner "akin to a tiger hunt" now that they had served their purpose and had helped to expel the tsar.[18] Success in the east had only whetted the appetites of the German elite.

Lenin favored halting the German advance by giving them what they demanded at Brest-Litovsk. Trotsky, while he understood the futility in trying to fight on, nevertheless advocated stalling in order to increase the chances of a pro-Bolshevik revolt either among the troops of the German army or inside Germany itself. Trotsky's German revolution existed only in his mind, however; Lenin's arguments for capitulation therefore carried the day. On March 3, Russia submitted to the German delegation its intention to sign a peace treaty on German terms. Russian delegate Gregori Sokolnikov contacted General Hoffmann and asked him to halt hostilities immediately rather than await the formal signing of the treaty. Hoffmann refused. Sokolnikov then arrived at Brest-Litovsk and informed the Germans that he would sign a "peace which Russia, grinding its teeth, is forced to accept."[19] Russia's participation in the war was over; its civil war between the Whites and Reds was about to begin.

Along with the Treaty of Bucharest signed shortly thereafter, the Treaty of Brest-Litovsk demonstrated to the Allies the extreme cost of losing the war. Under the terms of the treaty, Russia surrendered its former territories of Finland, the Ukraine, Bessarabia, the Baltic States, Galicia, and the entire Crimean peninsula. In all, Russia lost one million square miles of territory and 62 million people. To be sure, many of those people were not ethnically Russian, although few were German, either. Russia also surrendered to Germany vast stores of oil, grain, locomotives, heavy guns, and ammunition, which the Germans planned to use to compensate for the British blockade and to prepare for a 1918 offensive on the western front.

The Germans expected Brest-Litovsk to improve their position in the west by enabling the transfer of large numbers of men and materiel to the western front. Their harsh treatment of the newly occupied territories, however, precluded a mass reassignment of troops. Hungry peasants refused to cooperate with the Germans in handing over grain, and many people simply refused to trade their old Romanov masters for new Hohenzollern ones. As a result of the unrest in the east, German plans to move 45 divisions from Russia to France in the period between November 1917 and March

Leon Trotsky (center, wearing white scarf) arrives at Brest-Litovsk to negotiate with Germany. Knowing that Russia was on the verge of collapse, the Germans offered harsh terms, which Trotsky had little choice but to accept. (© Corbis)

1918 had to be revised downward to 33 divisions. A more lenient occupation policy in the east would have freed up many more troops, but such a policy would not have been consistent with German expansionist goals. As a result, the Germans were still unable to solve their two-front dilemma.[20]

The situation in the Ukraine shows these problems most clearly. The unwillingness of the Bolsheviks to support Ukrainian desires for independence led to a civil war there and the establishment of several competing governments. In February 1918 Germany recognized one of them in exchange for nearly six months' worth of grain and minerals. The Central Powers also returned Ukrainian prisoners of war in German and Austrian prison camps. The Bolsheviks responded by invading the Ukraine, occupying

Kiev, and chasing the German-sponsored government out. In March, Germany and Austria replied with their own invasion, less out of concern for the Ukrainians than out of a desire to ensure the flow of the promised supplies.

The offensive worked, but Ukrainian peasants, expecting another army to come through their fields in the near future, proved reluctant to return to their farms. The Germans then decided to cut out the middleman and dissolved the same government they had played such an important role in creating. Field Marshal Hermann von Eichhorn and his assistant, Wilhelm Groener, declared martial law, then installed a new puppet government. Led by a former tsarist general of Cossacks, Pavlo Skoropadsky, the Germans and their Ukrainian allies attempted to restore order. Skoropadsky's social conservatism, antirepublican government, and obvious reliance on the Germans undermined these efforts and led to further violence.

Bolshevik agitators took advantage of Ukrainian displeasure with Skoropadsky, arguing that the Ukraine's future lay in a renewed relationship with the new regime in Russia. This option did not appeal to most Ukrainians, but the manifest failures of Skoropadsky's government continued to mount. Displeasure with the German occupiers also grew, culminating in the assassination of Eichhorn by a Ukrainian nationalist on July 30.

The upheaval in the Ukraine forced the Germans to spend more resources than they would have liked. In all, the Central Powers had 650,000 troops there, and they consumed far more food than the Ukraine exported to Germany. The disruptions in the Ukraine therefore both directly and indirectly prevented the Germans from reaping the tremendous harvests that they had expected. By one estimate, the Germans saw only one-tenth of the grain that they had anticipated.[21] Neither were the Ukraine's miseries over. The republic became an important battleground between White and Red forces in the Russian Civil War and was the scene of a horrible famine in the interwar years.

Abiding turmoil in the east notwithstanding, the Germans had still won a notable set of victories there. They had also tested a new tactical system that had yielded devastating results. Their task now was to adjust this system for the conditions of the remaining fronts, particularly Italy and the western front. Moreover, the Germans knew that they would need to win the war quickly, as masses of fresh, eager American troops were beginning to arrive in France. Fortunately for Germany, 1917 on the western front had been a terrible year for the Allies, giving the Germans the breathing room they needed to readjust and prepare for what they knew would be the year of decision.

9

SALVATION AND SACRIFICE

American Entry, Vimy Ridge, and the Chemin des Dames

> General Nivelle is convinced that he can and will obtain a decisive re-
> sult. Should one ask on what he bases his confidence? I asked him
> that, not because I did not believe him capable of the success that we
> all wanted, but because we had already heard the same language, be-
> fore other offensives which did not obtain any particular success. [He
> answered that] it has become possible to employ other methods.
>
> —British diplomat Lord George Curzon,
> reporting on a meeting held in London, January 15, 1917

FRENCH General Robert Nivelle, a rare French Protestant with a
half-Italian father and an English mother, had a competent, but
not spectacular, prewar career. He had risen to colonel in command of an artillery regiment in 1914 but was headed for retirement when the war led to an extension of his career. Nivelle had
been unpopular with many of his peers during his thirty-nine
years of service because of his reputed prejudice against Roman
Catholics, a problematic trait when so many senior French officers, like Foch and Castelnau, were devout Catholics. His reputation as one of the army's best horsemen served him well on the
parade ground, but it quickly became obvious that his equestrian
skills would not be needed on the modern battlefield.

Nivelle had, however, led and fought well in the war's early
months, leading to his rapid promotion. His artillery batteries
in the Sixth Army had played a critical role in the Battle of
the Marne in 1914. His superiors soon came to be impressed by
his creative tactical use of field artillery pieces, and promoted
him to division command in 1915. At Verdun, Nivelle became a

household word in France, recapturing critical positions like Forts Douaumont and Vaux at relatively light cost. He had handled each of his new assignments with talent, skill, and innovative thinking that backed up his claim that he had discovered a new formula for fighting modern warfare. This quality made him stand out next to more senior commanders like Foch, Franchet d'Esperey, and Castelnau, who lacked new ideas. Furthermore, Nivelle's confidence stood in marked contrast to the extreme caution of generals like Fayolle and Pétain. Only Nivelle argued that he could win the war quickly and at relatively low cost.

Nivelle also promised to improve the French army's relationship with its British allies. As a result of his having a British mother, Nivelle understood British social mores and spoke fluent, idiomatic English. That his maternal grandfather had been a British officer under the legendary Duke of Wellington only endeared him further to English officers and politicians. (For the sake of Allied harmony, it was best not to dwell on the irony that Wellington had been responsible for the defeat of Napoleonic France at Waterloo in 1815.) The British army's liaison officer to French headquarters thought Nivelle was "smart, plausible, and cool." David Lloyd George, then Britain's prime minister, thought him the finest soldier in the French army: "Here at last," he exclaimed, "is a general whose plan I can understand."[1]

Lloyd George also saw in Nivelle a chance to reduce the authority of his own commander, Douglas Haig. The prime minister had never been a supporter of Haig, but he felt that the field marshal's links to the royal family and the conservative politicians upon whom Lloyd George's coalition government depended made removing him impossible. The bloodletting at the Somme convinced Lloyd George that Haig was a "dunce" whose unimaginative plans needlessly wasted the lives of British soldiers.[2] He had publicly humiliated Haig by coming to France and meeting with Foch to ask him why French forces had advanced on the Somme further than British forces had (Foch refused to answer). If Lloyd

George had no choice but to retain Haig as commander of British forces, he could at least subordinate Haig by placing him underneath a joint Allied command led by Nivelle. "Nivelle has proved himself to be a Man at Verdun," Lloyd George told his confidential secretary, "& when you get a Man against one who has not proved himself, why, you back the Man."[3]

While willing to coordinate his actions with his French allies and even to accept their overall strategic guidance, Haig insisted on absolute control over British operations. Lloyd George prepared a trap for Haig at the Calais conference held on February 26, 1917. Lloyd George planned to use the conference, originally conceived for the prosaic but important function of coordinating railroad logistics, to give Nivelle control over all Allied operations on the western front. The British prime minister had already prepared a memorandum that gave Nivelle control over British operations, supply, and administration beginning on March 1. Before leaving for Calais, he had secretly attained the British Cabinet's approval of the plan, but he had kept the Chief of the Imperial General Staff, General William Robertson, entirely in the dark. At the start of the conference, Lloyd George summarily dismissed the railroad experts; then he and Nivelle introduced the joint plan together, leaving Haig with little authority but to carry out Nivelle's orders.

Haig, who had never fallen under Nivelle's spell, reacted with horror. He and Robertson, both of whom detested Lloyd George were dumbfounded. After the meeting concluded, Haig protested Lloyd George's plan to subordinate him to Nivelle through a personal letter to King George V. The king promised to support Haig but told him that on no account could he create a leadership crisis by resigning as he had threatened to do. Robertson intervened, obtaining Lloyd George's agreement to leave the conditions in place only for the duration of the planned spring offensive. In practice, Nivelle rarely insisted on overseeing British operations as long as the British stuck to his overall strategic vision.

Nivelle's political conduct served him better with French politicians than it did with British generals. To repay the initial confidence placed in him, Nivelle created an atmosphere of openness at his headquarters. He moved French headquarters out of Joffre's palatial Château de Chantilly and into smaller, less majestic quarters nearer to the front at Beauvais. Unlike Joffre, who had once threatened to arrest politicians who came to his headquarters unannounced, Nivelle welcomed them, leading tours of his headquarters personally and showing a political acumen and charisma that Joffre manifestly lacked. Nivelle also had a gift for symbols and language. In one of his most dramatic linguistic reforms, he changed the name of the GAR from Groupe d'armées de Réserve to the more aggressive sounding Groupe d'armées de Rupture.

Nivelle aimed to destroy the entire seventy-mile-long salient that jutted westward into Allied lines from Arras to Craonne. He asked the British to attack the northern shoulder of the salient just before French forces attacked the southern shoulder. The twin attacks would prevent the Germans from focusing on either one. By using the methods he claimed to have perfected at Verdun, he would achieve "a rupture in 24 to 48 hours with one blow by a brisk attack" in the German lines. Nivelle thus hoped to force an enemy withdrawal from the entire salient. His staff spent the first months of 1917 training men in the new methods, assembling the needed supplies, building roads, and instilling in French forces an ethos of "violence, brutality, and rapidity."[4]

As a show of its faith, the government reassigned generals in whom Nivelle had little confidence. It dispatched Foch, the former commander of Army Group North, to the busywork assignment of preparing a war plan in the extremely unlikely event of a German violation of Swiss neutrality. Marie-Emile Fayolle, a favorite of the men because he did not order needless attacks, received a promotion to commander of Army Group Center, Nivelle's old command at Verdun. In reality, Nivelle wanted

Fayolle in the Verdun sector because he did not envision attacking there. Thus Fayolle sat out 1917 in relative inactivity. By a happy coincidence, the French government decided to send Joffre on a speaking tour of the United States; thus the old commander would not be around to look over the new commander's shoulder.

Nivelle believed that the key to breaking the western front lay along a ridge between the Aisne and Ailette Rivers. There sat a panoramic country lane called the Chemin des Dames (Road of the Ladies), named after the daughters of Louis XV, for whom the area had been a favorite riding and picnic site. Here the front line ran west to east as the river ran, not north to south as on most of the western front. Nivelle hoped that because the region had been calm for much of the war, the German defenses there would be inadequate to resist men trained to carry out his new methods. While the lane's magnificent views of the nearby countryside had offered Louis XV's daughters a pleasant ride, they also offered German defenders a perfect crow's nest—as high as 600 feet over the plains below—from which to observe the French movements. The Germans, moreover, had defended the region since 1914 and knew its crevices and slopes intimately.

The Germans had already begun to undermine the principles of Nivelle's plan by retiring to a dominant set of prepared defenses known to them as the Siegfried Line and to the Allies as the Hindenburg Line. In places, the retirement to the Hindenburg Line forced the Germans to give as much as forty miles, but by straightening the line and moving back to more solid defenses, they freed up 13 infantry divisions from static defense duties. As they retreated, the Germans destroyed everything in their path, poisoning water wells, leveling buildings, setting booby traps, and dynamiting bridges. In February 1917 Australian forces entered the city of Bapaume, an important objective of the Somme offensive, without firing a shot. They found it a complete ruin.

The construction of the Hindenburg Line, largely accomplished by prisoners of war forced to perform hard labor, meant that by evacuating much of the salient voluntarily, the Germans had eliminated the strategic justification for Nivelle's offensive. Nivelle announced that his offensive would nevertheless go ahead as scheduled, even if it now meant that Allied forces would have to attack much stronger positions. He believed that his 49 infantry divisions and 5,300 artillery pieces, in combination with his new tactics, would prove sufficient to overcome both the defenses on the Chemin des Dames ridge itself and in the Hindenburg Line behind it.

Hubert Lyautey, a hero of French colonial operations named war minister in December 1916, thought the plan reckless and imprudent. Lyautey had had no part in the decision to give Nivelle command and was less enamored of him than the French politicians were. Upon being briefed about Nivelle's plan, he belittled it by calling it "a plan for the army of the Duchess of Gerolstein," an unflattering reference to an 1867 comic opera by Jacques Offenbach.[5] Lyautey considered replacing Nivelle, but ran into stiff opposition from powerful members of the French Parliament. In part to protest the offensive without making his objections public, Lyautey resigned as war minister in March 1917, returning to his post as governor-general of Morocco.

Lyautey's resignation contributed to the fall of the Briand cabinet. The new cabinet included mathematician and aviation expert Paul Painlevé as minister of war. Painlevé was France's seventh minister of war since 1914 and the first civilian to hold the post in that time. Painlevé told Nivelle of his concerns about the operation and informed the general that his staff had done a poor job of maintaining secrecy. Several elements of the plan, including its start date, had already become common knowledge in Parisian circles not normally privy to such information. Moreover, at least ten copies of the plan had already turned up in London.[6] Painlevé did not know that details of the plan were common in German circles as well. Two separate German raids on French trenches had captured complete copies of the plan, which had inexplicably been given to officers in dugouts on the front line. Nivelle continued to voice his optimism and Painlevé, unwilling to provoke a major political crisis so soon after taking office, yielded.

Painlevé soon learned that many French generals, including some charged with leading the attacks, did not share Nivelle's confidence. Pétain's opposition might be written off as a function of the general's customary pessimism and mistrust of anything favored by politicians, but that of the aggressive Franchet d'Esperey and the widely respected Joseph Micheler could not. On April 4, Painlevé met with Nivelle to share these doubts and ask the general to scale down the offensive and its goals. With the preliminary artillery phase of the British offensive just five days away, Nivelle raged at Painlevé and threatened to resign if the government forced changes in his plan. "The only thing I fear," Nivelle told Painlevé, "is that the enemy will evacuate. The more Germans there are, the greater the victory will be." The minister again yielded, but asked Nivelle to agree to halt the offensive if no breakthrough occurred at the Chemin des Dames within forty-eight hours. Nivelle promised that he would do so. "I do not intend to restart the Battle of the Somme," Nivelle said.[7]

Two days after the meeting, on April 6, 1917, the United States Congress overwhelmingly approved President Wilson's request for a declaration of war against Germany in response to the Germans' resumption of unrestricted submarine warfare. Although it would take time for the Americans to make their presence felt, the news sent a wave of emotion through France. To mark the event, Prime Minister Alexandre Ribot called for a special session of the French Chamber of Deputies. Several desks in the Chamber sat empty because the men who normally occupied them had left to serve in the army. Others had wreaths commemorating the deaths in battle of the men (like Emil Driant) who had formerly occupied them. When Ribot first spoke the word "Amérique," the Deputies "rose in unison" and turned to American Ambassador William Graves Sharp, bowing to him and cheering.

Feelings were no less strong in the army. Nivelle sent a letter to the American chief of staff, General Hugh Scott, which read:

> The French Army has heard with the deepest emotion the noble and moving words addressed by President Wilson to the American Congress. Her joy is immense on hearing that Congress has declared war with Germany. She recalls the memory of military fraternity sealed more than a century ago by Lafayette and Rochambeau on American soil and which will be made still tighter on the battlefields of Europe.[8]

The United States, in the words of Robert Bruce, "meant more to France than merely a new ally in the war; it symbolized salvation."[9] The entry of the United States seemed to many Frenchmen a positive sign for the offensive they were about to commence.

Nivelle's plan called for the British to begin the spring offensive with an attack near the city of Arras. The key to Arras and the Douai plain to the east lay at Vimy Ridge, a 250-acre crest of high ground held today in perpetuity by the Canadian government. The Vimy Ridge's obvious strategic value made it an important German prize during the race to the sea. Subsequently, it became the scene of three separate battles in 1915 and 1916. In 1915, the French lost almost 150,000 men in a futile attempt to retake the ridge. That fall, French forces finally succeeded in taking it back. In 1916, the Arras sector fell into British hands as part of a shortening of the French front, designed to free up more French units for combat at Verdun and the Somme. A German offensive in May of that year retook Vimy Ridge, embarrassing British generals, who had promised to hold it.

Although Haig remained displeased by the command arrangement for the spring, he saw the value in retaking both Arras and

Soldiers of the British Royal Field Artillery move pieces by hand in preparation for the Vimy Ridge assault in April 1917. Field artillery was responsible for damaging enemy wire and providing direct fire support during the offensive. (Imperial War Museum, Crown Copyright, P. 396)

Vimy Ridge. He assigned the task of seizing the latter to one of his protégés, General Henry S. Horne, who was commanding the British First Army. To capture an objective as powerful as Vimy Ridge, Horne turned to his best unit, the Canadian Corps, which was fighting as a quasi-independent force reporting to Ottawa, but under the command of a British general, Julian Byng. A veteran of the Boer War, the First Battle of Ypres, and Gallipoli, Byng had four divisions of Canadian troops who had acquired a reputation for efficiency and combat cohesion second to none.

The attack on Vimy Ridge showed the growing complexity of British military operations. The Royal Flying Corps first attained air superiority, allowing for careful British artillery spotting, thus greatly improving the accuracy of the British barrage. British gunners concentrated one heavy gun per 21 yards of the enemy front, as opposed to one per 57 yards at the Somme.[10] The one-week preparatory bombardment contained fewer duds and more high explosives, allowing the artillery to neutralize a much higher percentage of enemy artillery batteries than at any other point of the war thus far. Artillery also cut the German wire much more effectively than it had at the Somme. Staff work had also improved, demonstrating how well the British had internalized the lessons of the Somme and how much they had learned in the intervening months.

German preoccupation with the expected French attack near the Chemin des Dames offered possibilities for the British. The German redirection of forces to the Aisne River sector left the Arras sector lightly defended. As a result, the British enjoyed an advantage in infantry divisions of 12 to 8 on top of their already large advantage in artillery pieces. British artillery shelling, moreover, led German Sixth Army commanders to move their reserves so far to the rear that they could not effectively counterattack.

The infantry attack began on Easter Sunday, April 9, with careful preparations made by Byng and his staff. Gas shelling kept the Germans pinned to their positions and killed many of the unprotected German horses, impeding the resupply of ammunition and other supplies to the men at the front. A creeping barrage protected the infantry as it advanced, and 48 tanks provided even more cover, although many of the machines still suffered from mechanical problems. The Canadians charged the ridge and achieved remarkable results for an operation originally envisioned as a diversion. In the first hour, they captured the German first line, which sat just a few yards across No Man's Land.

The Canadians succeeded in advancing past all three German lines on Vimy Ridge. They captured 9,000 German prisoners and recovered the entire ridge where today stands one of the western front's largest memorials. The British Third Army, attacking closer to Arras, took another 4,000 German prisoners. Together they also took 200 German heavy artillery pieces and moved the line more than three miles. Nevertheless, no breakthrough occurred. While German lines proved to be vulnerable to initial piercings, they nevertheless retained enough strength to repulse a British cavalry charge and prevent a complete British breakthrough. Poor weather on April 11 slowed the British and gave Ludendorff a chance to address a situation that he considered critical.

The capture of Vimy Ridge represented the single largest territorial gain in one day for the British army to date. It had been a heroic and well-planned attack, but it did not lead to further gains. The Germans were able to stabilize their lines without taking men away from the Chemin des Dames sector, and the momentum of the British offensives soon slowed. Allied attempts to seize the communication centers of Douai and Cambrai failed. Nevertheless, the volunteer British forces had demonstrated a prowess that deeply impressed the Germans. Bavarian Crown Prince Rupprecht, in charge of all German operations north of the Oise River, confided to his diary, "Is it of any use to pursue the war further under such conditions?"[11]

For the Allied success at Arras to have greater meaning for the war, Nivelle would have to achieve a similar victory. As the start date of April 16 approached, French morale surged. The Americans had joined the war, and the Canadians had achieved one of the most dramatic Allied victories on the western front by retaking Vimy Ridge. Perhaps the momentum had turned, and the French attack on the Chemin des Dames would indeed be the final drive of the war. "An epic fever has taken a hold of us," noted one French soldier. "Officers and soldiers are refusing leave so as not to miss the great offensive."[12] One French divisional commander was so confident that he hired a band to play "La Marseillaise" upon the division's triumphant march into the town that

Like his Australian counterpart John Monash, Canadian Arthur Currie rose through the ranks despite not conforming to the British ideal. To underscore his separation from the British system, he refused to grow the mustache his British counterparts sported. (Australian War Memorial, negative no. H06979)

was their primary objective for day one. Nivelle and his supporters believed that circumstances had rarely favored a general so well in the history of warfare.

THE CHEMIN DES DAMES

Not all signs were positive. A German airplane had flown over French lines, dropping a note reading "When will this attack of yours begin?"[13] A mixture of snow, rain, and fog left the soil a morass of cold mud. The poor weather grounded the fleet of 500 French airplanes and 40 observation balloons, the largest air armada the French had yet assembled. Moreover, the diversion at Vimy Ridge had not succeeded, as Nivelle had hoped, in forcing the Germans to move forces away from the Chemin des Dames. As a final blow, a sergeant in one of the French armies who was carrying a complete copy of the latest plan for his regiment became a prisoner of war as a result of a German trench raid. Surprise was thus out of the question.

Having learned of the Allied plan in advance, the Germans not only knew when the French would attack, but they also knew how to stop it. German pilots had seen enough before the fog rolled in to give their staff an accurate picture of French dispositions. German troops proceeded to reinforce concrete emplacements in which they housed machine guns with interlocking fields of fire. They also strengthened the natural chalk caverns in which they planned to protect themselves from French artillery. They moved more men into the sector from the general reserve, increasing their forces in the Aisne sector by a factor of five. Whereas in February the Germans had had just nine divisions in the sector to meet forty-four French divisions, by April they had forty-three. Many of these divisions were specially trained to conduct counteroffensives, an indication of the confidence the Germans had in their ability to repulse the attack.

Still, Nivelle remained confident. He altered a famous call of Verdun, "On les aura" (We'll get them) to "On les a" (We've got them). He and the aggressive General Charles Mangin entrusted the first wave of the attack to veteran troops in units that had proved themselves at Verdun. They included in the first wave the colonials Mangin preferred. To keep up with the creeping barrage, these men would have to advance uphill in muddy terrain at a pace of 100 yards every three minutes across a total front of approximately 15 miles. Mangin's Sixth Army formed the westernmost portion of the attack and was responsible for capturing the most powerful single position on the line, the Fort de Malmaison. In the center sat General Denis Duchêne's Tenth Army. Duchêne, a graduate of the French military academy at St. Cyr, was of the old school, totally devoted to the offensive as the only means of conducting warfare. The easternmost part of the front belonged to the Fifth Army, which was under the command of a cavalry general whose lack of familiarity with either the infantry or the artillery had caused his subordinates to lose faith in him.

The day of the attack opened with more bad weather. Cloudy, snowy weather grounded the French aircraft once more, meaning that gunners had to fire against the last known positions of their targets. The Germans responded by moving many of their guns. Thus French artillery fire could neither hit targets where they were nor correct their fire from information provided by pilots. The cold, icy rain made the the French soldiers particularly miserable; most had not slept for days. Still, they left their trenches in relatively good spirits. One more battle and the western front might just break.

The great optimism that had swept over so many French soldiers helps to explain the disillusion that came next. Their attack soon withered in the face of intense German machine gun fire. "The regiments were taken almost immediately under the fire of innumerable machine guns protected from the bombardment by concrete casements and natural caverns," reported one general. There were so many machine gun nests in the Chemin des Dames defenses that photo reconnaissance "could not have suspected their presence."[14]

Under such fire, the infantry could not hope to advance at the pace set for them. Consequently, the rolling barrage moved too far forward to offer them any meaningful protection. The Germans had more than enough time to sight their weapons and take their pick from among the packets of French soldiers moving slowly toward them. The French medical service, receiving several times the number of wounded it had been told to prepare for, was soon overwhelmed, adding to the misery. By midday many French units had the additional problem of turning back the counterattacks that were part of the Germans' plan. The only French suc-

*In contrast to Nivelle's rosy proclamations, French attacks in
Champagne in 1917 were bloody disasters. They led to widespread
mutinies and the replacement of Nivelle by Henri-Philippe Pétain.
(National Archives)*

cesses of the first day had come from the casualties the Germans
suffered as a result of those counterattacks and the prisoners who,
as on the Somme, had taken refuge from the artillery in their deep
dugouts and surrendered to the first soldiers who overran their positions.

By nightfall, no French units sat on or even near their first day's
objectives. Even Mangin's colonials had failed. Nivelle decided to
resume the attacks on the second day. Even if he had intended to
stay true to his promise to Painlevé, he still had twenty-four hours
to rupture the German front. On the second day, the French attacked again, this time in units hastily formed out of the remnants
of those shattered the day before. Officers were in short supply,
and the artillery batteries lacked the shell reserves to support the
attack. Nivelle broke his pledge and attacked again on April 18,

leading Painlevé to try in vain to halt the attack on April 20. Finally, on April 23, President Raymond Poincaré took the highly unusual step of ordering a halt in the offensive.

In seven days of attacks on the Chemin des Dames position, the French lost 30,000 men killed, 100,000 wounded (the medical corps had been told to prepare for 15,000 wounded), and 4,000 prisoners. Because Nivelle's plan put France's best troops in the first wave, the losses hit elite units disproportionately. Nivelle announced, to the amazement of his staff and the government, that he would resume the attacks in May. He deflected blame onto his army commanders, charging Mangin with failures of leadership and relieving him of his command.

To protect the French army from an immediate concentration of German forces, the British attacked again at Arras. They continued their offensives well into May, suffering some of their heaviest casualties in the campaign as a result of these ad hoc attacks. Nivelle's failure had confirmed Haig's suspicions, but the losses the British took in protecting the French gave him little cause to gloat. Along with the Vimy Ridge success, however, it did solidify his position against Lloyd George and guarantee that the latter could not move to replace him unless he failed as spectacularly as Nivelle had done.

The failures on the Chemin des Dames created a crisis in the French army. The losses revealed Nivelle's charm to be mere naïveté, his charisma to be slick and cynical posturing, and his military acumen to be better suited to the Napoleonic period. He ignored calls for his resignation and insisted that he could still achieve a strategic breakthrough. But the man with the formula for victory had been unmasked as a snake-oil salesman. The time had come for a change in leadership, and Nivelle was sent to Algeria. The French government now had to find to a man who had the confidence of the troops and who would not advocate any more offensives.

France turned to Pétain; he was named commander of the

French army on May 15. His successful defense of Verdun made him a popular choice with both the troops and the French populace generally. He had never believed in the possibility of piercing the German lines at the Chemin des Dames or anywhere else in 1917. The politicians who supported naming him commander could therefore count on him not to resume the offensive prematurely. Pétain, however, came with some drawbacks, which were largely unknown outside the circle of French military and political leaders who knew him best. He held a deep suspicion of the French republican form of government and despised almost all of France's senior politicians, traits that would cost France dearly in 1940. Furthermore, he held an equally deep mistrust of the British. As a result, throughout 1917 and into 1918 the two armies fought two largely disconnected wars.

The French armies Pétain now commanded faced a tremendous crisis in morale as a result of the repulse on the Chemin des Dames. Shortly before Pétain took over, several units of the French army began what army officials called "acts of collective indiscipline." They did not desert and they did not refuse to leave their positions unguarded, but they did refuse to resume the offensive or, in many cases, even to advance into the front lines.

In his excellent study of the French Fifth Infantry Division, Leonard Smith argues that the mutinies resulted from the belief among French soldiers that proportionality had broken down. The soldiers, he argues, had risked their lives in the past and would continue to risk their lives to expel the Germans from French soil, but they refused to do so under the circumstances they had seen at the Chemin des Dames. Men understood that in war soldiers die; they failed to understand, however, how their deaths in senseless operations such as that on the Chemin des Dames brought France any closer to victory.[15] In the words of one soldier, "I can no longer believe in a victory of arms after what I have just seen."[16]

The soldiers of the French army came increasingly to see their lot as a choice between a seeming eternity of "incarceration in the trenches" or a series of bloody failures like the Chemin des Dames. The mutinies were an attempt to find a third way. They were an expression of the soldiers' unwillingness to continue to fight the war the generals' way.[17] In their eyes, the French state and the French army had ceased to see them as individuals and as citizens of the republic. From their miserable pay, food, and housing, they concluded that their officers had come to see them as little more than animals. In the words of one song sung by mutineers:

> Adieu la vie, adieu l'amour
> Adieu, toutes les femmes
> C'en est fini et pour toujours
> Dans cette guerre infâme
> C'est à Craonne sur le plateau
> Qu'on va laisser le peau
> Car nous sommes tous condamnés
> C'est nous les sacrifiés
>
> Goodbye life, goodbye love
> Goodbye to all the ladies
> It is over forever
> In this vile war
> It is on the plateau of Craonne
> That we will leave our skins
> For we are all condemned
> We who are sacrificed[18]

French headquarters originally blamed pacifist agitators for the outbreak of the mutinies. It soon became obvious to Pétain and others, however, that the mutineers came from some of the best units in the French army. Many of them were highly decorated veterans of Verdun and the Somme. Writing them off as cowards or malcontents would not do. Sixty-eight divisions became unavailable for service at one point during May and June, making the mutinies far too common to dismiss as a series of isolated incidents. Later French army studies identified the most common features of the mutineers: service in infantry units (artillery and cavalry were not affected); service in units that had served at the Chemin des Dames or in one of the supporting attacks; and service in units whose officers had performed poorly in the recent offensives. Married men were more likely to mutiny than single men, a reflection of the lack of leave that caused men to go months or even years without seeing their families. The studies found no correlation between the mutinies and units believed by French headquarters to include pacifist elements.

The French mutineers had taken great care not to reveal their activity to the Germans or give the enemy a chance to exploit the situation militarily. "Soldiers have their grievances," said one, "but the Boche is still there, and we must not let him pass." Ludendorff later recalled that he had received only "faint echoes" of the disturbances happening just a few miles from German positions. As a result, the mutinies had little impact on the overall strategic situation.[19]

The soldiers' complaints often had political overtones as well. A small number chanted "The Internationale" or showed their support for the Bolsheviks by waving red flags, but they remained a clear minority. Many mutineers openly supported an end to the war, but not peace at any cost. The mutineers commonly called for a peace without annexations; but, tellingly, many of them demanded that France regain Alsace and Lorraine as a condition for ending the war. These demands demonstrate that the French soldiers retained a careful link with the political goals of the French state and that they did not consider Alsace and Lorraine to be "annexations." Most often, they argued for the return of Belgian independence and German evacuation of all territory it had occupied since 1914.

The mutinies had a dramatic impact on the French army itself. Pétain managed to put the mutinies to rest with a combination of heavy-handedness and concern for the men's legitimate grievances. He authorized the executions of 27 men (out of 499 condemned to death by military tribunals) who had committed serious crimes, such as threatening officers or advocating mass desertion. Almost 3,000 others found guilty of lesser offenses received prison sentences or hard labor.

Pétain also changed conditions at the front. He authorized more regular leave and included extra time for men who lived far from the front so that they would not spend the majority of their leave time in train stations or en route home. He also ordered the preparation of better meals, including the addition of more fresh vegetables into the soldiers' diets. Citing a report that blamed drunkenness for many of the disturbances, he took steps to control the soldiers' access to their beloved *pinard,* a cheap, watered-down wine. He removed dozens of officers, including two generals, and told the remainder that they had to take a greater interest in the welfare of their men and had to be seen at the front more regularly. He gave the French army a much-needed rest by canceling an offensive scheduled for mid-June.

Pétain famously told his men that France would wait for tanks and the Americans before attacking again. He did, however, order three limited and meticulously planned offensives. The first used men from the north who were unaffected by the mutinies to support Haig's summer operations at Ypres. The second recaptured two important positions still in Germany hands at Verdun, Hill 304 and the Mort Homme ridge. In October, acting on intelligence that the Germans had seriously denuded their Chemin des Dames defenses in order to reinforce Ypres, Pétain even dared to try again in this notorious area. His attack succeeded, taking the entire ridge in one week at a cost of 2,240 French soldiers killed. No sign of mutiny appeared in any of the advancing units. The attacks, especially the one at the Chemin des Dames, gave the French army a badly needed morale boost.

Pétain also began the belated process of modernizing the French army. He started training soldiers in combined arms operations,

Aviation gave birth to anti-aircraft gunners, like these British soldiers on the western front. Gunners became more important as pilots learned to strafe ground positions from the air. (United States Air Force Academy McDermott Library Special Collections)

integrating infantry with artillery, air, and armor. Larger artillery pieces and tanks provided heavy fire support, while trench mortars and light machine guns gave attacking infantry mobile weaponry. Pétain ordered the creation of elastic defenses in depth such as the one the Germans had used at the Somme. First lines would slow down attacking Germans, while second lines offered the main resistance, and third lines counterattacked where practicable. French offensives, limited and local, would proceed only with proper intelligence and logistical support. Whatever his faults, and however great his crimes in the next world war, Pétain had brought the French army back from the edge of mutiny. Morale improved, and Pétain restored "dignity to the individual soldier, if not his sense of isolation from society."[20] The French army had survived.

THE SIXTH TO ELEVENTH BATTLES OF THE ISONZO

The Italian Cadorna did all he could to rival the French Nivelle for stubbornness and insensitivity to the welfare of his men. Between August 1916 and August 1917 he launched six more attacks in the Isonzo River valley. While none of these battles yielded the results necessary to allow Cadorna to perform his promised walk to Vienna, each produced just enough success to justify a sequel. Cadorna therefore saw each bloody battle not as a setback, but as a victory and proof of the developing fighting capability of the Italian army. Each new offensive that he planned seemingly held out the prospect of being the last.

The August 1916 attack, the Sixth Battle of the Isonzo, yielded Italy's first substantive gains of the war. The Brusilov offensives had distracted Austrian attention, and the ability of the Italians to hold their positions on the Asiago Plain had led to a noticeable rise in morale. Italian troops, moreover, "thirsted to avenge" 6,900 of their comrades, victims of a surprise Austro-Hungarian gas attack in late June. The high winds of the mountains created unpredictable weather conditions for gas, and the Austrian use of gas represented the first attack of its kind on the Isonzo. Italian troops, who had few gas masks, died "horribly and slowly," in the words of one historian of the battles, their eyes and lungs burning.[21]

Thus motivated, Italian soldiers fought well. They captured Mt. San Michele and Mt. Sabotino as well as the region's largest town, Gorizia. Although the town was largely abandoned and badly damaged by August 1916, its capture, the first Austro-Hungarian city to fall to Italian forces, nevertheless marked an important victory. The Italians now had control of the east bank of the Isonzo River, forcing the Austro-Hungarians to assemble a new defensive line.

Cadorna attacked in September (the Seventh Battle of the Isonzo), hoping to catch the Austrians before they could establish their new defenses. The Italians achieved some successes, but could not break through. Two more offensives in the fall gained the Italians three more miles, but at very high cost. Italian war weariness became a serious problem, but no signs of a mutiny appeared. Lloyd George, watching from London, was sufficiently impressed by the Italian gains to support the dispatch of British soldiers and artillery pieces to reinforce Cadorna and give the Italians a chance at a major breakthrough.

Winter weather slowed the pace of operations and gave Haig and Robertson sufficient time to stop Lloyd George's scheme. Cadorna attacked again in spring 1917 with the largest Italian effort to date. In May, after the Nivelle offensive and the British Arras offensive had ended, Italy launched the Tenth Battle of the Isonzo. Italian forces moved into the Bainsizza Plateau northeast of Gorizia, but at a heavy cost. The Italians suffered 157,000 casualties to Austria-Hungary's 75,000. Believing that the Austro-Hungarians were at the limits of their capabilities, Cadorna decided to try yet again.

The Eleventh Battle of the Isonzo in August nearly accomplished Cadorna's goals. The attack involved more Italian soldiers than had been in the entire Italian military in 1915. More than 530,000 men attacked along a thirty-mile front. The aggressive General Luigi Capello, once banished by Cadorna, had returned to command the Second Army. His men had the responsibility of capturing the remaining Austro-Hungarian positions in the Bainsizza Plateau. The Duke of Aosta, from whom Capello had stolen the credit for the capture of Gorizia, would attack to the south with his Third Army, offering Capello support and moving between Gorizia and Monfalcone.

Amid heavy losses, Boroević's forces stopped the Third Army. Capello, however, captured the entire Bainsizza Plateau, stopping only when his men outran their supplies. The highlight of the battle for the Italians came when the soldiers in the valley below

Italian soldiers on the Isonzo front peer from behind bulletproof screens at the Austrian lines, visible in the background. Note the mountainous terrain and the shallowness of the trenches dug into the rock. (United States Air Force Academy McDermott Library Special Collections)

Mt. Santo heard Italian martial music coming from the summit above. The band played on, despite Austro-Hungarian shelling. The cheers from the valley drove on the band's leader, world-famous conductor Arturo Toscanini, who at age fifty had climbed the 2,250-foot mountain to rouse Italian troops to victory.[22] It marked the high point of the Italian war effort.

Not for the first time in the war, the defeated Austrians turned to the Germans. They could no longer hold their lines without support. If the British and French reinforced the Italian sector, the Austro-Hungarian position would quickly become hopeless. After eleven efforts and casualties estimated at 460,000 Italian dead and another 960,000 wounded, Cadorna had finally worn out the Austro-Hungarian army. He was still a long way from Vienna, but he had seemingly won a great victory of attrition. The Germans, however, had other ideas. They formed a new Fourteenth Army under General Otto von Below. The new German forces, containing heavy concentrations of storm troops, soon began to plan an Isonzo offensive of their own. It was to produce one of the most lopsided victories of the war.

10

A FEW MILES OF LIQUID MUD

The Battle of Passchendaele

And Will ye go to Flanders, my Mally-o?
To see the chief commanders, my bonny Mally-o?
You'll see the bullets fly,
And you'll hear the ladies cry,
And the soldiers how they die, my Molly-o.

—Song sung by the soldiers of the Duke of Marlborough,
early eighteenth century

For the Allies, the disaster of the Nivelle offensive and the accompanying slump in French morale that culminated in the mutinies placed the weight of winning the war in 1917 on the British army. Haig and his staff turned to a plan they had been developing since the petering out of the Somme campaign the previous autumn. They turned their sights north to Flanders and the Ypres salient, already the site of two bloody battles. Flanders, which was close to the British supply centers and guarded the critical English Channel ports, never lay far from Haig's strategic thinking. The Germans had remained relatively inactive in this sector since the Second Battle of Ypres in April 1915. Haig therefore believed that the Germans would be vulnerable to a major operation there in 1917.

German resumption of unrestricted submarine warfare provided additional motivation for an offensive in Flanders. In April 1917 alone, the Germans sank 250,000 tons of allied shipping. From May to December USW claimed another 500 British merchant ships, many close to home in the English Channel and off the south coast of Ireland. The sinkings placed Britain's food supplies in great jeopardy, leading American Admiral William Sims to remark, "I was fairly astounded, for I had never imagined anything so terrible."[1] Sims had watched the submarine war carefully and had formed close relationships with Royal Navy admirals, learning from their experience. He later became adept in forming the techniques necessary to fight antisubmarine warfare effectively. The allies needed those techniques, because the success of USW led many in Britain and the United States to wonder if the Allies could survive past the autumn.

Haig promised that his offensive would help to solve the USW menace. He planned a three-stage operation that would force the Germans out of Belgium as far as Zeebrugge and Courtrai. If successful, the operation would give Britain control of an important stretch of the Belgian coastline, thus denying submarine bases at Ostend and Zeebrugge to the German submarine fleet. In the first phase, British forces would create a major breakthrough at Ypres. In the second phase, the Royal Navy would land the Fourth Army behind German lines near Ostend. In the final phase, the two forces would exploit their success, driving toward Ghent and moving the line more than forty miles, thus permitting British control of vital German naval bases in Belgium.

As most people familiar with its details understood, the plan was far too ambitious for the realities of warfare in 1917. Lloyd George raised immediate objections. Chief of the Imperial General Staff Sir William Robertson helped convince Haig to cancel the amphibious phase, perforce necessitating the cancellation of the joint drive to Ghent. Robertson, the son of a tailor who had risen through the ranks to become Britain's senior soldier, had a commanding presence. Like Haig, he detested Lloyd George, whom he had once called "underbred swine" in a letter to Haig's chief of staff.[2] Despite their common enmity for Lloyd George, however, Robertson reined in Haig's unrealistic ambitions, believing that Haig's plan had no chance of meeting all of its ambitious goals.

The prime minister, understanding the need to impede the

William Robertson (left) and Ferdinand Foch (right) shared a deep suspicion of politicians and a desire to see the war to a successful conclusion. Both men began their military careers as privates and rose to become marshals. Robertson was the first man in British history to do so. (Australian War Memorial, negative no. H09473)

German submarine fleet by any means, lent his grudging support to the operation. He let it be known, however, that if the offensive did not succeed, he reserved the option of transferring British forces from the western front to Italy, Salonika, or Palestine. Anxious for the French army to take part in a successful operation, Pétain sent the reliable and effective French First Army to operate on the British left flank.

ALTERING THE GEOGRAPHY: PLUMER AT MESSINES

The geography of the Ypres salient made an offensive difficult. As it had in the last Ypres battle in 1915, the British salient jutted into German lines in a three-mile long backward C from Boesinghe to St. Eloi. To the south of the British salient sat a similar German salient based around the towns of Wytschaete and Messines. The German salient threatened any British operation to the east and impaired all communications to the south. It posed an enormous obstacle to the offensive's planners. The Germans held most of what high ground existed around Ypres, establishing their positions along a ridge that ran northeast from Messines to the village of Passchendaele. The ground in the sector rarely rose much higher than sixty meters, meaning that even these low rises held significant strategic importance. Most important, the Germans' possession of ridges allowed them to observe British movements.

Before any operation could go forward, the British had to neutralize the threat to their south posed by the Messines salient. The responsibility fell to a portly general who looked distinctly unmilitary in his appearance, but was so well loved by his men that he became known as "Daddy." Herbert Plumer had been in the Ypres sector since 1915, rising to command of the Second Army. Methodical and intelligent, Plumer and his brilliant chief of staff, Charles "Tim" Harington, had by summer 1917 built the Second Army into one of the finest large units on the western front. Philip Gibbs, who harshly criticized most of the British senior leaders, singled out the Second Army for "a thoroughness of method, a minute attention to detail, [and] a care for the comfort and spirit of the men" generally lacking, he believed, in most British units.[3]

Plumer and his meticulous staff had devised a novel plan to eliminate the German defenses on the Messines Ridge. If the first two battles at Ypres had shown the difficulty of destroying enemy positions from the surface, the British would destroy them from below. In 1915, Plumer's men had begun an immense tunneling operation underneath the German positions. By 1916, the British had constructed five miles of tunnels, capable of holding more than a million pounds of explosives. The painstaking work of tunneling continued at the rate of ten to fifteen feet per day. The success of the mining operations at the Somme gave Plumer more incentive to continue the project. After the Somme, however, British miners could no longer count on surprise. They therefore had to be careful not give away their plan to the German forces, which often sat as close as thirty feet above them. German countermeasures uncovered one of the tunnels and blocked it, but the discovery did not lead the Germans to suspect the massive scale of Plumer's project.

On May 21, 1917, the British began the offensive at Messines. More than 300 airplanes of the Royal Flying Corps cleared the skies and began the process of correcting the accuracy of the artillery. Plumer had concentrated 756 heavy guns and 1,510 field guns in the sector to oppose 400 German heavy guns and 344 field guns.[4] It amounted to one artillery piece for every twenty yards of ground over a nine-mile front. In all, the awesome British artillery fired 144,000 tons of shell. This firepower, however, was merely an adjunct to the main operation underground. On the night of June 6, Harington oversaw the final preparation of the mines, remarking, "I do not know if we shall change history tomorrow, but we shall certainly alter the geography."[5]

The next morning, residents in Lille, more than fifteen miles away, reported an earthquake to their German occupiers. In eastern England, Vera Brittain noted a "strange early morning shock." People in London heard the unusual noise as well. What they had heard and felt was no earthquake (although the earth did tremble as far away as the outskirts of London), but the simultaneous detonation of nineteen mines under the Messines Ridge, containing more than 500 tons of highly concentrated ammonal explosive in all. Fast on the heels of the detonations, the British opened up an artillery bombardment with their 2,266 guns.

The effects were devastating. One crater caused by the mine explosions measured more than 130 yards in diameter. The craters averaged 76 yards wide by 26 yards deep; some of them were large enough, as one commentator noted, "to hold a five-storey apartment building."[6] Almost 10,000 Germans were killed by the impact or buried alive by the upturned earth.[7] More than 7,300 German survivors, most of them too stunned to fight, surrendered. The first 1,500 yards of the German lines of defense at Messines crumbled. Fighting on the eastern slopes of the ridge and beyond continued for ten more days, with the British experiencing diminishing returns as they advanced. Once again, a breakthrough proved elusive and British casualties mounted as German resistance stiffened. In all, the British lost 17,000 men, while the Germans lost more than 25,000. The Second Army had achieved a phenomenal local success and certainly fulfilled Harington's pledge to alter the geography of the Messines Ridge, but at this rate Allied forces would reach Brussels, to say nothing of Berlin, in decades, not weeks.

The success at Messines meant that Haig now had his southern flank secured for the great drive out of the Ypres salient, but he moved with glacial slowness: he waited almost seven weeks to exploit the success of Messines. In doing so, he wasted valuable time and surrendered any hope of achieving surprise in the Ypres sector. It was the first of many mistakes Haig made in this campaign, which proved to be one of the most poorly commanded of the entire war. A breakthrough of enemy lines, so difficult to achieve un-

The Allied airfield shown here was still under construction when this photograph was taken in 1918. The hangars were still being built, but the fire pits designed to protect anti-aircraft machine gunners are visible at the bottom left and right. (United States Air Force Academy McDermott Library Special Collections)

der any circumstances, now became all but impossible. Messines, a one-time success more than two years in the making, could not be repeated. The Third Battle of Ypres therefore began under less than ideal conditions, and the problems were soon compounded by disastrous decisions made at the most senior levels of the British army.

Part of the delay came from Haig's imprudent decision to change commanders. Plumer's caution and attention to detail had been critical to the success at Messines. Haig believed, however, that those same qualities might keep Plumer from attacking and exploiting the opportunity with the kind of ardor he expected.

Thus, despite Plumer's unparalleled familiarity with the Ypres salient, the superiority of his staff work, and the confidence his men had in him, Haig changed commanders. He ordered Plumer's Second Army to the south, out of the Ypres sector it knew so well.

In place of Plumer's Second Army, Haig assigned the Fifth Army of Hubert Gough to occupy the Ypres salient. Gough came from a remarkable military family. One of his ancestors had commanded the British conquest of the Punjab. His father, brother, uncle, and cousin had all won the Victoria Cross, Britain's highest military decoration. A graduate of Eton and Sandhurst, Gough survived a serious wound in the Boer War, where he had fought with distinction. He later went on to teach at the prestigious British Staff College at Camberley. On paper, he was the ideal soldier.

Still, it was only due to Haig's intervention that Gough even had a job in 1917. In March 1914 Gough held the command of the Third Cavalry Brigade, stationed at Curragh Barracks, Ireland. When it appeared to Gough and the brigade's other officers that the government was ready to issue a declaration of support for Irish Home Rule, Gough and fifty-six other officers threatened to disobey the order and resign. When the government prepared to call their bluff, Haig protested, warning then Chief of the Imperial General Staff Sir John French that if the army punished Gough and the other mutineers, it would cause a flood of resignations from the army's officer corps. The resulting scandal, which King George V called a "disastrous and irreparable catastrophe," led to the resignations of both Sir John and Secretary of State for War, J. E. B. Seeley.[8] (Liberal admiration for Sir John's principled resignation contributed to his being named BEF commander in August of that year.)

Gough, however, had survived, thanks largely to the support of Haig. Indeed, instead of the dismissal from the army that he richly deserved as a result of his behavior at Curragh, Gough advanced rapidly through the ranks. He became successively more senior, quickly moving from the command of a division at

Festubert to a corps at Loos and then to the Fifth Army during the Somme campaign. Gough was the youngest of the British army commanders, six years younger than Rawlinson, nine years younger than Allenby, and thirteen years younger than Plumer. He had his own doubts about Haig's ambitious goals for the offensive and believed that Plumer, who understood Ypres and had recently experienced success at Messines, should have retained command of the operation.[9]

The problems in command were compounded by the tardiness with which Haig made his decision. Gough did not even set up a headquarters in Flanders until June 1, just six days before the opening of the attack at Messines. He had no experience with the Ypres salient, and his unpopularity with enlisted men, subordinates, and colleagues was rivaled only by that of his chief of staff, the sarcastic and hard-driving Neill Malcolm. Gibbs described Gough's staff officers as "arrogant and supercilious without revealing any symptoms of intelligence. If they had any wisdom it was deeply camouflaged by an air of inefficiency. If they had any knowledge they hid it as a secret of their own."[10] New to the region and unwilling to rely on Plumer's advice, Gough had much to do and little time.

The Germans took advantage of the delay on the British side to strengthen what was already one of the deepest defensive positions in the world. Because the high water tables of Flanders made entrenching difficult, the Germans had established an elastic system of defenses based on fortified farmhouses, concrete pillboxes, and reinforced redoubts. The Germans planned to absorb the weight of enemy attacks with three main belts 2,000 yards apart. Up to four more lines of defense protected key places. With the French army expected to remain inactive for the summer as a result of the Chemin des Dames disaster, the Germans moved additional forces into the sector. More than seventy German divisions eventually fought in the Third Battle of Ypres, also known as the Battle of Passchendaele.

Two recent historians of the campaign concluded that "the gap between the high command's aspirations and its power to accomplish them could hardly have been clearer."[11] Surprise was out of the question, with Robertson writing to Haig's chief of staff from Paris's famous Hôtel Crillon, "Everybody seems to know the [start] date, down to the lift-man."[12] Nevertheless, the British went ahead with the offensive, beginning with a ten-day pre-offensive artillery bombardment on July 22. Gough's Fifth Army had an impressive artillery battery, amounting to 3,000 pieces, over one-third of which were heavy guns. British pilots, however, had not attained air superiority, and poor weather kept many planes grounded. As a result, many German positions remained intact and most were still operating when the preparatory artillery phase ended on July 31.

The bombardment had failed to neutralize the Germans, but it had certainly chewed up the ground over which the troops had to advance. By destroying the drainage system of Flanders, British artillery left the terrain vulnerable to heavy rains. Those rains, soon to become so intimately associated with the Passchendaele offensive, fell heavily on day one of the infantry phase, July 31. The rain continued for all but three days of August. During that month, the Passchendaele sector, which averaged 70mm of rain in August, instead received 127mm. The ground quickly became a soupy quagmire in which men, horses, and vehicles struggled (often in vain) to avoid drowning.

The poor weather limited the fire support available to the advancing infantry. The mud prevented Gough's 136 tanks from joining the battle; only 19 of the 52 tanks assigned to the first wave were able to advance. The mud also tended to absorb the shock of artillery shells, and the continuous rain prevented aerial reconnaissance. On day one the British advanced the line a few hundred yards in most places, although on their left they managed to advance almost three miles, capturing the town of Pilckem. Still, they suffered 27,000 casualties on the first day and failed utterly

Torrential rains and the destruction of drainage systems flooded the Ypres salient during the Passchendaele campaign in 1917, leading some men to joke sardonically of seeing U-boats in the trenches. (Imperial War Museum, Crown Copyright, P. 396)

to pierce, or even significantly threaten, the German second line. The failure of the British right to penetrate into the Gheluvelt Plain left the British center dangerously exposed.

It should have been obvious from the first day that no breakthrough of the German lines would occur. Gough himself doubted that the battle could possibly result in the high hopes Haig held for it. Haig, however, did not entertain his officers' suspicions and was poorly served by his own staff officers. His chief of intelligence, John Charteris, insisted throughout the campaign that German morale was weak and that both German reserves and German combat effectiveness would soon reach their limits. Haig either wanted to believe what he was hearing, all evidence to the contrary notwithstanding, or he was misled by a poor staff whose assertions he did not bother to check personally.

The Passchendaele campaign underscores the difficulties involved in the command structures of modern warfare. A century earlier, in another corner of the small nation of Belgium, Wellington had been able to observe Napoleon riding across the battlefield through a field glass and talk with his principal field commanders about tactics. In the American Civil War a half century later, such a command arrangement remained the preferred style for Robert E. Lee and his Confederate generals. By 1917, however, battlefields had become so much larger and the flow of information so much greater that the personal style of command practiced in the nineteenth century had become impossible. Like most senior commanders, Haig saw little of the actual battlefield, not out of cowardice, but because he simply could not manage such an enormous battle from the front.

For this reason, senior commanders became more dependent than ever on the abilities of their staff officers. When staff officers performed poorly, they effectively left their commanders blind or operating on faulty information. Most of the war's great commanders, not coincidentally, had excellent chiefs of staff. Hindenburg's reliance on Ludendorff, Foch's on Maxime Weygand, and Plumer's on Harington all greatly improved their ability to make decisions based on the best information available. None of these chiefs of staff assumed army commands themselves, in large part because of the value they represented to their commanders. Haig, however, depended at Passchendaele on the entirely too optimistic Charteris and an inexperienced chief of staff, Launcelot Kiggell. The latter had never heard a shot fired in armed conflict in his entire thirty-five-year military career and gave Haig consistently poor advice throughout this campaign.[13]

The manifest weaknesses of the staff officers led to what Gibbs described as "a sense of deadly depression among many officers and men with whom I came in touch."[14] The mistrust between line and staff, ever present in any army, became a serious problem. The men eventually began to spread a rumor that the two sides

Kaiser Wilhelm II (center) tries to look competent while hiding his withered arm in a propaganda photograph. Paul von Hindenburg (left) and Erich Ludendorff (right) were by 1918 running the war without regularly informing the kaiser of their actions. (National Archives)

had secretly agreed not to shell each other's headquarters. "The German scores both ways," the story went. "His staff is spared, which is valuable to him. And our staff is spared, which is also valuable to him."[15] Another rumor had Kiggell leaving the safety of headquarters halfway through the campaign to see for himself why the men were not advancing. Upon reaching the edge of the battle area his car became stuck in the deep mud. He then turned to an officer and cried, "Good God, did we really send men to fight in this?" Without pausing, a veteran of the campaign replied, "It's worse further on up."[16] The incident never happened, but the assumption of the staff's incompetence gave the story credibility.

A second major effort by British forces in mid-August captured the rubble that had once been the town of Langemark and gained 1,500 yards for 15,000 British casualties. Gough grew frustrated, and his anti-Irish bias reemerged. He blamed the failures of his Irish troops for the inability to break the German lines. Haig himself showed an anti-Catholic bias, later attributing the War Office's pessimism about the Passchendaele offensive to its Catholic Director of Military Information, the cautious but capable George Macdonough.[17] Haig accused Macdonough of obtaining his information from suspect "Catholic" sources. The estimates coming from Macdonough's office certainly contrasted sharply to the rosy proclamations of Charteris.

To break the stalemate that Passchendaele had become, Haig reluctantly decided to reduce Gough's Fifth Army area of operations. He extended that of Plumer's Second Army, giving Plumer belated authority over the southern portion of the Ypres salient. Plumer went to work with his characteristic meticulousness. Rather than try to break the German lines, Plumer planned to leapfrog through the Gheluvelt Plain by three measured steps of roughly 1,500 yards each. Once the plain was in British hands, Gough would have his right flank secured for a renewed effort on the main obstacle, the Passchendaele Ridge. Plumer assembled a concentration of artillery three times greater than that used on July 31 and fired more than 1.6 million shells to support his first step. The British also employed a Livens projector, an electrically powered device resembling a slingshot for firing gas shells. Powerful but inaccurate, it could fling a 200-pound projectile almost 2,000 yards, far enough to avoid gas blowing back on friendly troops, a chronic problem with gas canisters.

Plumer directed two battles in September and October 1917, the first for control of the Menin Road and the second for control of Polygon Wood. The ensuing fighting became some of the campaign's most bitter. The Germans introduced mustard gas in large quantities, and the rains stopped, allowing for more accurate artillery fire. Plumer succeeded in capturing both goals by October 4,

*The Allies attacked on the western front in 1917 with disastrous results,
but the Germans suffered terribly as well. The Germans hoped for
troop transfers from the eastern front to make up for the losses. The
Allies counted on the Americans. (© Bettmann/Corbis)*

but the casualties had been horrendous. The first seven weeks of
the campaign had already cost Britain 86,000 casualties. Plumer's
attack on the Polygon Wood added another 15,000. In all, the
campaign had resulted in 4,400 British casualties per square mile
of ruined, water-logged Belgian territory.[18]

The tremendous costs for such minor gains led Lloyd George
and the War Office to consider making changes. The prime minister compared Haig's progress unfavorably with Nivelle's that
spring. Unwilling to question Haig's operational plan, which was
seen as the exclusive preserve of the military, Lloyd George con-
templated taking away many of the Fifth Army's heavy gun batteries and sending them to Italy. Doing so, he hoped, would prevent

Haig from resuming the offensive without placing British soldiers in a vulnerable position against a possible German counterattack. Haig, however, remained optimistic and had even told the Royal Navy to prepare for a landing on the Belgian coast to support the breakthrough he believed to be imminent.

Rain returned in October, dooming a rapid advance on Plumer's third step, the town of Broodseinde, just south of Passchendaele. Heavy downpours continued with no end in sight throughout the month, adding to the misery of the campaign. The battle had lost all strategic significance, but the symbolic goal of Passchendaele village, supposed to have been taken on day four, remained in German hands. On October 30, the British and Canadian forces took 2,000 casualties to move the line a mere 500 yards. Plumer continued his slow and bloody advance toward Passchendaele, finally taking it on November 4. By then it had become an insignificant prize that augured no further British gain. It had become, in the words of one British general, "a really untenable position" in a dangerously exposed salient.[19]

The Battle of Passchendaele stands as a symbol of futility. In the words of officer and historian Basil Henry Liddell Hart, it became a "synonym for military failure."[20] The British lost an estimated 275,000 men killed, wounded, and captured for negligible gains. As one veteran accurately summarized it, Passchendaele represented the seemingly pointless waste of men: "the Ypres battlefield just represented one gigantic slough of despond into which floundered battalions, brigades, and divisions of infantry without end, to be shot to pieces or drowned, until at last and with immeasurable slaughter, we had gained a few miles of liquid mud."[21]

Passchendaele had cost the Germans terribly as well. Their total casualties amounted to 200,000 men. The Germans had rotated 73 divisions through Passchendaele, but had surrendered no strategically significant territory.[22] More significantly, the German submarine pens remained secure.

"A TEMPORARY ILLUSION OF TRIUMPH":
THE BREAKTHROUGH AT CAPORETTO

The final stages of the bloody British setback at Passchendaele occurred at roughly the same time as another Allied setback: a major Central Powers breakthrough in Italy. The Central Powers had concluded that Cadorna's Isonzo offensives were succeeding in wearing down the Austro-Hungarian army. The Eleventh Battle of the Isonzo had forced Boroević and his men out of their main defensive positions and the Italians stood poised to attack again, with a numerical advantage of 608 battalions to 249 and 3,700 artillery pieces to 1,500.[23] Most Germans and Austro-Hungarians believed that another Italian push would break their lines and lead to the loss of the key port of Trieste. For the Austro-Hungarians, resuming the offensive seemed the only way to halt the Italian momentum, but with such a numerical inferiority, they would need to turn again to their domineering German ally. For their part, the Germans saw an offensive against Italy as of decidedly tertiary importance. They therefore agreed to offer only temporary support to relieve the immediate crisis. They would not devote major resources to the Italian theater.

The Central Powers created a joint Fourteenth Army, consisting of seven German and eight Austro-Hungarian infantry divisions under German command. As its commander, they chose Otto von Below, brother of the German commander at the Somme and a respected veteran of fighting in Russia, France, and Salonika. The German units included men familiar with the storm-troop tactics used with such great success at Riga; three of the German divisions had participated in that victory. The Fourteenth Army had three times the artillery support the Germans had enjoyed in that battle and also had more than 1,000 gas projectors modeled on the British Livens system.[24] The German air force provided one squadron for every kilometer of the front, a concentration of air power that the Germans had never known and a

Artillery dominated the Great War battlefield. Large pieces, like the one shown here, were too heavy to move by any method other than the rails. (National Archives)

valuable reconnaissance asset in the mountainous terrain in which they would fight.

The Central Powers' concentration of forces caught the Italians in an unusually exposed position. Although Italian intelligence had divined the size of the German forces transferred opposite them, the Italians did not anticipate a major enemy offensive. Cadorna expected the Austro-Hungarians to take winter quarters in late 1917 after the beating they had taken during the summer. This blindness continued even after deserters had provided key details of the Central Powers plan.[25] If the enemy did attack, Cadorna guessed that the blow would fall in the Trentino. To confuse matters further, Luigi Capello, commander of the unit the Central Powers had targeted, spent the days before the attack in Padua receiving treatment for a painful kidney disorder.

On October 24, the Central Powers opened a powerful artillery barrage that caught the Italians entirely unprepared. Two Austro-German corps advanced quickly to the town of Caporetto while two more corps moved to the south to capture high ground. Some Italian units fought much better than their reputation from this battle would suggest, but others simply crumbled. Panic quickly ensued, and the orderly retreat that Capello and Cadorna directed soon turned into a "wild bacchanalia" of drunkenness, rioting, and looting.[26] Within four days, the Austro-German forces had advanced as far as Cadorna's Udine headquarters, which Cadorna had deserted just hours before.

The astonishingly rapid collapse of the Italian army after the initial Austro-German breakthrough has forever tarnished the honor of Italian arms. In just four days, as Holger Herwig noted, Cadorna "abandoned all the territory that he had seized in the past 30 months" and much more.[27] Over 275,000 Italians became prisoners of war, and another 350,000 deserted. The Italians surrendered 3,152 artillery pieces (almost half of their total), 3,000 machine guns, 1,700 mortars, and 22 airfields. The entire Second Army, Italy's largest, ceased to exist as a military formation. Morale in other units and on the home front threatened to break as well.

But the Italians did recover. Cadorna ordered Italian forces to regroup behind the Tagliamento River, which ran unusually deep that autumn because of the heavy rains. If the Italian units could cross the river and destroy the bridges, they would have an excellent chance to refit and regroup. The Central Powers, moreover, had not planned to supply their men so far forward and had no cavalry with which to reach the bridges, destroy them before the Italians could cross the river, and thereby trap the Italians. Had they done so, the rout might have been complete. The Italians crossed the Tagliamento on November 3 and destroyed the bridges. The chase continued, however, when Central Powers scouts found places to ford the river. With enemy forces continuing to pursue them, the Italians decided to regroup farther to the south behind the Piave River.

The crisis at Caporetto led the Allies to implement a plan developed by Foch that spring in the event that just such an emergency presented itself. Within three days of the Central Powers breakthrough, the Allies rushed six French and five British infantry divisions as well as 44 artillery batteries to Italy. Foch himself assumed command of the French units; the British sent Plumer. Cadorna expected to use these troops in a counterattack along the Piave, but Foch and Plumer told him that the troops would remain outside the Italian chain of command and would primarily serve to secure the critical city of Venice and to guard against a suspected Central Powers offensive in the Trentino. They would not attack until the Italians themselves had proven that they could secure the Piave and restore order.

The Italians reached the Piave on November 9, the same day that the Italian government finally replaced Cadorna. In his place came Armando Diaz, a man little known outside the corps he commanded, but well loved by the men of that unit. Diaz took a

Italian troops cross a river during the Caporetto retreat in 1917. The collapse of the Italian Second Army sent Italian forces into headlong retreat, but the Italians rebounded and reformed under the command of Armando Diaz. (United States Air Force Academy McDermott Library Special Collections)

firm grasp of the situation, establishing a solid defensive line based on the Piave and the strategic high ground of Monte Grappa. The new Italian positions held off Central Powers attacks in December, and the battle came to an end on Christmas Day. The enemy had been stopped, and the important cities of Venice and Padua remained in Italian hands.

With the immediate crisis over, Diaz worked to restore his battered army. He offered amnesty to men who had become "detached from their units," an effective way of getting men to return

274

to their units with honor rather than face punishment for desertion. The move returned thousands of soldiers to service. Diaz then improved the soldiers' food, entertainment, recreation, and pay. He distributed medals to men who had fought bravely, supported giving soldiers the right to vote, and sponsored government programs to provide insurance and land to veterans after the war. One of Cadorna's staff officers who remained with Diaz remarked that "Diaz is taking decisions with calmness and coolness. . . . Trust is returning."[28] The Italian army had taken a terrible beating, but it had survived and would yet play a key role in winning the war.

CAMBRAI AND THE BIRTH OF MECHANIZED WARFARE

The immense losses at Passchendaele notwithstanding, Haig still believed that the opportunity for winning the war lay with Great Britain in 1917. By the spring of 1918 the Germans would have transferred sufficient forces from the east to make a major offensive in France possible. The French still needed time to regain confidence and incorporate new weapons into their training, the Italians could not possibly resume the offensive for several months if at all, and the Americans had not yet arrived in sufficient number to make a real difference on the western front. If the war were to be won in 1917, Haig contended, the British army would have to win it. Still, the bloodletting at Passchendaele forbade another large-scale infantry assault. Haig thus faced the dilemma of wanting to resume the offensive, but lacking the men with which to do so.

Two men believed that they had found the solution to Haig's problem. The more senior of the two was a brash, outspoken, thirty-six-year-old protégé of Robertson. Hugh Elles had been a member of a group Robertson had formed in 1915 to travel around the western front and report back to him on the conditions they saw. The men were so young relative to their responsibility that the group came to be known by the name "La Creche," from the French word for nursery. In 1916, Elles went back to England to become Haig's liaison officer to the group developing tanks. In September 1916 he was promoted to brigadier general and named commander of the tank corps.

The second man was a bookish and eccentric Sandhurst graduate who disliked most aspects of soldiering and had a fascination for the occult. Frustrated with the human cost of the war, J. F. C. Fuller developed ideas for winning the war by the assemblage of more than 3,000 tanks supported by masses of airplanes, ideas he codified in a study he called "Plan 1919." Named chief of staff to Elles, Fuller continued to work on ways to win the war by fighting with machines, not men. He finalized plans for a raid using tanks, not in small, detached groups as at the Somme, but as an arm of warfare all their own, with a tank corps commander and a staff trained in the doctrine of armored warfare.

Third Army commander Julian Byng took Fuller's initial idea and developed it into a full-scale offensive. Already widely respected as the man most responsible for the capture of Vimy Ridge that spring, Byng now envisioned using tanks to carve out a six-mile hole in the German lines on the dry, firm ground near the town of Cambrai. Though Cambrai had been quiet for much of the war, the Germans had six German infantry divisions in the sector. Byng concentrated nineteen infantry and five cavalry divisions as well as 400 tanks. The tanks assembled in the nearby woods in relative concealment. British planes flew overhead to cover the noise of the tanks' engines, thereby providing even greater secrecy.

The plan for Cambrai involved achieving surprise by using tanks in place of artillery to open a gap for exploitation. The British still planned to concentrate an enormous artillery battery of 1,000 guns to Germany's 34, but because the tanks would provide the shock, the guns could direct a brief but intense barrage on the German front lines before shifting to targets further to the rear.

Once the tanks had opened the gaps, the infantry would follow to mop up any remaining enemy units. Finally, the British cavalry would charge through, attack retreating German units, and turn the victory into a rout.

On November 20, the tanks moved out from their cover and fought as an independent unit for the first time in history. They advanced in 120 teams of three tanks each. The first tank in each team approached the enemy's first line and dropped a fascine, a large brushwood bundle, into the trench to fill it in for the next tank. It then turned left and moved parallel to the near side of the German line, flattening wire as it went. The second tank dropped its own fascine, crossed the enemy trench, turned left, and moved along the far side. The third tank followed to offer fire support or to take over the role of a tank that experienced mechanical failures.

The surprise was nearly total, and German infantry in the trenches had no weapon powerful enough to disable the thickly armored Mark IV tanks. Tank losses due to engine failure were much lower than on the Somme. German infantry broke and ran, often leaving British infantry in the unusual predicament of having no targets. Many British soldiers did not even fire their weapons on the first day. A five-mile gap in the enemy line opened, but the British lacked sufficient infantry reserves to exploit the success with the necessary speed because Passchendaele had drained the army of its manpower. Byng rushed his cavalry forward, but even under these relatively favorable circumstances, British faith in the tactical value of the horse remained misplaced. Forced to abandon their horses and fight on foot, the cavalry only managed to capture one German artillery battery and a handful of prisoners.

As Fuller himself later acknowledged, he had made a critical mistake by not leaving any tanks in reserve. The British therefore had no means with which to continue the battle on favorable terms. Even though he had no clear objectives in front of him, Haig ordered the battle to continue, in large part because he could not give up such an impressive advantage. He also needed to win at Cambrai to regain momentum after Passchendaele and to firm up his political position against Lloyd George. The prime minister, he knew, not only wanted him removed, he also wanted to remain on the defensive on the western front and refocus British offensive operations elsewhere.

Byng had not expected the Germans to have enough strength to counterattack, and therefore his forces sat vulnerable to a fierce twenty-division push by the rapidly reinforced German Second Army on November 29. German units soon improvised defenses against the tanks, including digging wider and deeper trenches and using field guns against the tanks themselves. They also introduced large numbers of low-flying aircraft to strike targets on the ground. The Germans eventually regained three-fourths of the territory they had lost in the battle. In some places, they even took ground that had been British on day one. By the time the battle ended on December 5, the British had little to show for their imaginative and innovative tactics.

Some observers of the Battle of Cambrai, including many Germans who played key roles in developing blitzkrieg tactics in the 1930s, quickly grasped the meaning of the new style of warfare. Winston Churchill became an instant convert. When asked after the war how the bloodletting of the western front could have been avoided, he answered: "Pointing to the Battle of Cambrai, [I say] '*This* could have been done.' This in many variants, this in larger and better forms ought to have been done if only the Generals had not been content to fight machine gun bullets with the breasts of gallant men and think that was waging war."[29]

Haig, whom Fuller called "wooden-headed," saw the value of tanks as an adjunct to the infantry, but failed to see Cambrai as a major watershed in military operations. "No change for the better will take place in the British army," Fuller concluded, "until it is given new brains in a new commander-in-chief."[30]

The consequences of Passchendaele and Cambrai led to a deepening mistrust between Lloyd George and the two men he held most responsible for the debacles, Haig and Robertson. A cabinet investigation into the problems at Cambrai singled out command and especially intelligence failures. Still lacking the political backing to replace Haig, Lloyd George instead forced the removal of Charteris and Kiggell from Haig's staff in January 1918. The following month, the prime minister also orchestrated the replacement of Robertson as Chief of the Imperial General Staff.

Haig and his supporters defended his actions in 1917 by arguing that, as a continuation from the Somme, the battles of 1917 had attrited the German army, thus helping to set the stage for the 1918 victory. But the British had taken more casualties on the western front in that year than they had inflicted on their German foes, meaning that the macabre logic of attrition could only work if the British could replace their dead faster than the Germans could. As Haig knew, the British had tapped their last manpower reserves by introducing conscription in 1916. The Germans, however, did have a source of manpower in the tens of thousands of soldiers on their way west from the Russian front. Haig's claims of attrition thus ring hollow, in part because attrition did not figure in his original plans for either the Somme or Passchendaele. His bloody calculus, moreover, killed his own men at too large a rate to make attrition a viable long-term strategy. Only the arrival of the Americans promised to make good the Allied losses of 1917. It remained to be seen, however, whether the Americans would arrive in time.

11

NOT WAR AS WE KNEW IT

The U-Boat Menace and War in Africa

> D. [David Lloyd George] also saw Gen. Haig, & had a very serious
> talk with him. He made it quite plain that the time had come when
> he was going to assert himself, & if necessary let the public know the
> truth about the soldiers & their strategy.
>
> —Diary of Frances Stevenson, November 5, 1917

Allied battlefield frustrations in 1917 led to the creation of new forms of civilian control over the war effort. Before 1917, Allied generals had largely been able to argue that, given their specialized knowledge, they, and only they, could make the military decisions necessary to obtain victory. After the bloodletting of 1915–1916 and the tremendous defeats of 1917, however, the generals lost the monopoly of military decision-making that they had theretofore possessed. In Britain and France, and to a lesser extent in Italy as well, civilians came to share important roles with the military and even began to have an effect on the formerly military preserves of operations and strategy. Although the growth of civilian authority created friction between the "frocks" (politicians) and the "brass hats" (generals), it allowed for the expertise of the civilians to complement that of the military. The result was a dynamic, if occasionally confrontational, relationship that helped the Allies win the war.

In Germany, no such system developed. Instead, the military came to assume greater and greater power over all elements of German society. By late 1917, Hindenburg and Ludendorff had become virtual dictators over Germany and the lands under German occupation. Intelligent and industrious civilians such as Walter Rathenau, head of the War Materials Department, saw their influence fade. The kaiser played little real role in governing Germany, becoming more of a figurehead as the war developed. In July 1917 Hindenburg and Ludendorff neutralized the office of chancellor as well, when they forced the resignation of influential Chancellor Theobald von Bethmann Hollweg. In his place the two generals chose the pliable Georg Michaelis, a commoner whom the kaiser did not even know. Michaelis thus assumed the chancellorship, "a post," one scholar noted, "to which his subservience to Ludendorff was his only qualification."[1] Germany had become a military dictatorship in everything but name.

The German system, moreover, relied on principles that proved ill suited to the rigors of modern warfare. The first cracks in the German political organization became apparent as early as the period of mobilization. The kaiser had demonstrated a fundamental misunderstanding of the needs of mobilization and the nature of modern warfare. As the war continued, it became increasingly apparent to the German elite that only the military really understood the issues facing wartime Germany. The German parliament, the Reichstag, was weak; even before the war, it had held significantly less power than its western European counterparts. During the war, it played only a minor role in directing German war efforts. With no other institution capable of controlling the reins of power, the German military, specifically the army, stepped in.

The democratic British and French systems, by contrast, had a flexibility and adaptability that allowed them to change with circumstances. At the outset of the war, both governments yielded much of their authority to the generals. By 1916, however, parliaments in both nations had begun to reassert control, forming committees to oversee various aspects of the war and creating entirely new governmental agencies to solve specific problems. The British creation of a ministry of munitions proved to be especially important, ameliorating the serious problems caused by the shell crisis and providing British soldiers with the weapons they needed. Civilians such as Sir Eric Geddes in Britain and Albert Thomas in France played critical roles in reorganizing governmental and economic structures to better serve the needs of the war.

THE GOAT AND THE TIGER

The most important changes came at the highest executive level. Britain's David Lloyd George (named prime minister in December 1916) and France's Georges Clemenceau (named prime minister in November 1917) provided powerful, energetic civilian leadership that was virtually absent in Germany. Both men held the portfolio of their nation's ministry of war as well, giving them legal authority over the military. Unlike most of their predecessors, these two men did not hesitate to use that power. They remained determined to see the war to its finish, reordering their nations for the total war that had emerged by 1917. Their leadership, controversial at times, became a critical factor in the eventual triumph of the Allies.

Both men had abiding adversarial relationships with their nation's senior military leaders. Lloyd George's opposition to the Boer War, advocacy of Irish Home Rule, and support for increased spending on domestic programs set him at odds with the military in the years before the war. His political background in Welsh mining communities led him to develop to a deep suspicion of the British elite. Known as "the goat" to his detractors, Lloyd George popularized the term "Establishment" as a pejorative. He saw Britain's generals, including Haig, as representatives of the Establishment, wasting the lives of the working-class men under their care.

Similarly Clemenceau, nicknamed "the tiger" for his tenacious and combative political style, had been a vigorous opponent of French army leadership during the infamous Dreyfus Affair. At the height of the scandal, he played a leading role in exposing the

French army's cover-up of evidence that would have cleared Jewish Alsatian Captain Alfred Dreyfus of the charges of espionage that had sent him to the notorious prison on Devil's Island. Clemenceau saw most generals as too conservative, too Catholic (Clemenceau was a leader of the French anticlerical movement), and too unimaginative. He supported an all-out effort to win the war, but he offered scathing criticism of French military leaders, especially Joffre. Unlike many French politicians, Clemenceau was not intimidated by soldiers and was not afraid to take them to task in public if he deemed it necessary to the national defense.

Their suspicions about their own militaries notwithstanding, both prime ministers were ardent patriots and firm supporters of national defense. As Chancellor of the Exchequer in 1909 Lloyd George consistently found the money to meet and exceed German appropriations during the naval arms race of the prewar years. He was one of the first government officials to understand that the war would last years, not months, and would require a massive change to the Asquith government's "business as usual" philosophy. Clemenceau was the last surviving member of the 1871 National Assembly that had voted to cede Alsace and Lorraine to Germany as a price for ending the Franco-Prussian War. Clemenceau had voted with the minority against the measure, preferring to fight on, whatever the cost. He had played a key role in uniting French public opinion against the kaiser's efforts to increase German influence in Morocco in 1911 and had stood with the army in supporting the 1913 extension of universal service from two years to three.

Perhaps most important, neither man held military officials or military operations inviolate. "War," Clemenceau often said, "is too important a business to be left to generals." Both men had their own ideas about how the war should be waged and did not shirk from making their views known. Clemenceau had been a journalist during the American Civil War and mayor of the Montmartre section of Paris during the Franco-Prussian War and the Paris Commune. He believed that he had seen more of war than most of the generals had. He frequently reminded them that he held the constitutional responsibility for national defense and, even at age seventy-six, he insisted on going to the front line on an almost weekly basis, talking to the men of both the British and French armies to get their views unfiltered by the military chain of command and earning the soldiers' respect by entering positions so far forward that he occasionally came under fire.

Despite their controversial political postures and their often unpopular decisions, Lloyd George and Clemenceau were the men for the hour. British General Charles Grant thought Lloyd George had an air of "unsavoury intrigue," but noted that this trait could be forgiven "if the ends justify the means." Lloyd George, Grant knew, enjoyed tremendous popularity among the British rank and file. "Soldiers who did nothing but abuse Lloyd George in 1912 or 1913," Grant wrote to his father-in-law, "now look upon him as the saviour of his country, a part I imagine he is not unwilling to play."[2] Another British general noted that after the "muddle of the Asquith government, it was time a strong man should rule the country and all felt that in Lloyd George we had the right man."[3] Neither of these generals would likely have supported Lloyd George before 1914; the national emergency of the war, however, led them to overlook partisan and personal preferences in the name of the needs of the nation.

Clemenceau might have had more domestic political enemies than any politician in Europe. Over the years he had been responsible for bringing down one French cabinet after another. Like Lloyd George, however, he had charisma and the leadership skills to make people forget their grievances in the face of a national crisis. In words strikingly reminiscent of those of Winston Churchill twenty-two years later, Clemenceau told the French people during the crisis of spring 1918 that even the loss of Paris would not force France out of the war. "After Paris, we will fight on the Loire; after the Loire, on the Garonne, and after the Garonne, in the Pyrenees; finally, if there is no more earth, we will fight on the water."[4] His most famous speech came in the French parliament in March 1918 in response to a pacifist proposal to end the war:

> The first importance is freedom. The second is war. Therefore we must sacrifice everything to the war in order to assure the triumph of France. . . . You want peace? Me, too. It would be criminal to have any other thought. But it is not by bleating the word "Peace" that one can silence Prussian militarism. . . . My formula is the same everywhere. Domestic politics? I make war. Foreign affairs? I make war. I always make war.[5]

Although both Lloyd George and Clemenceau made mistakes, their strategic judgment proved to be no worse than that of most of their generals. Both men were ardent nationalists and saw the alliance as primarily a means to serve state and national interests. They enjoyed a cordial professional relationship, although they disagreed on many issues, especially on matters pertaining to their visions of the postwar peace. Still, together they energized the British and French governments, maintained morale by demonstrating their determination to see the war to a successful finish, and formed important linkages between the allied nations. The goat and the tiger thus ensured the viability of their nations and played critical roles in the final victory.

Informed by their shared suspicion of Allied generals, Lloyd George and Clemenceau worked together to create an overarching governing body to run the war. The Italian disaster at Caporetto and the dispatch of British and French troops to stop the resulting Italian collapse underscored the need for some sort of inter-Allied organizing body. Lloyd George took the lead in planning a meeting at the Italian city of Rapallo in November 1917 to discuss the formation of such a body. The Rapallo meeting resulted in the formation of a Supreme War Council with inter-Allied committees to govern finance, food, munitions, transportation, and naval (particularly antisubmarine) warfare. Its official mission was to "watch over the general conduct of the War" and to prepare "recommendations for the decisions of the Governments."[6] In other words, the Supreme War Council would serve as an alternative to the French and British general staffs, which both Lloyd George and Clemenceau distrusted.

The real goal of the Supreme War Council, therefore, was to reestablish civilian control over the military by creating a body above the traditional general staffs. The Supreme War Council included the head of government, one other politician, and a Permanent Military Representative from Britain, France, the United States, and Italy. Politicians thereby outnumbered generals by two to one. Lloyd George and Clemenceau naturally selected their nation's political representative from among their most trusted political allies. The generals were on the Supreme War Council to provide advice on "technical matters" only.

Haig and Pétain, occupied with the daily needs of running their armies, had no direct voice on the Supreme War Council, which met far from the front lines at Versailles. As Permanent Military Representative for France, Clemenceau chose the French army's chief of staff, Ferdinand Foch, a man whose personality and temperament had often set him at odds with Pétain. Clemenceau quickly moved to ensure that Foch would not play a major role in the Supreme War Council. Upon Foch's first contribution to the Supreme War Council's deliberations, Clemenceau leaned toward him and said, "Be quiet. I am the representative of France."[7] Lloyd George moved in a similar direction. He chose Field Marshal Henry Wilson as Britain's Permanent Military Representative, a man who had heavily criticized both Haig and the British general staff. Haig had expected Lloyd George to name Haig's close ally, William Robertson; the appointment of Wilson thereby isolated Haig from the deliberations of the Supreme War Council—as, of course, Lloyd George had intended.

The generals of the Supreme War Council, however, had no intention of sitting idle while politicians decided their fate. Wilson and Foch were old friends and had been discussing possible Franco-British wartime cooperation for more than a decade. Both men agreed on the need for greater coordination between the French and British armies. They also agreed on the importance of creating a general reserve of men from all of the Allied nations, to be dispatched to any point where their presence was needed, either to hold off a German attack or to reinforce an Allied one. The concept received the Supreme War Council's approval, but both Haig and Pétain vigorously opposed the idea. Haig had even threatened to resign if troops under his command were placed under the general reserve and commanded by anyone but him. As a result, the general reserve existed only on paper.

Wilson and Lloyd George also used the Supreme War Council to argue for a redirection of Allied efforts away from the western front. Both men believed that greater results might be obtained by forcing a decision against Turkey or by pressing through the Balkans against the dying Austro-Hungarian empire. Wilson had concluded that the Germans would attack east toward the Black Sea in 1918 before attacking in France, an idea that Haig called "laughable but for the seriousness of it."[8] Foch, whose own intelligence reports suggested that the Germans were preparing a massive western front operation for 1918, agreed with Haig and staunchly opposed any operations outside of France. The Americans, who were not officially at war with the Ottoman Empire, also opposed any eastern operations.

Although the Supreme War Council created much acrimony and demonstrated the fault lines between nations and between frocks and brass hats, it served several important roles. Even though they disagreed more often than not, the various national representatives had a chance to work through their divergence and toward compromise. The Supreme War Council also helped to initiate the Americans into the complex issues of running a multinational war on a massive scale. America's delegation was led by President Wilson's most trusted adviser, Edward House, and the United

States Army's intelligent and capable chief of staff, General Tasker Howard Bliss. The Supreme War Council thus gave the Europeans and the Americans a chance to get to know each other and to work on joint solutions to common problems.

The Supreme War Council represented a step toward the creation of a single Allied war effort, although Haig and others argued that this particular step might have been worse than none at all. The true value of the Supreme War Council became obvious in spring 1918, when the German offensive Foch and others had foreseen began. The personal relationships that had developed and the professional discussions that had taken place in the meetings of the Supreme War Council laid the groundwork that allowed the Allies to meet the challenge of German offensive as a single entity. It also allowed the United States to integrate itself rapidly into the Allied war effort, despite continued disagreements over the exact role the Americans should play.

BREAKING THE SUBMARINE MENACE

Before the Americans could hope to play a decisive role on the battlefield, the Allied navies had to find a way to neutralize the German submarine threat. In the third quarter of 1916, the German navy had sunk 600,000 tons of Allied shipping; the Allies and the Americans together had built only 450,000 tons of merchant shipping in that same period. Sinkings of Allied shipping rose dramatically as German submarine officers became more aggressive at the end of 1916. Allied shipping losses for the first quarter of 1917 climbed to 1.65 million tons while new construction only rose to 600,000 tons. On February 1, 1917, the Germans officially resumed unrestricted submarine warfare, leading Allied shipping losses to reach a wartime high of 2.2 million tons in the second quarter of 1917.

The admirals may have overstated the seriousness of the U-boat menace to Allied war efforts, but given the need to transport

Germany's prosecution of unrestricted submarine warfare caused supply problems for the Allies, but it also led to American belligerency. Despite the claims of some of its senior leaders, the German U-boat fleet could not stop the Americans from arriving in France at the rate of as many as 20,000 men per day. (National Archives)

American soldiers safely across the Atlantic, their concern was understandable. The American naval mission to Great Britain had been following the problem for months before American belligerency. Upon American entry into the war, American Admiral William Sims asked British Admiral John Jellicoe what solution could solve the U-boat problem. "Absolutely none that we can see now," Jellicoe replied.[9] Jellicoe grew increasingly despondent about Britain's chances to survive past November 1917 if the submarine menace did not end quickly. Great Britain's near-total dependence on secure shipping lanes for food, fuel, and raw materials concerned him even more than the need to secure the safe transportation of American troopships across the Atlantic.

Fortunately for Jellicoe and the Allied war effort, Sims had a solution. He urged the British to adopt the convoy system, whereby merchant vessels were, as the system's name implied, escorted across the ocean by warships to protect them from submarines. The British had considered convoys for years, but the system posed several problems. Ships traveling in convoy obviously moved at the same speed, limiting the entire convoy to the speed of the slowest ship. Once they arrived at a port en masse, they overwhelmed the unloading and docking facilities, meaning that some ships were forced to sit idle with their needed, and sometimes perishable, cargo on board while other ships unloaded. Most important, the pride and strength of the Royal Navy was in its battleships, and most of them were too slow for escort duties.

Sims worked with the Allied Naval Council, an arm of the Supreme War Council, to solve all of these problems. He dedicated America's fleet of destroyers to escort missions. Fast and powerful enough to deal with submarines, the destroyers proved to be reliable escort vessels. Sims and the Allied navies then created convoys in three speeds to accommodate different types of vessels and to ease port congestion. By May 1918 the Allies had gained enough faith in the Canadian-born Sims to name him commander of all Allied escort and antisubmarine vessels in European waters. The system produced immediate results. During an experimental convoy in the last two weeks of May, losses of merchant vessels on the Gibraltar-to-Britain route (normally 33 percent when unescorted) fell to just 1.5 percent when escorted. The experiment convinced the remaining doubters and led to the immediate use of convoys on a larger scale.

The escort system grew increasingly complex as its experimental success led naval leaders to dedicate more resources to it. Large convoys included as many as fifty merchant ships and troop transports escorted by one cruiser, six destroyers, eleven trawlers, two torpedo boats, and aerial balloons to look for the telltale wakes caused by submarine periscopes. Eventually, eight separate escort stations were developed in far-flung places: Hampton Roads, Vir-

Despite an inconsistent performance at Jutland, Admiral David Beatty replaced John Jellicoe as commander of the Grand Fleet. Along with American Admiral William Sims, he endorsed the convoy system that protected Allied shipping and helped to end the submarine menace. (Imperial War Museum, Q19570)

ginia; Halifax, Nova Scotia; Panama; Rio de Janeiro; Murmansk; Port Said; Gibraltar; and Dakar.[10] Better than almost any other single factor, the convoy system reveals the truly global nature of World War I.

Working closely with Jellicoe, Grand Fleet Commander Admiral David Beatty, and the French naval staff, Sims used these bases to extend the convoy system across the entire Atlantic Ocean. From the high of 2.2 million tons lost in the second quarter of 1917, shipping losses for the third quarter fell for the first time in a year to 1.5 million tons. In the fourth quarter they fell again, to 1.24 million tons and again the following quarter to 1.1 million tons. In the spring of 1918 Allied shipbuilding exceeded losses for the first time since early 1915. Between the time of the first convoy and the signing of the armistice, allied navies escorted 88,000 ships across the Atlantic and lost just 436. Of the 1.1 million American soldiers sent across the Atlantic, only 637 were lost to German submarines.

Offensive warfare against submarines matured as well. By 1916, the British had developed and deployed the first successful depth charge. Destroyers equipped with depth-charge projectors could lay down a ring of charges set to different depths. If one of the charges exploded within forty feet of a submarine, it would damage the vessel; if the charge exploded within fifteen feet it would destroy its target. Depth charges accounted for twenty-eight U-boat sinkings, more than any other cause for sinkings between 1916 and 1918. The mere presence of destroyers laden with depth charges often sufficed to keep a submarine harmlessly submerged. The British also worked on a system (known as asdic to the British and sonar to the Americans) to make depth charges more accurate by determining the depth and bearing of an enemy craft. The system, not operational until 1919, had no significant outcome on the antisubmarine campaign of World War I, but had a critical effect on that of World War II.

Allied efforts did not end the German U-boat problem, but

The American declaration of war provided a morale boost to the French and British, but the Americans had to turn their desire to fight into an ability to fight. These American soldiers keep a watch for U-boats during their crossing of the Atlantic. (United States Air Force Academy McDermott Library Special Collections)

they succeeded in keeping losses to a manageable level. Allied mastery of the war at sea meant that the German underwater blockade had been broken while the Allied surface blockade of Germany continued, effectively shutting off all imports from overseas and adding to the misery of the German people. Jellicoe's fears of Britain being starved out before the end of November faded as quickly as German Admiral Henning von Holtzendorff's pledge to the kaiser in January 1917 that the U-boats could assure that "not one American will land on the continent."[11] Two planks of German strategy, starving Britain and stopping the Americans from landing in force in Europe, had thus failed.

So had a third plank, that of inciting a rebellion in Ireland.

The First World War began at a critical time for British-Irish relations. In the weeks before the assassination of Archduke Franz Ferdinand, the controversy over Irish Home Rule had assumed center stage in British politics. Home Rule would transfer domestic Irish governance to the Irish parliament based in Dublin. Upon the implementation of Home Rule, the Dublin parliament would have control over Ulster as well, where the majority of the population were Protestants. Home Rule would thus give effective control over all of Ireland to Irish Catholics, although foreign affairs and military policy would continue to be governed from London. As a compromise solution it had much to recommend it, mostly because it offered the best hope of heading off another round of violence.

Many Irish nationalists saw Home Rule as the first logical and peaceful step on the road toward total independence from England. For this reason, Ulster unionists, including many of the army's most senior generals, feared that Home Rule would lead to the beginning of bloody reprisals against Ireland's Protestant population and, eventually, the end of a Protestant presence in Ireland. In order to resist what they often derided as "Rome Rule," Protestant groups, many with close ties to the army, began to arm themselves. These groups, known as the Ulster Volunteers, were illegal, but had tremendous sympathy among the Protestant population as a whole and among many people in key governmental positions.

John French, Hubert Gough, and Henry Wilson were among those generals of Anglo-Irish stock who saw Home Rule as dangerous. Other senior generals, while not Anglo-Irish, saw Home Rule as an ominous omen for the future of the British Empire. Gough and Wilson made it clear to the government that Home Rule could create a potential powder keg if the government asked Anglo-Irish officers to disarm their fellow Protestants in order to give power to Catholics.

A Home Rule bill had already passed Parliament in 1913 and

was scheduled to go into effect in June 1914. In April 1914 Gough, then commander of a cavalry brigade at Curragh barracks in County Kildare, announced to his officers that he would resign if the government ordered him north into Ulster to disarm the Ulster Volunteers. Fifty-eight of his brigade's seventy officers agreed to stand with him. Gough's younger brother was then serving as Haig's chief of staff. He told Haig that he would resign if his brother did. The "Curragh mutiny" sent shock waves through the British army. Haig warned the government that any attempt to punish Gough for his actions might be met with massive resignations across the British officer corps. The king, furious over the incident, nevertheless urged Parliament to suspend Home Rule pending further investigation.

The July crisis and the start of World War I pushed Irish issues to the back burner. The war temporarily rallied Irish opinion to British colors as Irishmen, both Catholic and Protestant, volunteered for the British army. The Irish nationalist group Sinn Fein initially supported Catholic participation in the war in the hope that the British government would see Ireland as an ally and therefore be more inclined to enact Home Rule once the war had ended. A number of Irishmen, however, saw the war not as a chance to be granted Home Rule by a reluctant government in London, but to seize independence with their own hands. Led by Roger Casement, Irish separatists raised money among the Irish community in the United States, gathered arms, and opened up channels of communications to Germany.

Like the 1917 insertion of Lenin into Russia, Germany hoped to insert Casement into Ireland at a time when such a move might produce important results. Inciting a rebellion in Ireland promised many benefits. A rebellion could tie down thousands of British soldiers and deny Britain the services of thousands more Irish volunteers. It might also serve as a source of inspiration to nationalists across the British Empire, most notably in India. Given the tensions of the Curragh mutiny, a rebellion in Ireland might also set the British army's senior leaders in opposition to their own government. The Germans therefore pledged support and weapons to Irish nationalists. In April 1916 British warships captured a German ship laden with arms destined for Ireland, raising British concern about a rebellion.

Two other events in 1916 added fuel to the already tense situation in Ireland. Early in the year, the British government granted a more limited version of Home Rule to the Dublin parliament, but did not extend that rule to Ulster. Sensing that they had been betrayed, Irish nationalists saw the move as the beginning of a permanent division of their island and reacted with anger. Shortly thereafter, Britain introduced conscription to meet the enormous manpower needs of Haig's attrition strategy. While Irish nationalists acquiesced in the voluntary service of Irishmen into the British army, they were aghast at the prospect of the British government's compelling such service. Britain did not attempt to conscript men from southern Ireland until 1918, but the introduction of conscription elsewhere nevertheless increased tensions dramatically.

These issues came to a head in April 1916, when police arrested Casement and two others after they were discovered landing in Ireland with the assistance of a German U-boat. Casement claimed that he had had grown disenchanted with the Germans and was coming to warn the authorities of the German plan to foment rebellion. The British naturally suspected him of treachery and presumed that a German-induced rebellion was imminent. The British army began preparations to meet such a rebellion in force. Three days later, on April 24, Irish nationalists seized the Dublin General Post Office and declared Ireland independent of the British Empire. Already on alert, British units responded in force, clearing Dublin block by block and using gunfire from riverboats to destroy nationalist strongpoints. The British quickly executed the rebellion's leaders by firing squad. By August, they had tried, convicted, and hanged Casement as well.

*British soldiers establish a barricade during the Easter Rising. Tensions
in Ireland distracted British attention in the war's final years, but did
not lead to massive troop rotations from the western front, as the
Germans had hoped. (© Bettmann/Corbis)*

The brutal crushing of what became known as the Easter Rising inspired a new generation of Irish nationalists. Led by Eamon
De Vallera and Michael Collins, they inaugurated a guerrilla war
against Britain, which replied by revoking limited Home Rule and
dispatching thousands of soldiers to Ireland. In 1918, Britain extended conscription to Ireland, setting off another round of violence. As a result, the end of World War I did not bring peace to
Ireland, but a civil war that by 1922 resulted in the fragmentation
of Ireland into an Irish Free State based in Dublin and a Republic
of Northern Ireland based in Belfast and remaining part of the
United Kingdom. Events in Ireland underscored the expanding
set of shock waves that resulted from the war.

"NOT WAR AS WE KNEW IT": THE WAR IN AFRICA

Those shock waves hit Africa as well. World War I in Africa was actually several overlapping wars. The declared war pitted Allied colonial interests against German colonial interests. British forces also fought against Boer separatists, who, as J. J. Collyer put it, saw the war "as a heaven-sent opportunity for an effort to regain the complete independence which they considered they had lost" during the Boer War at the turn at the century.[12] Both sides fought wars against nature as well, as Europeans succumbed much more often to disease than to enemy action. Lastly, the white powers each had to fight against the desires of Africans for greater autonomy or independence. Colonizing whites, a minority everywhere on the continent, had no intention of defeating their European enemy only to see native Africans grow more powerful as a result.

Africa had long been an area of interest to German expansionists. By the mid-nineteenth century, steamships, new weapons, and industrial production of medicines like quinine had enabled Europeans to push into the interior of Africa and extend their power there. Tensions created by the "scramble for Africa" led the great European powers to decide Africa's future by diplomacy. Many Germans felt that at the 1884–1885 conference on Africa (hosted in Berlin, no less) British and French diplomats had gotten the best territories. All four German colonies (Togoland, German Southwest Africa, German East Africa, and Cameroon) abutted a larger and more powerful British colony. Kaiser Wilhelm II railed at Britain's denial of Germany's "place in the sun," but could do little to change the situation until the outbreak of World War I offered him an opportunity.

Unfortunately for Germany, Britain held most of the advantages in Africa. Relatively secure sea lanes allowed Britain to transport men and materials along the African coast, alliances with Belgium and Portugal secured common borders, and Britain's greater

Boer commandos hoping to use the war to gain independence for South Africa assemble in 1914. The outbreak of hostilities in Europe led to a civil war between commandos like these and accommodationist white South Africans, who remained loyal to the British. (© Hulton-Deutsch Collection/Corbis)

manpower reserves in large colonies like Kenya, South Africa, and Rhodesia assured British primacy in Africa. The British also had far more white settlers in Africa than did the Germans. Most of these settlers feared that if Britain lost the war they might be transferred to German control as part of a peace settlement. They therefore volunteered to fight in large numbers (with the notable exception of many Boers) and gave generously of their money.

The vast, relatively underdeveloped territories of Africa made any thought of conquest and occupation absurd. Military operations therefore revolved around particular strategic goals such as wireless stations, ports, and railway lines. Distance, disease, supply, and reconnaissance problems all limited the ability of Europeans to operate in the African theater. No general staffs in the European sense existed in Africa, and most white soldiers there were trained to suppress Africans, not to fight other Europeans. German Southwest Africa, for example, had just 140 German officers and 2,000 trained enlisted men, enough to maintain control over the colony, but not enough to threaten British South Africa.[13]

The relative absence of Europeans meant that most of the fighting fell to Africans, whom both sides recruited in large numbers as both soldiers and porters. Europeans understood that in enlisting Africans they ran the risk of training for combat the very peoples they were subjugating. Still, given manpower constraints on other, more important, fronts, they had no choice. One recently arrived British officer was given command of a platoon of sixty men who had been recruited from thirty different tribes. The language problems inherent in such a command turned his forces into what he called a "comic opera." Most of his European commanders, moreover, were Boer War veterans who were now too old to march through the difficult terrain of East Africa, so they directed his unit's movements via wireless from Dar es Salaam. This situation, he recalled, was far from ideal, as "the Boer War in the open veldt was as different from East Africa as it was from France." The paucity of supply systems meant that guerrilla-style forces and Boer-style trekkers often fought much better than conventional forces did. It was not, this veteran of the Somme recalled, "war as we knew it in France, but a constant fight against disease."[14]

Where the British could bring their conventional advantages to bear relatively easily, they achieved rapid success. Because relations between white colonies had been largely friendly in the years immediately before the war (neighboring colonies were often dependent upon one another for trade), Germany had only a small military presence in Togoland and Cameroon. Both colonies bordered larger and more populous British colonies and had no field de-

British soldiers escort Germans out of Togoland in 1915. Before the war,
British, French, and German settlers in Africa bore little animosity
for one another. (© Hulton-Deutsch Collection/Corbis)

fenses along their frontiers. The British therefore seized effective
control of Togoland and almost all of Cameroon's coastline within
a matter of weeks. By the end of the war's first summer the wireless transmitters in both colonies were in British hands. With
those goals secured and the surrender of the small German force
in Togoland concluded, Britain and France divided the German
colonial possessions between them and focused their efforts on
Germany's other two African colonies.

The war in German Southwest Africa was more complex because of the British belief that the colony, in Hew Strachan's
words, had provided "a haven for diehard Boer rebels."[15] British
entry in the war led South African Prime Minister Louis Botha,
who had once fought against the British, to send South African
soldiers to the western front as part of the larger British effort.
The British request that South African forces invade German

301

Southwest Africa created the potential of civil war between Boers, like Botha, who had made peace with the British in South Africa, and those who had fled to German Southwest Africa. The official British history of the campaign in southwest Africa estimates that 11,000 Boers took up arms against Britain during the war.[16]

The existence of a mutual enemy brought the anti-British Boer community together with the Germans. The *South West Messenger,* a Boer newspaper, declared the war a "chance to get even" with the British Empire, which it hoped would "now receive the deathblow, the stab right through the heart." These sentiments were later echoed by Boer commander Andries de Wet, who urged his fellow Boers to "accept the hand of the German government to free yourselves."[17] In the Boers, the Germans had a relatively large population with experience fighting the British. The open spaces of southwest Africa, moreover, were ideal for the kinds of guerrilla and trekker tactics for which the Boers were so well known.

The threat of a Boer uprising notwithstanding, Botha and General Jan Smuts were determined that South Africa would support the British Empire. They justified their position on the grounds that South Africans of Boer and English descent alike had to unite to defeat a German takeover of their land. Botha hoped that the war might serve to unite the white settlers of South Africa, thus ensuring his larger goal, the subjugation of the region's majority black population. He envisioned a rapid defeat of the Germans, followed by the mutual cooperation by the region's whites to collaborate in the suppression of the much more numerous blacks. Using horses and mules for mobility, and fighting fellow Boers much more often than Germans, Botha's forces easily captured the southern parts of the German colony. The absence of a major Boer uprising inside South Africa freed up additional troops to invade deeper into German Southwest Africa. In June 1915, Botha won an important battle that forced Germany to admit defeat. He gave the Germans generous surrender terms, which they accepted in July. He then began a series of policies designed to replace Southwest Africa's Germans with Boers. For Botha, the military victory was one step in a larger scheme to create a white-dominated South African empire.

The final theater of the war in Africa, German East Africa, lasted the longest. There, a talented German guerrilla fighter, Paul von Lettow-Vorbeck, led a force of African Askari soldiers into Kenya, tying down British forces and moving across East Africa "practically unmolested" by unprepared and outmatched British forces.[18] Lettow's African soldiers were hardy, experienced fighters who had brutally suppressed native rebellions by the Herero and Maji-Maji nations. The Askari fought well for Germany, withdrawing into their own territory and thereby forcing the British to extend their supply lines and expose their flanks as they pursued.

Although later histories written by Europeans rained glory on Lettow and the German officers of the African *Schutztruppe* unit, the Askari proved to be ideally suited for guerrilla warfare. They were seasoned veterans of numerous African campaigns and knew how to move quickly and safely through the difficult terrain of East Africa. As Michelle Moyd has pointed out, German soldiers, many of whom were raised among European theories of racial difference, found themselves having to demonstrate a "flexibility, receptivity to ideas outside the mainstream of the Prussian officer's training, and a willingness to cooperate with their black troops" in order to succeed in this unfamiliar environment.[19]

In 1916, frustrated at their inability to locate and destroy the Askari, the British named Smuts, himself a veteran guerrilla fighter, to command British forces in East Africa. Using lessons learned from the fighting in German Southwest Africa, Smuts chased the Askari into Portuguese Mozambique. Limited by supply problems and ravaged by disease, Smuts's forces nevertheless pressed Lettow onto the defensive, although Lettow's troops continued to inflict damage on Allied interests through 1917 and 1918. Lettow's troops, never more than 3,000 Germans and 11,000 Askaris, required 130,000 Allied soldiers to follow and contain.

German officers train local militia in New Guinea. Australian forces captured German colonies south of the equator; Japanese forces captured German colonies north of the equator. (Australian War Memorial, negative no. A02544)

British forces pursued the Askaris into Tanganyika and then into Rhodesia. Lettow did not surrender until November 25, 1918, when he at last heard of the armistice on the western front.

The war in East Africa was far from the minds of most Europeans in 1918. That spring, the Germans launched their final effort to win the war. Since the surrender of the Russians in 1917, the Germans had transferred 48 infantry divisions to France, bringing their total infantry strength on the western front to 191 divisions. These reinforcements masked a deeper problem in the German system, however, as 10 percent of the German soldiers in November 1917 alone used the rails to get close to home, then deserted. The desertion problem grew through the winter, with military leaders powerless to stop it. Nevertheless, the German soldiers who remained maintained high morale, as they hoped to end the war, "the cause of all the grief," within a few weeks.[20]

As the German forces in France built strength, the war's secondary theaters faded to insignificance. Everyone involved in the war understood the meaning of the German transfers from the eastern front. The outcome of the war, privates and generals alike knew, rested not in Africa or Salonika or Italy. It depended on the Allied ability to throw back a determined German effort to win the war in the first months of 1918, or not win at all.

12

JERRY'S TURN

The Ludendorff Offensives

A message came down about getting ready to move shortly, which way it did not say. . . . As soon as I got out [of my trench] I found we were under heavy concentrated machine gun fire which seemed to come from all directions. Men were falling all around but no help could be rendered as it was a case of every man for himself.

—Private M. F. Gower, British Fourth Infantry Division,
to his sister, April 1918

Lt. Pat Campbell, an artillerist with the British Fifth Army, had spent the early part of 1918 responding to a series of false alarms. Occasional German shelling and trench raids had played with his nerves, but there had been no indication from headquarters that anything larger was afoot. Rumors had spread that a great German attack would begin in late February, on or around the second anniversary of the start of the massive German offensive at Verdun. But late February passed without incident, as did early March. Campbell, like virtually all soldiers on the western front, knew that the Germans had to attack in order to win the war with their transfers from the Russian front before the Americans landed in France in force. In fact, he almost wished for a German offensive. "It might be an agreeable change if they did [attack]," he wrote later; "we had done all the attacking in 1917. One failure after another. Now the Germans could have their turn."[1]

Even by mid-March, however, the German attack had not materialized, and Campbell had started to think that his superiors doubted the Germans were coming at all. "If our generals really thought they were [attacking], then the back areas would have been full of our reserves. But we saw no one." A brief trip to the rear indicated to Campbell that the multilayered defense lines marked on his map existed on paper only; no troops were there to man them. The first line of trenches represented the only resistance the Fifth Army could offer. As a result of the many false alarms and rumors, the army seemed to Campbell less well prepared to meet an attack than it had been in the previous weeks. More men were on leave in March than in February, partly explaining the empty rear areas Campbell saw. The front was so calm that Campbell had taken to wearing his comfortable soft cap. "No need to wear a steel helmet in a war like this."

The morning of March 21 brought German shelling, itself not an unusual occurrence. The fire that morning, however, was heavier than that of the previous weeks and, for the first time in Campbell's sector, much of the shelling was falling behind British lines, aimed, he soon discovered, at British rail junctures and command posts. Campbell quickly realized that the shelling had cut the telephone line connecting his forward observation position to divisional headquarters. He could not see what was happening in front of him because of a thick morning fog and the general chaos of the day. Neither could he get an accurate general picture or even fresh orders from his divisional headquarters. "I felt alone and lost," he later recalled.

As the morning wore on, British soldiers retreated past him in increasingly large numbers, but he still had no clear idea of the overall picture. Campbell and his battery could not assist the retreating British soldiers because they did not know the positions of either the Germans or British units. Directing artillery fire at prearranged coordinates might only hit empty space, and firing randomly at the front might kill British soldiers instead of German ones. "Something *was* happening up front," he later wrote, "and I did not know what it was."

That night, Campbell's unit managed to hold its line despite a lack of reserves and no information whatsoever about the general

The city of Arras, which for most of the war sat within artillery range of the front line, suffered tremendously during the war. The Germans failed to capture it during their spring 1918 offensives.
(Imperial War Museum, Crown Copyright, P. 396)

situation in the Fifth Army. Campbell knew that if the enemy attacked in force the next morning "we should not be able to hold him." The full magnitude of the situation dawned on him and a fellow officer who told him, "O my God! It will be another Sedan," a reference to a French disaster in the Franco-Prussian War.[2] Unable to direct artillery fire because he lacked telephone communications with his divisional headquarters and unwilling to retreat because he did not want to leave British soldiers without vital artillery support, Campbell and his men hung on, hoping for a miracle.

On the afternoon of the second day of the offensive, Campbell's signallers succeeded in restoring contact with headquarters, and Campbell could see advancing German units in the valley in front of him. He immediately directed fire onto new coordinates only to be told that the division had already packed up all of its guns and ammunition for an immediate retreat. Campbell eventually convinced his superiors to allot him two guns, but his commander warned him to be careful with his ammunition. "Careful with ammunition!" he later wrote. "For weeks past we had been firing hundreds of rounds every night without knowing whether we were inflicting a single casualty. Now in broad daylight when I had the whole German army to shoot at he told me to be careful with ammunition." Campbell ranged his guns and prepared to fire his limited shells, but before he could do so he received an order to retreat. His unit was in imminent danger of being surrounded and cut off. Campbell had just enough time to destroy his guns, but had to leave more than 2,000 rounds of ammunition behind. "Jerry's turn today," one of his men told him. "Our turn again tomorrow."[3]

Tomorrow would be a long time coming. The confusion in Campbell's unit repeated itself all along the line of the British Fifth Army. Ludendorff had targeted the Fifth Army as part of a massive operation code-named Michael. It aimed at slicing through both the Fifth and the Third Armies, cutting off their communications and avenues of retreat, destroying them, and then advancing on the British First and Second Armies from their rear. The Germans had assembled forty-four divisions to lead the attack, spearheaded by men from the German Seventeenth Army, most of whom were veterans of Caporetto. The Germans planned to use the same storm-troop tactics that they had used in Italy and Russia the year before. German artillery would target supply centers and communication nodes, while elite troops bypassed enemy strong points to cut off main enemy units from behind. Only then would conventional German infantry units advance and attack the isolated enemy front line. Speed, skill, and surprise would carry the day.

Concentration proved to be another key. Ludendorff had targeted the Fifth Army with good reason. Its commander, Hubert Gough, the man who had led the Curragh mutiny and mismanaged the Passchendaele offensive, had failed to implement an elastic defense-in-depth system. His army had just eleven divisions to cover forty-two miles of front. Gough judged that he did not have the reserves to develop a deep defense. Once the Germans broke through, therefore, the Fifth Army had no choice but to retreat those units still capable of movement. Thousands of British soldiers did not have that chance. They had no choice but to surrender when their units became cut off and surrounded.

The Germans found the Fifth Army's neighbor, the Third Army, under the command of General Julian Byng of Vimy Ridge fame, to be a tougher foe. With a shorter area of front to cover, Byng had developed a much more sophisticated system of defense. His Third Army still took heavy losses, but gave less ground. Ludendorff decided to reinforce his success, redirecting units designated for operations against the Third Army and sending them instead to inflict as much damage on the crumbling Fifth Army as possible. If the Germans could destroy the Fifth Army, Ludendorff calculated, they could force the exposed Third Army to retreat even if it did take fewer casualties than Ludendorff had envisioned.

Haig had expected French commander Henri-Philippe Pétain to meet the emergency by sending French troops under his command north. Instead, Pétain feared an attack on his own front and held his units in place, meaning that the Fifth Army's south (or right) flank received no support from its neighboring French allies. Consequently, the Fifth Army's heavy losses and its inevitable retreat had to be followed by the orderly retreat of the exposed Third Army. The Germans advanced rapidly into the area the British evacuated and took advantage of the opportunities in front of them. By early April, the German offensive had advanced as far as Montdidier, retaking the entire Somme River area and costing the British 170,000 casualties (including 21,000 prisoners of war on the first day), 1,000 heavy guns, and, by one estimate, more than 2 million bottles of whiskey, a loss that later provided a critical unexpected benefit to the British.[4]

The German attack had taken Haig and his headquarters inexplicably by surprise. Less than a week before the attack, Haig's headquarters had told the Fifth Army not to expect a "serious" attack in the Somme sector and Haig's staff had authorized leave for more than 88,000 men, causing some of the absences that Campbell had noted.[5] The heavy losses of 1917 had led Haig to reduce the size of his infantry divisions from twelve battalions to nine. The attrition upon which Haig had built his strategy had cut both ways, leaving the British army too weak to defend the line in the strength necessary to turn back a German offensive.

British lack of preparation had enormous consequences as the British Fifth and Third Armies moved west, abandoning all of their forward defenses and most of their armaments. Retreating across the ground of the Somme battlefields that they won at so high a price two years earlier proved to be especially demoralizing. Journalist Philip Gibbs, then traveling with the Fifth Army, recalled that losing the Somme positions "struck a chill in one's heart," although he also noted that it did not cause a general panic.[6] The situation was one of the worst the Allies had faced since 1914. "It seemed," Campbell thought, "as though we should go on retreating forever, I could see no end to it."[7]

The Germans had won a tremendous local victory, moving at a speed not seen in the west since 1914. Ludendorff had seemingly designed another masterpiece, exporting the tactics that had worked so well in Russia and Italy to France. The British had been his main target, and now two of their armies were in headlong retreat. Once the British had been defeated, the Germans assumed, the French would have no choice but to follow them out of the war. The Americans, who then had just three infantry divisions in line in the relatively quiet area south of Verdun, would have to retreat across the Atlantic, leaving Germany master of Europe. The kaiser confidently predicted a complete and total victory. He told his entourage that when the English delegation came to sue for peace, "it must kneel before the German standard for it was a question here of a victory of the monarchy over democracy." He ordered schools closed in celebration and bestowed Hindenburg with the Iron Cross with Golden Rays, last given a century earlier to Field Marshal Blücher for, ironically, helping the English rid the continent of Napoleon.[8]

The British were bruised, but far from considering kneeling before the kaiser. They continued to retreat, but at both the upper and lower levels of the British army, leaders took hold of the situation and prevented the retreat from becoming a rout. Dissociated men found their way to the nearest unit and regrouped. In some cases, British units managed local counterattacks that kept the Germans off balance. Key points, like Vimy Ridge at the extreme northern end of the German offensive, remained in British hands, providing reasonably secure places for the British to regroup and refit. As a result, the German attack pushed the British armies back almost forty miles, but did not break them as an offensive army.

Gough lost his job as commander of the Fifth Army on March 28, a victim of both poor circumstances and even poorer decisions. He blamed his defeat on the failure of the French units to his south to stretch their positions north, which would have allowed him to shorten the amount of front his Fifth Army had to cover. Pétain had seen the danger to Gough, but, fearing an attack on his own positions, had decided that protecting the approaches to Paris took precedence over Haig's request to maintain contact between the French and British lines. This situation highlighted a growing problem. The absence of a single commander for the western front gave the Germans fault lines to exploit and created the possibility of British units retreating north to the Channel ports and French units retreating south to cover Paris. If the two

This oversized German tank in 1918 gives a false impression of the strength of German armor. Allied success in building tanks and developing a doctrine for their use provided a tremendous advantage over Germany in the war's final months. (Imperial War Museum, Crown Copyright, 83/23/1)

armies retreated in opposite directions, it would open an enormous gap and provide exposed flanks in both armies for the Germans to attack.

Every general on the western front saw the danger, but only the French had proposed a remedy. Their solution, naming a single western front commander, had been vigorously opposed by the British and the Italians. Because the French army held the longest portion of the line and had the most men in uniform, a single commander would perforce have to be French. Haig and his colleagues remained haunted by their memories of the Nivelle experiment from the year before, which even Clemenceau admitted was a "very strong argument" against a joint command.[9] The British War Office's Director of Military Operations, General Frederick Maurice, a close friend to both Haig and Robertson, reflected the general British sentiment when he called the idea "rubbish" and wrote that a joint command was "nothing more than an attempt on the part of the French to get control, which they now find is slipping out of their hands."[10] Lloyd George had opposed the idea as well in a speech to the House of Commons in December, and the influential Italian politician Giorgio Sonnino called a joint command "the sharpest wound ever aimed at Italian honor and pride."[11]

The shocking German breakthrough at the Somme dramatically changed British opposition to a joint command. The danger of a lack of Franco-British cooperation outweighed the organizational concerns and national pride inherent in a joint command. On March 26, the Supreme War Council met in an emergency session at the town of Doullens, close enough to the fighting for participants to hear the sound of artillery fire. The situation could hardly have been more dire. The day before, the French government began preparations to evacuate to Bordeaux for the second time in the war. Also that week, the Germans had advanced their line close enough to Paris to begin random terror bombardments of the capital with the "Paris gun." A 210mm giant with a 130-foot barrel, the Paris gun could fire a shell almost seventy-five miles. It was too inaccurate to target individual points inside Paris. Its only mission was to frighten the capital and induce panic. It failed to do so, but eventually killed 256 civilians and wounded 620 more. A single shell from the Paris gun killed 70 Parisians gathered in a church for Good Friday services, provoking renewed charges of "Hun brutality."[12]

Doullens had once hosted the headquarters of Foch when he had worked to fuse British, Belgian, and French efforts during the Ypres and Yser campaigns of 1914. He and Clemenceau had guessed that the British would change their minds about a joint command if the French promised to move reserves north to halt the immediate crisis caused by the Fifth Army's collapse. Clemenceau initially favored giving the job to Pétain, but the French general arrived at Doullens pessimistic about the ability of the Allies to win the war. Instead of focusing on ways to reorganize Allied defenses, Pétain urged Clemenceau to consider abandoning Paris. Haig, who had already concluded that the initial German successes had left Pétain a "broken reed," saw Amiens, the juncture of the British and French armies, as much more important than Paris.[13]

Haig had already decided to support the feisty Foch for the job of commander-in-chief because he knew from experience that Foch would fight. Foch had many supporters inside the British army, including his close friend Henry Wilson, Chief of the Imperial General Staff at the time of the Doullens meeting. Foch's reputation inside the British army might have then been even higher than it was in his own army. British General Beauvoir de Lisle recalled meeting Foch in 1916 when he was then "out of favor [with the current French government], but even at that time, we looked upon him as the greatest soldier in the French army."[14] To most British generals at the time of Doullens, he seemed the best choice to lead the Allied armies.

For his part, Foch promised to repeat his performance from 1914 and unify the various Allied efforts into a coherent whole. His promises to fight for Amiens ("I would fight in front of Amiens. I would fight in Amiens. I would fight behind Amiens," he told the conferees) and not retreat the French armies toward Paris led Haig and Lloyd George to drop their opposition to a joint command and support Foch for the job. Haig helped to draft the final memorandum, which entrusted Foch with the "co-ordination of the action of the Allied armies on the western front."[15] Haig remained the commander-in-chief of British forces and Pétain the commander-in-chief of French forces, but Foch now sat in a position to direct the efforts of both. He quickly took control of the forces Pétain had set aside for the defense of Paris and moved them north to help close the gaps in the British line. He made it clear that the Allied armies would not choose between defending Paris and the Channel ports, but would fight for both.

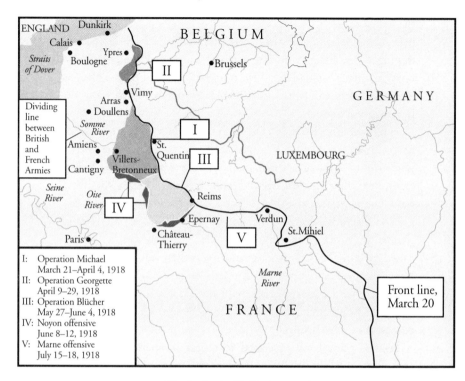

ENGLAND Dunkirk
Calais •   B E L G I U M
Straits   Ypres •
of Dover Boulogne •   • Brussels

II

GERMANY

Vimy
Arras •
Dividing   • Doullens
line   Somme
between   River
British   Amiens •
and   Villers-   St.
French   Cantigny Bretonneux Quentin III
Armies

I

LUXEMBOURG

Seine
River   Oise
River   IV   Reims

Epernay   Verdun
Paris •   Château-   St.Mihiel
Thierry   V

I: Operation Michael
     March 21–April 4, 1918
II: Operation Georgette
     April 9–29, 1918
III: Operation Blücher
     May 27–June 4, 1918   Marne
IV: Noyon offensive   River
     June 8–12, 1918   Front line,
V: Marne offensive   F R A N C E   March 20
     July 15–18, 1918

The Ludendorff offensives, 1918

"I fought for them [the Channel ports] in 1914," he told the British liaison officer to his headquarters, "and will do so again."[16]

Foch's appointment did not immediately solve the problems and mutual suspicions that had arisen between the French and British. Just four days after Doullens, Haig told a colleague that he thought the "French were bloody people to fight with, and that it was just the same now as in 1914, that they ran away."[17] Pétain continued to show great reluctance to move French troops out of his sector in order to help the faltering British. Nevertheless, the creation of a single command in the person of the confident Foch had produced such obvious benefits that the Allies, this time including the Americans, extended Foch's power on April 3, giving him "strategic direction of military operations," meaning the power to direct counterattacks when Foch deemed them appropriate.[18]

Two days later, Ludendorff closed the first phase of his operation. Given the general stasis on the western front for four years, Germany's ability to move the lines more than fifty miles in two weeks shocked the Allied commanders. The British had suffered an estimated 178,000 casualties and the French 70,000. Untold numbers of Allied artillery pieces, tanks, and ammunition rounds lay in German hands. But the Allies had not panicked and they had not broken, thanks in part to Foch's calm handling of the overall situation.

In fact, Ludendorff's great offensive plan had already failed. It had lacked a grand strategy from the beginning, with Ludendorff famously announcing that his only intention had been to "punch a hole into [the allied line]. For the rest, we shall see."[19] Having punched a rather considerable hole, Ludendorff sat at a crossroads. He had inflicted heavy casualties, but his own forces had suffered more than 239,000 casualties, many from Germany's elite units; March 21, 1918, had been Germany's costliest day of the war so far. Even with the odds in their favor, the Germans found that their attack had been very costly. Even worse for the Germans, the will of the French and British had not broken and the offensive had led the Americans to promise to move more men to Europe more quickly.

German soldiers had, in addition, broken discipline to loot French towns and eat and drink from British and French stores. Compared to the Germans' own often meager rations, the Allies appeared to have limitless supplies, leading many Germans to doubt their commanders' proclamations that the U-boat campaign was strangling Great Britain. The 2 million bottles of whiskey that the British left behind proved to be valuable weapons, as thirsty German soldiers stopped to drink their fill, producing what one German Army Group commander called "repulsive scenes of drunkenness."[20] One British medical officer noted that the mighty German army had been beaten by "something Ludendorff and his staff officers had not foreseen," namely "the abundance of Scottish drinking spirit!"[21]

ANOTHER HUNDRED YEARS WAR

Ludendorff himself understood that his territorial gains notwithstanding, his grand plan could not possibly produce the desired results. He had subordinated grand strategy to the tactical superiority that the German army had developed with elite infantry and artillery units. Ludendorff saw that the German army's most elite unit, Oskar von Hutier's Seventeenth Army, "had lost too heavily" in the first two days of the offensive to remain as the lead formation in future attacks. He also understood that his tactical success had not yielded results commensurate with winning the war. "Strategically," he noted, "we had not achieved what the events of the 23rd, 24th, and 25th [of March] had encouraged us to hope for."[22]

Despite the disappointments of the first days, Ludendorff could not switch to the defensive at this juncture. His overall mission, to win the war before the Americans could appear in large numbers, had not changed. He therefore launched his second major offensive in Flanders on April 9. Once again he targeted the British in what became known as the Battle of the Lys to the British and Operation Georgette to the Germans. Ludendorff was after the area defended by two divisions sent to the western front by Britain's "oldest ally," Portugal. The German attack caught the unfortunate Portuguese as they were being relieved. The line in their sector crumbled and dissolved within hours.

British efforts in 1918 to blame the outmanned Portuguese provide only a partial explanation for the setback. The Germans also infiltrated the British line near Ypres, capturing most of the ground to south of the town, including the strategically important Kemmel Hill and the symbolically important Messines Ridge. This German breakthrough threatened the nearest major Channel port, Dunkirk, which sat just twenty-two miles from the newly mobile front line. Operation Georgette therefore posed a serious threat to the BEF's supply lines. While British commanders reorganized their men and set up new lines of defense, the joint command structure provided immediate help. Foch dispatched ten divisions of French troops to the Flanders front he knew so well and ordered Pétain to assume seventy-five more miles of the western front in order to permit the British to concentrate their efforts.

Haig and his staff had been caught by surprise once again. They had expected a renewed German offensive farther south in the Arras–Vimy Ridge sector. They had underestimated the danger to the Lys sector in part because they had presumed that the Lys valley would not dry out until May, as had been the case in previous years. The relatively dry winter of 1917–1918, however, had produced firm soil in the Lys region by March, a fact that Haig's staff was unaware of. His headquarters, therefore, had not ordered the creation of an elastic defense in depth in the region. Some local commanders had taken the initiative to order such defenses on their own and, where they existed, they generally offered greater resistance to the Germans.[23]

Haig attempted to rally his men with his "Backs to the Wall" order of April 11. It read, in part, "There is no course open to us but to fight it out. Every position must be held to the last man: there must be no retirement. With our backs to the wall and believing in the justice of our cause we must fight on to the end. The safety of our homes and the freedom of mankind alike depend upon the conduct of each one of us at this critical moment."[24] The order was an extraordinary statement from a man not normally given to public eloquence; it reflected the urgency of the situation.

To many of his men, however, Haig's order suggested desperation or even panic, adding to fears that the situation might be even worse than many had dared to fear. Most soldiers, noted one corps commander, had had "their backs to the wall since March, and did not need to be told," especially by a general sitting in relative comfort behind the lines.[25] Most men, fighting for their lives and those of their comrades, did not even hear of the order for days. Pat Campbell noted laconically that he "never saw any of our men reading it."[26] Inspired by Haig or not, British soldiers fought with increasing determination, containing the Lys offensive and holding both Ypres itself and the critical railroad juncture of Hazebrouck to the southwest.

Farther to the south, the Germans renewed their efforts to seize Amiens. The town sat on the Somme River and commanded a vital railway link. It was also the meeting point of the French and British armies and was therefore always at the center of German thinking. On April 24, the Germans concentrated their meager tank assets (mainly captured British models) and captured the town of Villers-Bretonneux, just ten miles east of Amiens. Hindenburg said that the town had to be held "whatever happens, so that from its heights we can command Amiens."[27] Australian troops retook the town the next day, with a determined surprise attack unsupported by artillery. The retaking of Villers-Bretonneux marked one of the war's great achievements, leading one admiring British officer who witnessed the attack to comment about the Australians, "I am glad they were on our side."[28] For the Germans, the loss of the town took the steam out of Operation Georgette. On April 29, Ludendorff called off part two of his great offensive, having once again failed to drive a breach between the British and French armies.

Territorial losses notwithstanding, the British had held their lines. With reinforcements from Foch, they would be able to secure the Channel ports. Some officers even spoke optimistically of resuming the offensive in the near future. Haig's headquarters shelved emergency plans to demolish Calais and flood the region

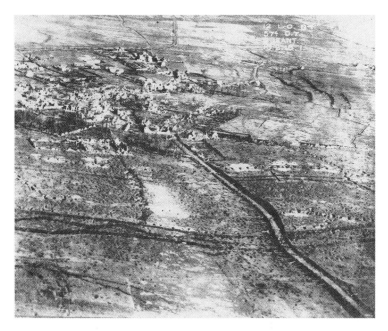

This aerial photo shows Queant, a Hindenburg Line strongpoint. Note the three belts of interlocking barbed wire (foreground, left to right) designed to protect German forces in the town itself. (Courtesy of Andrew and Herbert William Rolfe)

west of Dunkirk. The first two German attacks of 1918 had been tremendously costly, but they had not appreciably altered the strategy of the war. It appeared to many British soldiers that the Germans had the power to inflict great damage, but not enough power to force a decision. The British, for their part, could hold on, but could not deliver a knockout blow of their own. "I suppose," one officer told Campbell, "it will be another Hundred Years War."[29]

The human costs of Ludendorff's first two attacks were appalling. The German army had suffered 257,176 casualties in April on top of the 235,544 they had suffered in March. Germany was simply unable to replace manpower losses on this scale. The German army began to experience higher desertion rates, and some units reported that they could not expect their men to obey orders in the future. Sixth Army headquarters bluntly warned Ludendorff that "the men will not attack."[30] Still Ludendorff pressed on. He switched his attention south to Champagne, hoping to inflict a major defeat on the French that would impel the British to stretch their line in support. After dealing with France, Ludendorff then planned to strike the extended British again in Flanders.

Ludendorff launched his third offensive, code-named Blücher, in late May. His target was the infamous Chemin des Dames sector, where French forces were packed in between the ridge and the Aisne River. The French commander, Denis Auguste Duchêne, had commanded a corps in this sector during the failed French attempts to capture the ridge in April 1917. Now, as Sixth Army commander, Pétain had urged him to establish a defense in depth. Duchêne had resisted, arguing that the terrain in the Chemin des Dames sector did not allow for such a defense. Three British divisions, badly beaten in the first two German offensives, had moved down to his sector for what they hoped would be a rest period. The three British division commanders had seen firsthand the dangers of a forward defense such as the one Duchêne had in place. When they raised their concerns and asked him to consider the creation of an elastic defense, Duchêne dismissed them with an inelastic "J'ai dit" ("I have spoken").

The dense formation of French defenses in Duchêne's Sixth Army provided a mass of targets for the experienced German artillery, which opened its most deadly fire of the war on Sunday morning, May 26. Ludendorff had concentrated an astonishing 2 million artillery shells and 1,100 batteries in this sector. Even more astonishing, the Germans fired almost the entire allotment of shells in less than five hours, annihilating French defenses and stunning the French forces into a stupor. Thirty-six divisions of German infantry, twenty-seven of which were veterans of the spring's operations, then moved forward against twenty-four dazed and decimated Allied divisions that were covering the sector between La Fère and Reims. In the ensuing days, the Germans advanced as far as forty miles, severing French rail lines and coming within sixty miles of Paris.

The Germans had scored another monumental tactical success, but that success had brought them no closer to winning the war. The French had held the key cities of Reims, Château-Thierry, and Epernay, thereby containing the damage. The ground over which the Germans had advanced, moreover, offered few resources. The Germans had scorched this same ground during their retreat to the Hindenburg Line. Thus German forces, now as far as ninety miles from their railheads, were operating without regular food, water, or ammunition. The only strategic goal in this region, Paris, obviously lay outside the ability of the German army to capture or even seriously threaten. Still, Ludendorff was so taken with his success that he reinforced it, taking resources away from the original strategic goals of his offensives, Flanders and Amiens. That decision left the German army weaker in the area of greatest strategic importance, leading Foch to tell the British liaison officer to his headquarters, "I wonder if Ludendorff knows his craft."[31] All the German army had to show for its efforts in the south were two dangerously exposed salients and an exhausted army with which to defend them. By June 4, Ludendorff had to halt the offensive while he reorganized and decided on his next move.

"RETREAT, HELL! WE JUST GOT HERE"

Foch could afford to be cavalier about his adversary despite the latter's string of tactical successes, because he knew that he had a weapon Ludendorff could never hope to match. The American army, under its formidable commander General John Pershing, was at long last ready for action. A consummate professional with a reputation for working hard and holding stubbornly to his be-

American Expeditionary Forces (AEF) commander John J. Pershing (right) stubbornly resisted seeing his army placed under European commanders. With him is Benjamin Foulois, who became brigadier general and chief of the Air Service in the AEF. (United States Air Force Academy McDermott Library Special Collections)

liefs, Pershing had been a fast riser since his appointment as First Captain during his days as a cadet at West Point. His marriage to the daughter of the longtime head of the Senate Military Affairs Committee and patronage from President Theodore Roosevelt provided Pershing with needed political connections in the Republican party, although he was always careful to stand above partisan politics. Despite his failure to find and capture Pancho Villa, his political acumen during the operation had won him admiration from the Democratic Wilson administration as well, making him an obvious choice to command American forces in Europe. Pershing was also an excellent judge of military talent. His early appointments for positions in France included future five-star general George Marshall as well as the brilliant and enigmatic George Patton.

Almost one year after entering the war, the United States had finally solved enough of the myriad problems involved in waking from its isolationist slumber to enter the fray. One of the most serious of these problems involved determining the exact relationship between the United States and its allies. America had refused to sign the Treaty of London, which formed the legal basis for the alliance, preferring to call itself an "associated power." President Wilson had made it clear that he did not see American war aims as being entirely synonymous with those of France, Britain, and Italy. He and Pershing had made it equally clear that the Americans would fight only as an independent and visibly American entity. Both men firmly resisted European plans to "amalgamate" the American army at the company or battalion level into French and British divisions. America's inexperience, lack of suitable doctrine, and shortages of modern war materiel contrasted sharply with its principled resistance to amalgamation, but Pershing held firm.[32]

In the end the amalgamation controversy produced more smoke than fire. The Americans had agreed early on that limited and temporary amalgamation would be acceptable if it were needed to meet an emergency. "We do not desire loss of identity of our forces," Secretary of War Newton Baker wrote to Pershing in December 1917, "but [we] regard that as secondary to the meeting of any critical situation by the most helpful use possible of the troops at your command."[33] At the height of the crisis in late March 1918, Pershing had come to Foch to make an extraordinary offer that contrasted sharply with American resistance to amalgamation. Pershing, in his uncertain French, told the new commander-in-chief that "the American people would consider it a great honor for our troops to be engaged in the present battle. . . . Infantry, artillery, aviation, all that we have is yours; use them as you wish."[34]

The Europeans, for their part, agreed to the creation of an independent American army under American commanders, but not, as Clemenceau told Pershing, "while my country's fate was every moment at stake on the battlefields, which had already drunk the best blood of France."[35] Foch and Pétain had argued that a separate American army made operational sense because American troops could be expected to fight better under American officers. Still, the emergency created by the German offensive had to be stopped by any means necessary before an independent American army could be created. As a result, the two sides agreed to the temporary inclusion of American divisions (under American commanders) into French corps and armies until the immediate crisis had passed.

The Americans, British, and French also agreed to a system to transport and equip the Americans as quickly as possible. On May 2, Foch negotiated an agreement with Pershing whereby the Americans agreed to ship only infantry to Europe, thus maximizing the number of "doughboys" available to meet the German offensives. The British agreed to provide the necessary shipping to transport half of the Americans, ensuring that almost 500,000 Americans would be in Europe by July and another 500,000 would cross the Atlantic by the end of the year. In the end, the Americans exceeded those goals, landing as many as 300,000 men

American light tanks advancing. Compare these tanks to the cumbersome German tank on page 313. (National Archives)

per month. By the terms of an earlier agreement, the French provided the needed munitions in exchange for American steel and raw materials. France became the most important supplier of arms to the American army, eventually giving the Americans 3,532 field artillery pieces, 40,884 automatic weapons, 227 tanks, and 4,874 airplanes.[36] Without these weapons, the Americans would have been hard pressed to conduct offensives at all.

The close personal friendship that developed between Pershing and Pétain furthered the connection between the American Expeditionary Forces (AEF) and the French army. In late May, the two armies cooperated in the first large combat operation the AEF faced, at the town of Cantigny. A joint Franco-American force took the town, then held off six separate German attempts to retake it. The Americans made tactical mistakes, but showed the kind of élan that soon made their reputation in both the Allied and German armies. They may have been clumsy and dependent on the French for many support operations, but their battlefield immaturity would solve itself with experience. As the French, British, and Germans saw them firsthand, few doubted that the Americans had the "stuff" to fight on the western front. Their numbers (on average a division a day arrived in France) and their healthy, well-fed appearance led their allies to see them as "splendid" men with the highest morale and spirit.[37] The psychological effect alone of the appearance of so many fresh reinforcements can hardly be underestimated.

The Americans soon proved to be a formidable battlefield weapon in the war against Germany. They played key roles in shutting off two of the German approaches toward Paris. American troops filled in a gap near a hunting preserve held in force by the Germans called Belleau Wood. According to Marine Corps legend, a German attack on June 2 sent French units retreating, with French officers urging the Americans to retire to stronger positions. A Marine Corps officer, Captain Lloyd Williams, is supposed to have replied, "Retreat, hell! We just got here." Like all great one-liners from history, this one may be apocryphal, but its persistence over time reflects the ardor and spirit with which the Americans fought at Belleau Wood and elsewhere.

On June 5, the Americans attacked the wood as part of a general advance by the French XXI Corps. Nearly three weeks of deadly combat ensued before the Marine commander could signal "Woods now U.S. Marine Corps entirely." The vast cemetery next to the wood, now officially renamed "Bois de la Brigade de Marine," stands as evidence of the tremendous losses suffered by the U.S. forces to halt the German advance. The Marines lost 4,600 men, almost 50 percent of the men engaged. The victory at Belleau Wood, however, stopped the Germans at their closest point to Paris, just thirty-five miles away. They would not come as close again for the rest of the war.

Just a few miles from Belleau Wood, the Americans played the leading role in stopping another German drive, this time at the

American troops, like these men using a light machine gun, struck allies and enemies alike as eager, reckless, and idealistic. The realities of the war caused American commanders to abandon their preconceptions and learn from the French and British. (National Archives)

town of Château-Thierry on the Marne River. While their comrades were fighting off German attacks at Belleau Wood, the men of the Second and Third American Divisions denied the Germans the chance to cross the Marne at Château-Thierry. Other American units entered the battle as well. Their insignia can be seen today on the massive monument above the town dedicated to "the friendship and cooperation between the French and American armies." One American regiment defended a bend in the river so fiercely that it acquired the nickname the "Rock of the Marne." The AEF's forceful presence on the battlefield stood as conclusive evidence that Ludendorff's strategy had been an abject failure. "You Americans," one French officer said in mid-June, "are our hope, our strength, our life."[38] Even the defeat of the British that Ludendorff had so ardently sought would not stop the Americans from arriving en masse and fighting with more skill each month they were in France.

Despite June losses exceeding 200,000 men, Ludendorff decided on a fourth offensive. He held out the hope of seizing Reims and then advancing on Paris. The German army, wracked by defeatism, desertions, and the mysterious illness soon to be known as the Spanish influenza, could not repeat its previous successes. Duchêne's disaster on the Chemin des Dames led all Allied units to redouble their efforts to create elastic defenses. The Allies had finally seen enough of the Germans to know how to counter their tactics. German deserters (many of them from Alsace) gave the French the exact time and location of the attack. As a result, German advances were negligible and the kaiser watched in frustration as his men failed once again to capture Reims. Ludendorff responded by blaming his staff officers and announcing his hope to defeat the French in the near future, then continue his pursuit of the British, into India if necessary.[39]

Ludendorff's fifth offensive, on the Marne River east of Reims, surprised no one. German deserters, French intelligence reports, and Foch's own intuition had enabled the Allies to divine Ludendorff's plan. Foch had prepared a rude reception for the Germans, assembling infantry, air, and armor from four nations, including six American divisions that fought under the French Sixth Army. The German losses in the Second Battle of the Marne (July 15 to July 18) included 30,000 demoralized prisoners. The Allied victory definitively ended any German hope of capturing Paris and led Ludendorff to cancel his sixth offensive, aimed at the British in Flanders. On July 24, Foch announced to the Allied generals that the time had arrived "to cease our generally defensive attitude imposed until now by our general inferiority of numbers and pass to the offensive" in order to press the Germans every day along the entire front and "not allow them the time to reform their units."[40] Germany's last gamble had failed, and the Allied armies were ready to resume the offensive. The war's final phase had begun.

13

ONE HUNDRED DAYS
TO VICTORY

Amiens to the Meuse-Argonne

[Captured German] officers in particular inform us of the weakness of their forces, the youth of their recruits, and the influence of the American entry. They are depressed by their heavy losses, by the poor quality of their food, and by the crisis inside Germany. They are worried and begin to doubt German power. . . . The German is beginning to understand that he cannot win, but he is not ready to give up and he can continue to resist.

—French headquarters report on German army morale,
September 4, 1918

AFTER the victory at the Second Battle of the Marne, the Allied armies began a general offensive of their own. The Allied soldiers' progress was better than their senior generals had expected. The German army offered little resistance beyond a determined rear guard, preferring instead to move to more defensible positions further east. The most serious impediment to Allied movements was the Germans' scorched-earth policies, in accordance with which they felled bridges, leveled villages, and mined roads. The French army's first sight of French territory so brazenly destroyed by their enemy reenergized its desire to make Germany pay for its crimes. The men of the 77th French Infantry Regiment recalled their feelings as they passed through damaged French towns in August 1918:

> The destroyed and pillaged villages showed the vandalism of the Germans in their rage at having been forced to retreat, down to the last chair, the last broken window, [and] the last torn-up floor.

There were depots of gas shells [with fuses timed to release the gas after the Germans had cleared out] hidden among woods, cadavers of horses killed by Germans when they retreated over the Marne, fruit trees upturned, [and] unripe wheat cut down. This well-designed spectacle only increased our hatred of the Boche.[1]

In the view of the men of the 77th, these deliberate German actions lay outside the bounds of war. The destruction of livestock and crops in the summer of 1918 threatened a very difficult winter for the farmers and villagers of eastern France. The Germans, the French believed, should be punished for what they had done.

The men of the 77th were assisted in their pursuit of the Germans by a welcome novelty, motorized transportation. Where French engineers could rebuild bridges and secure the safety of roads from mines, the 77th traveled by truck, a positive change for any infantryman. This innovation underscored the importance of the mechanization of the Allied war effort. The use of tanks at the Second Battle of the Marne had proved to be a crucial deciding factor, allowing the Allies to bring mobile firepower forward to open holes for the infantry to exploit. Aviation, too, played an important role.

These successes were in large part a product of the economic reforms overseen by civilians in the war's first years. Britain's Sir Eric Geddes, among others, reformed the administrative capabilities of the British system to allow the right supplies to be produced in Britain, shipped to the various theaters of war, and used by the units that needed them. Geddes brought his expertise in railway management to the problems of temporarily rededicating Britain's essentially civilian railway network to military purposes. He eventually rose to become First Lord of the Admiralty, where he used his skills to solve Royal Navy problems as well. Allied economic and political reforms of 1915 and 1916, combined with the unhindered cooperation of American industry after April 1917, began to change the face of modern warfare in 1918, greatly to the Allies' favor.

The modernization of war did not extend to all parts of the battlefield. Every army continued to rely on animal and human power for moving supplies. (National Archives)

These successes notwithstanding, none of the Allied senior leaders thought that their victory at the Second Battle of the Marne in mid-July or their rapid pursuit of the Germans at the end of the month would lead to the defeat of Germany in 1918. The most optimistic among them envisioned that victory would follow a massive spring 1919 campaign led by fresh American divisions and spearheaded by thousands of tanks, trucks, and airplanes. More pessimistic leaders, including David Lloyd George, began to plan for a continuation of the war into 1920. Lloyd George had heard too many rosy predictions of easy victory in the past. He was unwilling to count on them in the summer of 1918 only to find himself unprepared to lead Britain into a longer war if one developed.

German leaders, by contrast, were much more likely to believe that the war might end, unfavorably for them, by the end of the year. Operationally, they believed they could overcome the setback at the Marne, but the defeat only underscored the bankruptcy of the Germans' strategy. After the Second Battle of the Marne, with their spring offensives a failure, Germany had no obvious strategic alternatives and no fallback plan. Germany's allies, moreover, required massive assistance just to keep them from collapsing. Austria-Hungary, Bulgaria, and the Ottoman Empire all sat at the extreme end of their operational capacities. Few Germans expected much help from them in the weeks and months to come. As their own allies began to collapse, the Germans knew, the Allied powers would be free to shift even more assets to the western front or to operations designed at attacking Germany from other directions. The latter included plans by Lloyd George and Henry Wilson to commence large-scale operations in the Balkans. Allied success in such theaters could have important consequences. Russia and Romania might even reenter the war if they sensed German weakness, placing at risk the eastern conquests that the Germans expected to hold after the war even if they lost the war on the western front.

Materially, the Germans' position gave them little cause for hope. The appearance of the Americans, combined with the economic strength of Britain and France, tipped the balance sheet on the western front against Germany for the first time in the war. In the summer of 1918 Germany faced a western front manpower deficit of 4,002,104 Allied soldiers to 3,576,900 German soldiers. Those numbers included 786,489 fresh Americans in France on August 1; throughout the summer the Americans augmented that number by almost 30,000 more men per day. The Allied numbers, therefore, would continue to grow as the German numbers fell. American divisions, moreover, were twice the size of German divisions, providing greater punch and endurance on the battlefield.

The crisis of 1918 led the Americans to send troops as quickly as possible, often without supplies. Many American units relied on French and British supplies, such as the French 75mm artillery gun shown here. (National Archives)

Scores of German units were in no condition to fight. Exhausted by the spring fighting, they needed several weeks or months to rest and refit before they could resume offensive operations. Resupplying these units would not be an easy task, as Germany also faced insurmountable deficits in tanks (1,572 Allied to 10 German), airplanes (5,646 Allied to 2,991 German), machine guns (37,541 Allied to 20,000 German), and gasoline reserves.[2] The Allies had the ability to add large numbers of newer models of all of the weapons of modern warfare throughout 1918 and, if necessary, into 1919. The Germans, by contrast, would need to rely on dwindling stocks of their increasingly outdated weapons, most notably tanks and airplanes.

Despite massive Allied casualties in the first half of 1918, Foch wanted to press his advantages as rapidly as possible. Consequently, having turned back the last of Germany's spring offensives, he directed the Allies to assume the offensive. The Marne sector offered an enticing opportunity because the German advance there had left them with a salient that jutted sharply into Allied lines, thereby exposing the Germans on three sides. The western tip of the salient, marking the point of Germany's furthest advance, lay at the town of Château-Thierry on the Marne River. The center of the salient lay at the Plateau of Tardenois, about ten miles to the east. Pétain hoped to attack the salient with twin drives at its northern and southern shoulders, with the drives meeting at Tardenois. The ultimate goal, according to Pétain's orders, was not only to "chase [the Germans] from the Château-Thierry pocket, but to cut off their retreat toward the north and to capture the mass of their forces."[3]

Pétain had eighteen French infantry divisions, three American infantry divisions, and two British infantry divisions at his disposal for the operation. Sensing the danger, the Germans abandoned the entire Château-Thierry salient on July 20 and 21. Their need to refit and replace their losses had reduced their available reserves from sixty-two divisions on July 17 to forty-two divisions just a week later. German headquarters also reduced the size of battalions from 980 men to 880 men, a further indication of the serious depletion of German manpower. German headquarters knew it could neither resist an Allied attack on the Château-Thierry salient nor afford the catastrophic losses that would have been suffered if the Allies cut off the salient.

The Allied reoccupation of the Château-Thierry salient had several important ramifications. With the threat to Paris eliminated, the two British divisions were now free to return to British command near Amiens in order to support offensive operations in that sector. They were replaced by three fresh American divisions, bringing the American total in the sector to six double-strength divisions, enough to lead to the landmark creation of the Ameri-

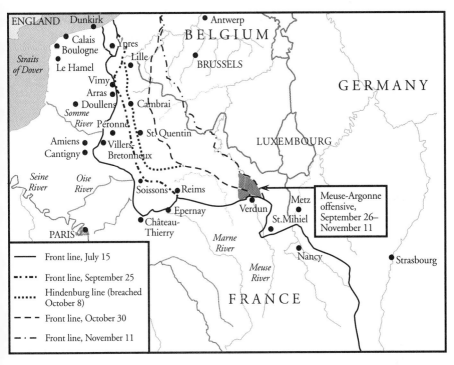

Allied advances, July 15–November 11, 1918

can First Army, approved by the Supreme War Council on July 25 and implemented on August 10. Together with the Americans, the French pursued the retreating Germans in the Marne sector from July 15 to August 5, capturing 29,000 German soldiers, 612 artillery pieces, and 3,330 machine guns. They also recaptured 177 French guns and 393 French machine guns lost during the spring. In all, they captured more than 6 million rounds of small arms ammunition and almost 1 million artillery shells.[4] Germany could not afford these losses.

After the Germans' failure to take Château-Thierry and push on toward Paris, Ludendorff became increasingly distant from both the realities of the war and from his own staff. He refused to read the signs of an army that had become completely exhausted, most notably the higher desertion rates, the propensity of the Germans to surrender, and increased instances of men refusing the orders of their officers. He denied that the Spanish influenza was having any effect on German soldiers, nor did he accept the reality that his offensives had killed most of Germany's elite soldiers, leaving the army with hundreds of thousands of poorly trained reservists to meet the determined Allied attacks he knew were imminent. Lacking a strategy and a way to turn Germany's fortunes, he yearned for a German victory without being able to effect one.[5] The strain reached across the entire German command structure. Hindenburg's second-in-command suffered a nervous breakdown, and several other officers lost faith in Ludendorff and his grandiose schemes.

On the Allied side, faith in the commanders and a belief in the possibility of victory were rising. Foch, Haig, and Pétain all understood the need to pressure the Germans before they could recover and reorganize. They knew how tired their own forces were, but believed that time lost in July and August could have critical ramifications. Pétain remained the most cautious of the three, arguing that his men needed more rest before driving east. Foch drove him on, telling him on July 23 that "it is important to resume the mastery of operations vigorously and without delay."[6] Haig soon urged a similar effort from his troops, telling them that "risks which a month ago would have been criminal to incur ought now to be incurred as duty."[7] By moving quickly and pressing on all fronts, the Allies could turn the war around and maybe even win it before winter set in.

THE BLACK DAY AND THE DRIVE
TO THE HINDENBURG LINE

In early July, the Germans had received a seemingly minor battlefield setback when Australian and American forces captured the

*American soldiers fought at Le Hamel alongside their Australian comrades.
Despite Pershing's demand that his units have absolute independence,
the Americans relied heavily for leadership on the experienced
Australian "diggers." (Australian War Memorial, negative no. E02690)*

nondescript village of Le Hamel. The battle for Le Hamel, although hardly noticed by most men on the western front, had two important ramifications for future combat. The first was its originality and improvisation. The genius behind the battle, a Jewish Australian general named John Monash, used his customary careful preparations to design a "textbook" victory.[8] Monash united air, armor, and infantry operations more smoothly than anyone had previously been able to do. At Le Hamel, tanks supported infantry advances more efficiently than they had done at Cambrai or the Second Battle of the Marne, allowing important communications problems that had previously limited the cooperation of armor and infantry to be overcome. Monash and his air commanders even arranged for Royal Air Force pilots to drop ammunition to men involved in the battle, allowing for resupply "on the fly."

The second innovation involved the incorporation of the Americans. Monash integrated two American regiments into the battle under the overall control of the veteran Australian 4th Infantry Division. Pershing had asked that the Americans not be included in the battle because they were not under overall American command, but after considerable debate Haig and Foch overruled him in the interests of ensuring that the Australians had the power to win the battle. The eager Americans fought extremely well (on July 4, no less), impressing their Australian allies. Pershing, however, remained irritated about his lack of control over American units and vowed to ensure that "nothing of the kind could occur again."[9] The angry reaction of the American commander marred an otherwise successful use of American units into the battlefield. Pershing's outrage, however, did not prevent a solid rapport from developing between the Australians and the Americans, which paid great dividends later in the year.

With American help, Monash's masterpiece worked as he had intended. The main portion of the fighting ended in a little over an hour and a half. Allied soldiers seized all of their objectives with astonishingly light losses. They also captured more than 1,500 German soldiers, many of them unwounded, indicating a growing willingness of the Germans to surrender at the first opportunity. The Australians who fought at Le Hamel noted the difference in German fighting strength. They concluded that the German army was "no longer the formidable foe in defence that it had been in 1916 and 1917."[10] Monash therefore argued that the Australian Corps' parent unit, the British Fourth Army, should take advantage of the momentum gained by the victory at Le Hamel. His new scheme of combined operations, he contended, should be tried out on a much larger scale and be aimed at a much more strategically important target.

Monash played a key role in developing the subsequent battle, which was directed at securing the lateral lines of communication running east of Amiens. These lines supplied most of the German units in Picardy and Artois. The plan counted on catching the Germans by surprise. There would be no preparation bombardment by a massive artillery park to give away the attack; instead, the British planned to mass tanks to provide local firepower. Foch ordered that all details of the plan be hidden from anyone who did not need to know, including several key members of Allied war ministries. Allied commanders continually shifted the location of conferences and meetings so that they would never be seen together in the same army or corps headquarters twice.

To ensure secrecy on the ground, the British restricted their movements to nighttime and flew airplanes overhead to mask the noise of tank engines. British troops found a slip of paper in their pay books that reminded them to "keep your mouths shut" about the operation when in rest areas. Signposts on the roads to and from forward areas carried the same message. British radio operators also made phony broadcasts to suggest that a British attack in Flanders was imminent. They knew that the decoy had worked when the Germans sent reinforcements to Flanders instead of the Amiens sector.

The careful preparations paid off; the British attack on August 8 took the Germans almost completely by surprise. The attack was led by the British Fourth Army, under its widely respected commander, General Henry Rawlinson. Rawlinson had taken over Gough's broken Fifth Army in late March, renaming it, reorganizing it, and restoring its confidence. Its role as the lead army in the offensive at Amiens showed that it had recovered from the losses it had received in the spring. The solid Canadian and Australian corps came under the Fourth Army as well, adding veteran leadership and some of the best soldiers in the Allied armies. The Canadians, moreover, had not been involved in the bloody fighting of

March and April and were thus fresh. The Australians brought lessons learned from Le Hamel and played a critical role at Amiens, occupying the center of the line.

Rawlinson had a total of 14 infantry divisions, 2,000 artillery pieces, and 450 tanks, the most yet assembled for one battle. The tanks included 342 of the new heavy Mark V models, which were, in the words of the Fourth Army's historian, "handy to maneuver, being able to twist and turn with a rapidity which a year before would have been thought impossible." The new tanks were also less vulnerable to low-trajectory fire, allowing them to be brought further forward. To this arsenal the British added 800 aircraft, some of them dedicated to supporting the advance of the tanks. In the weeks before the battle, aerial photography had spotted and marked all of the German defenses, making the German strongpoints "easily discernable" for the tanks and supporting aircraft. The planning had been done so thoroughly and the secret assembly of forces so efficiently that it was said that "the Battle of Amiens was really won before the attack began."[11]

For the men of the Allied armies who led the attack it was "glorious once again to be in the rush of an advance" after the months of retreating.[12] With near-total surprise and with the Fourth Army's careful preparations leaving little to chance, the advance was Britain's most successful of the war on the western front. By 11:30 on the morning of August 8, the Canadians had seized the first two lines of German defenses. By the end of the day, they had advanced a remarkable eight miles in some places, opening holes that allowed the British to use cavalry to attack the lines of communication of the retreating German units. The French First Army, operating under British control to ensure unity of command, experienced success as well, capturing men from eleven different German divisions.

The final balance sheet of Amiens proved two points. First, the Germans had experienced what their own official monograph on the battle called "the greatest defeat the German Army had suf-

This rare photograph shows a bomber dropping its payload on target sets, numbered on the photograph. Strategic bombardment suffered from problems of accuracy and identification of proper targets, but became a fundamental part of Allied plans by the end of the war. (United States Air Force Academy McDermott Library Special Collections)

fered since the beginning of the war."[13] On day one, the Germans had lost on average six miles of territory along the line of the attack and 28,000 men, the vast majority of whom surrendered rather than fight. Ludendorff famously called August 8 the "black day" of the German army and concluded that Germany could no longer hope to win the war. One week later, the kaiser authorized the German foreign ministry to approach the royal family of Holland in the hopes that the Dutch government might serve as a sympathetic intermediary in armistice negotiations with the Allies.

Second, Amiens proved that the Allies had mastered the art of the large set-piece battle. Air and armor working in tandem with infantry provided the mass of firepower needed to overcome enemy defenses. Sophisticated artillery techniques, such as flash spotting and sound ranging, allowed British gunners to locate German artillery batteries with considerable accuracy. Using these new tactics, Allied counterartillery batteries could efficiently destroy German artillery batteries, thus eliminating one of the main threats to advancing infantry. At Amiens, the crude tactics of 1916 and 1917 had given way to a mechanical style of war that allowed the Allies to move men faster, support their advances with accurate and overwhelming fire support, and allow operations to continue behind the enemy's lines. The Germans had no answer to this new way of war. Unable to hold on near Amiens, they retreated to the high ground around St. Quentin and Péronne, bringing them once again to the line of the 1916 Somme battles.

This retreat placed the Germans along some of the same ground that they had once defended so well. The terrain may have been similar two years later, but the armies were not. The inexperienced British New Armies that fought in 1916 with insufficient materiel had now been replaced by veteran units well served by stocks of modern weapons and men well schooled in the techniques needed to use them. The Germans, by contrast, were now tired, with some divisions at one-quarter of the manpower strength they had had in the spring. They could not hope to hold the British off the high ground around the Somme River in 1918 as stubbornly as they had in 1916.

The Germans held just one bridgehead west of the Somme River, at the town of Péronne. Ludendorff envisioned holding the town temporarily while his forces established new defensive lines east of the Somme but west of the line of defenses known as the Hindenburg Line, which ran intermittently south-southeast from Lille to Metz. His plan was complicated by two factors. First, of the forty-five divisions in the German reserve, only nineteen were classified as "fresh." Fifteen reserve divisions were in the process of being reconstituted, meaning that they were being pieced back together from among the survivors of other units; and eleven were "tired," meaning that they were unable to engage in offensive operations and could only engage in emergency defensive operations.[14]

The Germans' second problem was that the Allies had no intention of giving the Germans any time to rest and refit. Foch had already told Allied commanders to "give the enemy no respite" from a general Allied offensive and to "respond to the situation of the moment" in directing local attacks.[15] To accomplish these goals he moved the French Sixth Army out of the general reserve to add to the mass of Allied units available to attack. He also moved six other French infantry divisions out of the reserve and assigned them to the Army Group Center. French units were told not to expect reinforcements before "a delay impossible to determine," but Foch's actions gave the French maximum ability to pressure the Germans all along the western front.[16] To add weight to the British attack, Foch also moved six heavy artillery brigades from the French First Army to British efforts in Flanders.

Once again, the Australians led the way in putting Foch's orders into action. On the night of August 30, before the Germans could secure their defenses around Péronne, the Australians severed the rail lines south of the town. Without a rail link, the Germans could not resupply a sufficient garrison inside Péronne. The next night, British troops approached the heights of St. Quentin—"a veritable bastion," as the Fourth Army's historian wrote, "the capture of which would enable us to enfilade the enemy's positions . . . and threaten the safety of his whole line."[17] Australian troops once again led the attack, seizing the heights despite a variety of obstacles, both natural and man-made. Rather than fight another battle he knew he could not win, Ludendorff ordered German forces to abandon the Somme positions, retreat to the Hindenburg Line, and prepare to make a stand there. Ger-

The town of St. Quentin formed a main center of resistance on the Hindenburg Line in 1918. These ruins testify to the intensity of the fighting there. (National Archives)

man reserves then sat at just nine divisions capable of offensive operations.

Farther to the south, the Allies undertook the task of eliminating another salient, this one just south of Verdun and based around the town of St. Mihiel. Since the start of the war, this salient had protected the approaches to the economically vital Briey iron basin and the critical rail center at Metz. The responsibility for the St. Mihiel attack fell to the Americans, to whom Pétain had loaned four French infantry divisions, showing "the vast faith he had in the military abilities of the AEF and in the leadership capabilities of Pershing and his corps commanders." Pétain's decision, a function of the close friendship he had developed with

Pershing, was an example of amalgamation in reverse: French units now sat under an overall American command. The American First Army that attacked at St. Mihiel thus included 110,000 French soldiers, 3,010 French artillery pieces, and 113 French tank crews.[18] The Americans also had command of the entire Allied air fleet, the war's largest, which included 1,400 planes from four different air forces.

With this arsenal, the Americans simultaneously struck the southern and western faces of the St. Mihiel salient on September 12, 1918. The Germans had seen the danger to the salient and, as they had done at Château-Thierry, decided to evacuate it rather than fight. The American attack caught the Germans in the first stages of this withdrawal; nevertheless, the Germans lost 16,000 prisoners and more than 460 heavy guns. By nightfall on September 13, the American First Army had cleared the salient; by September 16 the Americans had recovered more than 200 square miles of French territory. The roads to Sedan and Metz were opened, the southern threat to Verdun had ended, and the Americans had gained immensely in confidence. They soon began the difficult process of planning a follow-up operation north of St. Mihiel in the Meuse-Argonne sector. Few generals on either side dared any longer to question the value of the Americans to the overall Allied war effort.

The attack on the St. Mihiel salient was the last in the series of limited offensives envisioned by Foch in his memorandum of July 24. After the victory at St. Mihiel, he directed an all-out attack aimed at pressuring the Germans on every front with maximum force. Foch was now certain that the Allies could win the war in 1918. To do so, he believed that they had to cut the lateral Antwerp-to-Metz railway that supplied German forces in France, place Allied forces across the Rhine River, and attrite German units to the point that they could not offer significant resistance. The most important obstacle to all of these goals was the

Hindenburg Line. Unless the Allies breached that line before the onset of winter, Foch knew, his hope of winning the war in 1918 would be dashed.

"MAKE IMMEDIATE PEACE OVERTURES"

By September 11, 1918, Allied forces had cleared most of the obstacles that guarded the approaches to the Hindenburg Line, including the Somme, Oise, Aisne, and Vesle River valleys. French and British units had established contact in the heights just west of the line itself. Excellent weather permitted the rapid movement of men and supplies as well as frequent reconnaissance overflights. These flights, combined with captured German documents, gave the Allies solid intelligence on the strong and weak points of the line's defenses. On September 18, the Australians seized important high ground opposite the Hindenburg Line east of St. Quentin. They moved the line forward 5,000 yards along four miles of front and captured 4,243 German soldiers, 87 artillery pieces, and 300 machine guns.

The line itself, however, remained unbreached. It was designed, according to the Germans who built it with labor from Russian prisoners of war, to afford "the most favorable conditions for a stubborn defense by a minimum garrison."[19] It contained thick belts of barbed wire, solidly constructed concrete machine-gun outposts, and a sophisticated trench network as deep as 2,000 yards in places. In the Australian-American sector, this set of defenses was augmented by the presence of the four-mile-long St. Quentin canal tunnel, which ran behind the main Hindenburg Line defenses. Once drained of its water, it formed a spacious underground bunker that offered protection from even the most powerful artillery bombardment. The tunnel was an ideal place for the Germans to locate storehouses. Once enhanced with ventilation, heat, electricity, and underground passageways to the trenches, the tunnel also provided an ideal location for barracks.

The steep slopes of the canal and German antitank ditches made the ground difficult terrain for Allied tanks, leaving many units without the armor support to which they had grown accustomed. Tanks therefore were used only to crush barbed wire on the near side of the canal.

The task of breaking the line at St. Quentin fell again to Monash and his Australians. The American II Corps, composed of the 27th Division from New York and the 30th from Tennessee and the Carolinas, came under Australian command for the duration of the operation. Due to the inexperience of so many American officers, Monash assigned an Australian officer or senior NCO to each American company. Because British artillery could not penetrate the tunnel, Monash planed to target tunnel entrances with gas and high-explosive shells in order to keep German soldiers pinned down inside. The Americans would then advance and capture initial objectives. Once the Americans had their goals in hand, the Australians would follow them to the second line in "leapfrog" style.

Powerful British artillery began its work on September 26. The British had concentrated one artillery piece for every three yards of front, double the ratio they had had at the Somme on July 1, 1916. From September 26 to October 4, the British fired 1.3 million high-explosive and gas shells. The raw power of the British shelling forced many Germans to seek deeper and deeper hiding places, neutralizing their effectiveness to resist the coming assault. On the night of September 28, the men of the two American divisions assumed their positions, received rations, and wrote letters home, some of them for the last time.

As they had in their previous campaigns, the Americans fought with an enthusiasm that compensated for their inexperience. On the first day of the ground phase, September 29, the 27th Division opened a hole 6,000 yards deep by 10,000 yards long in the German defenses and crossed to the far side of the canal. In parts of the attack sector, American inexperience proved to be costly. Some units failed to account for all German machine-gun positions before passing them by. This failure to "mop up" caused one unit, the 107th Regiment of the 27th Division, to sustain the highest casualty rates of any American regiment in the war. Still, by the morning of day two the southern entrance to the St. Quentin tunnel and the northern strongpoint known as the Knoll were in Allied hands. The Australian 5th Division then leapfrogged the Americans and continued the attack.

Ground combat in this sector continued for several more days until, on October 4, the Germans ordered a general retirement. The Hindenburg Line, which Ludendorff had expected would delay the Allies through the winter, had fallen in just days. The decision to retire from the Hindenburg Line sector left the Allies, noted one historian, in an area with "no prepared lines of defense" in front of them. The terrain, "well suited to the employment of cavalry and tanks," presented the kind of possibilities for pursuit that generals on the western front had been seeking for four years.[20]

Farther to the south, the Americans had launched a concurrent offensive in the Meuse-Argonne sector northwest of Verdun. A successful offensive in this region would cut the remaining railroads that serviced the German forces on the western front and might divide the German forces in two. Because of the importance of this sector, the Germans had no intention of voluntarily surrendering it as they had the Château-Thierry and St. Mihiel sectors. Their defenses, moreover, were anchored by the heavy woods of the Argonne forest on the west, the heights of Montfaucon in the center, and the Meuse River to the east. To reinforce these natural defenses, the Germans had built three solid belts of trenches defended with mutually supporting machine-gun nests and artillery positions. It represented one of the most formidable defensive arrangements on the western front.

The American First Army attacked the Meuse-Argonne sector on September 26 with 2,700 artillery pieces and nineteen divi-

This aerial view of trenches on the Meuse-Argonne front in 1918 shows the characteristic zigzag pattern of trench networks. The Americans hoped to move quickly through this sector to prevent the Germans from entrenching too deeply, but were frustrated by supply problems. (United States Air Force Academy McDermott Library Special Collections)

sions, six of which were French. The unenviable task of the First Army in the Meuse-Argonne was compounded by a poor road network, which greatly complicated supply and movement. The battle for the Meuse-Argonne turned into a massive campaign of attrition that the Americans could afford to fight, but the Germans could not. The fighting continued until the signing of the armistice, eventually engaging Americans from twenty-two divisions, 4 million artillery shells, 324 tanks, and 840 airplanes. In the offensive's first week, the Americans advanced to a maximum depth of eight miles and captured the commanding heights of Montfaucon. They approached the German third defensive line, which was actually an extension of the Hindenburg Line. There they temporarily stalled on October 4, but despite its logistical and tactical shortcomings the Meuse-Argonne offensive had already served its purpose. The American advance had proven that the Germans could not even hold the ideal defensive country of the Meuse-Argonne in the face of the materiel and human superiority of the Allies.

Sensing the hopelessness of their military situation, the Germans began to look for a diplomatic solution. On October 1, Ludendorff had directed the German foreign ministry to "make immediate peace overtures." He told them that "the troops are still holding on, but no one can predict what will happen tomorrow. . . . The front could be pierced at any moment."[21] Like most senior German officials, Ludendorff hoped to negotiate with the less vengeful Americans. Woodrow Wilson's Fourteen Points seemed to hold out the hope of a peace with some honor. Although Ludendorff had not bothered to read the actual text of the Fourteen Points for himself, he hoped that the president's call for national self-determination might allow Germany to keep the German-speaking parts of Alsace-Lorraine and the portions of eastern Europe then under German military control.

The Fourteen Points, which Wilson had first publicized in a presidential address of January 8, 1918, in fact held out no such hope. Point 8 specified that "the wrong done to France by Prussia in 1871 in the matter of Alsace-Lorraine . . . should be righted," and Point 6 called for German evacuation of all Russian territory. The real diplomatic value of the Fourteen Points to Germany lay in the disagreement that it caused between the Americans and their European allies. The British were uncomfortable with the anticolonial tone of Point 5, the removal of economic barriers called for in Point 3, and the demand for "freedom of the seas" in Point 2. The latter two points in particular threatened the very cornerstones of the British Empire. Clemenceau, who distrusted Wilson's idealism and disliked his arrogance, was more blunt.

Upon first seeing the Fourteen Points he declared, "God Himself was content with ten."[22]

On October 6, the new German chancellor, Prince Max of Baden, asked Wilson to arrange an armistice and organize peace negotiations based on the principles of the Fourteen Points. Wilson replied that he needed assurances that the Germans were truly willing to accept the Fourteen Points as the basis for discussion. The American response infuriated Clemenceau and Lloyd George, who were astonished that Wilson would engage in bipartisan talks with the Germans. They were also fearful that Wilson might conclude an armistice that was against their interests. Given British and French reliance on the United States for credit, manpower, and resources, they might be left with no choice but to accept an armistice Wilson negotiated without their input. The polite tone of Wilson's reply, however, was warmly received in Berlin, where the German government grasped at it "like a drowning person reaches for a lifeline."[23]

On October 12, Prince Max sent Wilson a carefully worded message that made no commitments, but left German desires for a peace based on the Fourteen Points quite clear. It indicated German willingness to abandon unspecified occupied territory and underscored that the chancellor, not the kaiser (with whom Wilson had refused to deal) was the head of the German government. German military headquarters had approved the text of the message, indicating how serious they believed the situation to be. At approximately the same time that Wilson received the second German note, he also received word that a German U-boat had sunk the civilian liner *Leinster,* killing 200 people.

The sinking, plus the pressure placed on him by Lloyd George and Clemenceau, put Wilson in a less conciliatory mood. His reply to the second note demanded an immediate end to submarine warfare and an immediate evacuation of all territory seized by Germany since 1914. The president also implied that unless the kaiser abdicated, Germany could not hope to open negotiations.

*For most of the war, northeastern France remained under harsh
German military government. These French peasants welcome their
liberators after four years of occupation. (National Archives)*

The contrast in tone between Wilson's first and second notes
caused a panic in Berlin, where German officials now knew that
they could not use the moderation of Wilson to avoid the harshness of the French and British.

The long-anticipated collapse of Germany's allies had begun as
well. On October 24, a reenergized Italian army struck the Austro-
Hungarians at Vittorio Veneto. By November 3, they had captured 80,000 Austro-Hungarian soldiers and taken 1,600 of Austria-Hungary's 2,000 remaining artillery pieces. On October 26,
Count Mihály Károlyi declared Hungary independent. Czecho-
slovakia, Slovenia, Bosnia, and Croatia all followed suit. Bulgaria
surrendered to the Allies on October 29. The Ottoman Empire
surrendered the next day.

The German state itself began to unravel as conditions on the home front approached desperation and the army could no longer hide the seriousness of the military position. On October 29, a mutiny by 600 sailors broke out in Kiel, followed by a massive mutiny on November 4 by 100,000 sailors in ten ports. The mutineers seized control of ships, took over town governments, and demanded an end to the war. The mutinies had distinctly pro-Bolshevik overtones, as did the creation of a "Free State of Bavaria" under socialist Kurt Eisner on November 7. Several members of Germany's nobility had already fled the country, fearing an outbreak of Soviet-style Bolshevism that the army was in no position to quell.

Nor could the army stop the Allied steamroller. The only factor slowing the Allied armies was their inability to provide food and ammunition to units moving so quickly that they had advanced far ahead of the rail centers designated for their resupply. The German units, by contrast, were increasingly beset by disease, malnutrition, lack of ammunition, and a crisis of demoralization that left no doubt about the war's outcome. A letter found on the body of a German officer in the war's final week described his unit:

> The men have been in the same clothes, dirty, lousy, and torn, for four weeks, are suffering from bodily filth and a state of depression due to living continuously within range of the enemy's guns, and in daily expectation of an attack. The troops are hardly in a fit state to fulfill the task allotted to them in the case of an attack.[24]

The Germans faced a stark choice. They could agree to whatever armistice terms the Allies offered, thereby fending off the invasion of Germany itself that Pershing and others were urging, or they could fight on. The absolute futility of sustaining an armed struggle combined with the nightmarish prospect of an Allied victory march through Berlin led the Germans to send a radio signal to Paris on November 7, indicating their willingness to discuss armistice terms.

Foch had argued forcefully that the Allies should conclude an armistice as soon as the Germans agreed to his conditions. Fighting on to make the symbolic gesture of invading Germany struck him as unnecessary. "I am not waging war for the sake of waging war," he told Edward House. "If I obtain through the armistice the conditions that we wish to impose on Germany, I am satisfied. Once this object is attained, nobody has the right to shed one more drop of blood."[25] Upon receiving the German signal, he reiterated his belief to Clemenceau that an armistice was a purely military affair and therefore fell under his purview, not Clemenceau's. The French prime minister reluctantly agreed and left the arrangements for the armistice to Foch. The Allied commander-in-chief assembled his staff, gave them precise instructions for delivering the Germans through Allied lines, and warned his army commanders to look out for a German trick. With victory so close at hand, Foch left nothing to chance.

CONCLUSION

An Armistice at Any Price

At ten minutes past eight on the evening of November 7, 1918, five automobiles appeared along Route Nationale 2 and approached the line guarded by the Third Company of the 171st French Infantry Regiment. A large white flag flew from the first car, and from somewhere in the caravan the French soldiers heard a trumpet blaring "cease-fire." The arrival of the five large German cars had been prearranged for 8:30 that morning, nearly twelve hours earlier, but the poor state of the roads in the sector and the masses of retreating German soldiers had caused unavoidable delays. Many of the delays were the result of German demolition teams that had felled trees and mined intersections in the hopes of slowing down the pursuing Allied armies. At each barricade, the German drivers had to convince local commanders to clear the roads and indicate a route free of mines.

The arrival of the German delegation suggested to the men of the Third Company that rumors of an imminent armistice might be true. They watched as a large man in a German general's uniform got out of the second car and apologized to the French captain in command of the company for his tardiness. The general then tried to make introductions, but the French officer cut him short, saying, "General, I have no authority to receive you officially. Please get into this car and follow me." The general then got into a car driven by a French corporal and the convoy disappeared.[1]

The general was Detlef von Winterfeldt, the liaison officer between German army headquarters and the chancellor's office. Before the war, he had served on the German military mission to

France as military attaché and therefore seemed a logical choice to undertake the awesome responsibility of being the senior military figure on the German armistice team. Since mid-September, he had advocated an armistice and had observed the growing pessimism in German higher headquarters. He had hoped that a late German victory on the battlefield might create the conditions to get an armistice favorable to Germany; such an armistice, he and many other German officers hoped, might leave Germany in control of its eastern conquests and leave the fate of Alsace-Lorraine up to a plebiscite. The woeful state of the German army, with some German divisions now down to less than 500 healthy men, had dashed all of these expectations. Now Winterfeldt sat in a car driven by a French soldier, unsure of his exact whereabouts, on his way to Marshal Foch to negotiatiate an armistice.

Behind him, in another car, was the head of the German mission, Mathias Erzberger, a key figure in the German Catholic Center party who had recently assumed office in the new German government. Neither the kaiser, who was then preparing to abdicate, nor Ludendorff, who had resigned and fled to Sweden, was present to take responsibility for ending the war they had prosecuted with such ferocity. Instead, that job fell to Erzberger, who on November 5 had been named by the cabinet as head of the armistice mission. Erzberger later recalled that the government had given him no official papers and no orders. "Despite my desire," he wrote shortly after the war, "they gave me no instructions other than the general one of concluding an armistice at any price."[2] He, too, sat in a car somewhere in France headed for an unknown destination.

Erzberger and his delegation eventually came to a clearing in a forest near Compiègne, where Foch and the Allied delegation were waiting for them in a vintage Second Empire railroad car. Foch, expecting a much higher level delegation, demanded introductions from the unfamiliar faces in front of him. He also asked for formal presentation of evidence that the delegates had

358

Londoners celebrate news of the armistice in November 1918. Perceptive leaders on both sides knew that the armistice only halted hostilities and that creating a lasting peace would require a Herculean diplomatic effort to match the military effort of the Allies in 1918. (National Archives)

authority to speak for the German government. Upon seeing Winterfeldt, Foch demanded that the German officer remove his French Cross of the Officer of Legion of Honor, which he had been awarded before the war. Foch then told the delegates that he had not come to negotiate, but to give them the conditions by which they could obtain an armistice. His chief of staff, Maxime Weygand, then read the conditions aloud to the Germans.

The terms included a complete German evacuation of Belgium, France (understood to include Alsace and Lorraine), and Luxembourg within fifteen days of the signing of the armistice; the creation of three Allied military bridgeheads across the Rhine River at Coblenz, Mainz, and Cologne; the surrender and internment of the German battle fleet; and German surrender of 5,000

The men charged with making peace meet in Paris. From left to right: David Lloyd George of Britain, Vittorio Orlando of Italy, Georges Clemenceau of France, and Woodrow Wilson of the United States. (National Archives)

heavy guns, 30,000 machine guns, 5,000 locomotives, 150,000 railway cars, and 150 submarines as insurance against the Germans' using the armistice as a respite before resuming the offensive. Foch then told the Germans that the terms were unalterable, that combat and the British blockade would continue until the Germans agreed to the terms, and that the terms expired in seventy-two hours. He then dismissed them.

Erzberger sent the terms of the armistice back to the German government by radiogram. After the war, German officials disingenuously expressed shock at what they claimed was the harshness of the terms Foch had presented. In November 1918, however, they knew that they had no choice. The winter of 1918–1919 only promised more suffering from the Allied blockade, more political turmoil, even a possible revolution. The Americans would continue to arrive in force, and if there were to be a 1919 military campaign, the Allies would prosecute it with tanks and airplanes in numbers the Germans could not possibly hope to match. On November 10, Hindenburg replied to Erzberger with a coded telegram asking him to ameliorate Foch's terms, most notably in allowing Germany to keep more machine guns in order to quell the Bolshevik rebellion then taking place inside some German cities. "If you cannot obtain these points," Hindenburg concluded, "you must sign all the same."[3]

Shortly thereafter another telegram arrived, this one unencoded. It informed Erzberger that the kaiser had abdicated and was in exile in Holland. Despite this development, the telegram informed Erzberger that he retained the authority to negotiate and sign an armistice. Although Hindenburg had written the text, the telegram was signed "Reichskanzler Schluss." The French officer who received the telegram demanded to know who Chancellor Schluss was (no politician named Schluss was familiar to the Allies) and by what authority he had empowered Erzberger to continue the negotiations. Erzberger explained to the French officer that Schluss meant "stop" in German and only indicated the end of the telegram.

At 2:15 on the morning of November 11, Erzberger sat across from Foch and asked for the number of machine guns and airplanes to be modified. Foch agreed to only the most minor of changes, and at 5:12 Erzberger agreed to sign. The armistice was to go into effect almost six hours later, on the eleventh hour of the eleventh day of the eleventh month. The war was over. Foch telegraphed to Clemenceau to tell him that the Germans had signed and that he was on his way to Paris to present the armistice to the French government. At 8:00 a.m. Clemenceau telegraphed to the

Emir Faisal stands at the Paris Peace Conference with his close advisors.
His wartime ally, British colonel T. E. Lawrence, stands to Faisal's left.
Despite the wishes of both men, Arabia did not achieve full
independence after the war. (© Corbis)

heads of the other Allied governments to tell them of the signing. "I do not yet know the details of the deliberations with the German plenipotentiaries," he told them. "As soon as I have been informed, I will communicate them to you."[4]

It had been 1,597 days since Archduke Franz Ferdinand entered Sarajevo on an official state visit. The events of those days had forever transformed Europe and, with it, the world. The Hohenzollern, Romanov, Habsburg, and Vahdeddin (Ottoman) dynasties were gone. In their place came Bolshevism, authoritarianism, the beginnings of fascism, and fragile democracies. The infrastructure of Europe lay in shambles, and the economies of the continent were in a precarious state. Perhaps worst of all, the emo-

NOTES

ABBREVIATIONS

IWM   Imperial War Museum, London
LHCMA   Liddell Hart Centre for Military Archives, Kings College, London
SHAT   Service Historique de l'Armée de Terre, Château de Vincennes

INTRODUCTION

1. Alexei Brusilov, *A Soldier's Notebook, 1914–1918* (Westport, Conn.: Greenwood Press, 1930; 1971), p. 4.
2. Cambon quoted in Francis Halsey, *The Literary Digest History of the World War*, vol. 1 (New York: Funk and Wagnalls, 1919), p. 101.
3. Moltke quoted in Robert Asprey, *The First Battle of the Marne* (Philadelphia: Lippincourt, 1962), p. 34.
4. Brusilov, *A Soldier's Notebook*, p. 1.
5. Douglas Porch, *March to the Marne: The French Army, 1871–1914* (Cambridge: Cambridge University Press, 1981), p. vii.
6. Wilson quoted in Asprey, *The First Battle of the Marne*, p. 40.
7. The Triple Entente refers to a prewar diplomatic arrangement between Great Britain, France, and Russia. In September 1914 these nations signed the Pact of London, creating the Entente Alliance. Thereafter, these nations and the nations that fought alongside them became known as the Allies.

1. A CRUEL DISILLUSION

The epigraph is from Bulletin des Opérations, September 21, 1914, "Opérations du 2 au 25 août 1914," SHAT Fonds BUAT 6N9, carton 8, dossier 5.

1. Hew Strachan, *The First World War*, vol. 1, *To Arms* (Oxford: Oxford University Press, 2001), p. 211.

2. John Horne and Alan Kramer, *German Atrocities, 1914: A History of Denial* (New Haven: Yale University Press, 2001), p. 53.

3. Bethmann Hollweg quoted in Francis Halsey, *The Literary Digest History of the World War,* vol. 1 (New York: Funk and Wagnalls, 1919), p. 255.

4. Sophie de Schaepdrijver, "The Idea of Belgium," in Aviel Roshwald and Richard Stites, eds., *European Culture in the Great War: The Arts, Entertainment, and Propaganda, 1914–1918* (Cambridge: Cambridge University Press, 1999), pp. 267–294, quotation at p. 268.

5. Diary of A. Reeve, IWM 90/21/1, p. 1.

6. Quoted in Robert Asprey, *The First Battle of the Marne* (Philadelphia: Lippincourt, 1962), p. 42.

7. General Sir Henry de Beauvoir de Lisle, "My Narrative of the Great German War," 1919, LHCMA, de Lisle Collection, Part 1, p. 5.

8. Diary of A. Reeve, p. 2.

9. Diary of John McIlwain, IWM 96/29/1, entry for September 2, p. 12.

10. For an excellent overview of Plan XVII, see Robert Doughty, "French Strategy in 1914: Joffre's Own," *Journal of Military History* 67 (April 2003): 427–454.

11. Joffre quoted in Halsey, *History of the World War,* vol. 1, p. 279.

12. For more on Foch see Michael Neiberg, *Foch: Supreme Allied Commander in the Great War* (Dulles, Va.: Brassey's, 2003).

13. Ministère de la Guerre, *Les Armées Françaises dans la Grande Guerre,* series 1, vol. 2 (Paris: Imprimerie Nationale, 1925), p. 587.

14. French quoted in Asprey, *The First Battle of the Marne,* pp. 80–81.

15. *Les Armées Françaises,* series 1, vol. 2, p. 627.

16. Frank Pusey, "A Long and Happy Life," 1978, IWM 79/5/1, p. 12. Emphasis in original.

17. *Les Armées Françaises,* Tome 1, vol. 2, p. 681.

18. Falkenhayn quoted in Asprey, *The First Battle of the Marne,* p. 126. Count Alfred von Schlieffen had been Moltke's predecessor as Chief of the German General Staff. His detailed notes and planning remained influential in German thinking, as did Schlieffen himself, whom Moltke consulted regularly until Schlieffen's death in 1913.

19. Moltke quoted in Asprey, *The First Battle of the Marne,* p. 153.
20. Rupprecht quoted in GQG des Armées de L'Est, "La Bataille des Flandres," 19 Novembre 1914, SHAT Fonds BUAT, 6N9, p. 4.
21. French quoted in Martin Gilbert, *The First World War: A Complete History* (New York: Henry Holt, 1994), p. 97.
22. Robert Cowley, "Albert and the Yser," *Military History Quarterly* 1, no. 4 (Summer 1989): 106–117.

2. LOOSED LIKE WILD BEASTS

The epigraph is from a quotation in Francis Halsey, *The Literary Digest History of the World War,* vol. 7 (New York: Funk and Wagnalls, 1919), p. 40.

1. Norman Stone, *The Eastern Front, 1914–1917* (London: Penguin, 1975), p. 36.
2. Alexei Brusilov, *A Soldier's Notebook, 1914–1918* (Westport, Conn.: Greenwood Press, 1930; 1971), pp. 22, 37.
3. See Dennis Showalter, *Tannenberg: Clash of Empires,* rev. ed. (Dulles, Va.: Brassey's, 2003), pp. 63–65.
4. Stone, *The Eastern Front,* p. 63.
5. Hoffmann quoted in Francis Halsey, *The Literary Digest History of the World War,* vol. 7 (New York: Funk and Wagnalls, 1919), p. 89.
6. Jaroslav Hašek, *The Good Soldier Schweik,* trans. Paul Selver (New York: Doubleday, 1963, [1930]), p. 21.
7. Holger Herwig, *The First World War: Germany and Austria-Hungary, 1914–1918* (London: Edward Arnold, 1997), p. 12.
8. C. R. M. F. Cruttwell, *A History of the Great War, 1914–1918* (Oxford: Clarendon Press, 1934), p. 4.
9. John R. Schindler, "Disaster on the Drina: The Austro-Hungarian Army in Serbia, 1914," *War in History* 9 (2002): 159.
10. John Reed quoted in Martin Gilbert, *The First World War: A Complete History* (New York: Henry Holt, 1994), p. 111.
11. Halsey, *History of the World War,* vol. 1, p. 93.
12. Quoted in Stone, *The Eastern Front,* p. 114.
13. Brusilov, *A Soldier's Notebook,* pp. 93–94.

14. Quoted in Halsey, *History of the World War,* vol. 7, p. 93.
15. These numbers are from ibid., pp. 94–97.

3. THE COUNTRY OF DEATH

The epigraph is from LHCMA 2/1/1–41. Grant's father-in-law was Lord Rosebery.

1. Extracts from a German soldier's journal, 160th Infantry Regiment, VIII Corps, found in a trench near Souain, SHAT 19N159, Carton 1, Dossier 6, entry for September 9, 1914.
2. See especially Gary Sheffield, *Forgotten Victory: The First World War, Myths and Realities* (London: Headline, 2001) and Brian Bond, *The Unquiet Western Front* (Cambridge: Cambridge University Press, 2002).
3. Jean-Pierre Guéno and Yves Laplume, eds., *Paroles de Poilus: Lettres et Carnets du Front, 1914–1918* (Paris: Librio and Radio France, 1998), p. 90.
4. Grand Quartier Général [Headquarters] Army of the East, "The war of February to August, 1915," SHAT Fonds BUAT, 6N9, pp. 2 and 10.
5. Sheffield, *Forgotten Victory,* p. 43.
6. Philip Gibbs, *Now It Can Be Told* (New York: Harper, 1920), p. 69.
7. Ibid., p. 13.
8. Francis Halsey, *The Literary Digest History of the World War,* vol. 2 (New York: Funk and Wagnalls, 1919), p. 283.
9. General John Charteris quoted in Martin Gilbert, *The First World War: A Complete History* (New York: Henry Holt, 1994), p. 133.
10. General Sir Henry de Beauvoir de Lisle, "My Narrative of the Great German War," 1919, LHCMA, de Lisle Collection, Part 1, p. 59.
11. Normally, Germany's eastern position proved to be a great advantage: allied attacks at dawn had to move directly into the bright, rising sun.
12. Dennis Showalter, "Mastering the Western Front: German, British, and French Approaches," paper presented at the Second European Conference in First World War Studies, University of Oxford, England, June 23, 2003.
13. C. R. M. F. Cruttwell, *A History of the Great War, 1914–1918* (Oxford: Clarendon Press, 1934), p. 158. Other sources put the percent-

age of shells that contained shrapnel at 75 percent, but the overall idea of British overreliance on shrapnel remains true.

14. Brigadier General Oxley quoted in Gilbert, *The First World War,* p. 160.

15. Albert Palazzo, *Seeking Victory on the Western Front: The British Army and Chemical Warfare in World War I* (Lincoln: University of Nebraska Press, 2000), p. 55. The French were producing 100,000 per day.

16. Quoted in Pierre Miquel, *Les Poilus: La France Sacrifiée* (Paris, Plon, 2000), pp. 209–210.

17. Cruttwell, *A History of the Great War,* p. 167.

4. Ordered to Die

The epigraph is from a quotation in Dennis Showalter, "Salonika," in Robert Cowley, ed., *The Great War: Perspectives on the First World War* (New York: Random House, 2003), p. 235.

1. Richard Hall's *The Balkan Wars, 1912–1913: Prelude to the First World War* (London: Routledge, 2000) is an excellent introduction to these critical, and often understudied, wars.

2. Edward Erickson, *Ordered to Die: A History of the Ottoman Army in the First World War* (Westport, Conn.: Greenwood Press, 2001), p. 8.

3. Ibid., pp. 76–77.

4. W. L. Berridge to his parents, March 4, 1915, IWM P73.

5. Kemal quoted in Andrew Mango, *Atatürk* (London: John Murray, 1999), p. 146.

6. Tim Travers, "Gallipoli," in Robert Cowley, ed., *The Great War: Perspectives on the First World War* (New York: Random House, 2003), p. 191.

7. Dennis Showalter, "Salonika," in Robert Cowley, ed., *The Great war: Perspectives on the First World War* (New York: Random House, 2003), p. 235.

8. Ibid., p. 242.

9. Holger Herwig, *The First World War: Germany and Austria-Hungary, 1914–1918* (London: Edward Arnold, 1997), pp. 119 and 137.

10. Norman Stone, *The Eastern Front, 1914–1917* (London: Penguin, 1975), p. 187.

11. Alexei Brusilov, *A Soldier's Notebook, 1914–1918* (Westport, Conn.: Greenwood Press, 1930; 1971), pp. 170–171.
12. Falkenhayn quoted in Herwig, *The First World War,* p. 148.
13. Ulrich Trumpener, "Turkey's War," in Hew Strachan, ed., *The Oxford Illustrated History of the First World War* (Oxford: Oxford University Press, 1998), p. 85.
14. Erickson, *Ordered to Die,* p. 119.
15. Quoted in Margaret Macmillan, *Peacemakers* (London: John Murray, 2001), p. 454.

5. GORDIAN KNOTS

The epigraph is from a quotation in Francis Halsey, *The Literary Digest History of the World War,* vol. 9 (New York: Funk and Wagnalls, 1919), p. 257.

1. Churchill quoted in Geoffrey Parker, *The Cambridge Illustrated History of Warfare* (Cambridge: Cambridge University Press, 1995), p. 258.
2. C. R. M. F. Crutwell, *A History of the Great War, 1914–1918* (Oxford: Clarendon Press, 1934), p. 68.
3. Hew Strachan, *The First World War,* vol. 1, *To Arms* (Oxford: Oxford University Press, 2001), p. 393.
4. Crutwell, *A History of the Great War,* p. 188.
5. German Undersecretary for Naval Affairs Alfred Ballin quoted in B. J. C. McKercher, "Economic Warfare," in Hew Strachan, ed., *The Oxford Illustrated History of the First World War* (Oxford: Oxford University Press, 1998), p. 126.
6. "America and Britain," *Archives de la Grande Guerre,* Series 1 (Paris: E. Chrion, 1919), p. 381.
7. Roosevelt quoted in Martin Gilbert, *The First World War: A Complete History* (New York: Henry Holt, 1994), p. 158.
8. Robert Zieger, *America's Great War: World War I and the American Experience* (New York: Rowan and Littlefield, 2001), p. 44.
9. Wilhelm II quoted in John Keegan, "Jutland," in Robert Cowley, ed., *The Great War: Perspectives on the First World War* (New York: Random House, 2003), p. 167.
10. Holtzendorff quoted in Gilbert, *The First World War,* p. 306.

11. Wilhelm II quoted in Strachan, *The First World War,* vol. 1, p. 696.
12. Edward Erickson, *Ordered to Die: A History of the Ottoman Army in the First World War* (Westport, Conn.: Greenwood Press, 2001), p. 112.
13. This Hussein family is no relation to Saddam Hussein of Iraq.
14. Anthony Bruce, *The Last Crusade: The Palestine Campaign in the First World War* (London: John Murray, 2002), p. 80.
15. Lt. Gen. Sir Henry de Beauvoir de Lisle, "My Narrative of the Great German War," [1919], LHCMA, de Lisle papers, vol. 2, p. 36.
16. Allenby quoted in Erickson, *Ordered to Die,* p. 171.

6. Bleeding France White

The epigraph is from a quotation in Pierre Miquel, *Les Poilus: La France Sacrifiée* (Paris: Plon, 2000), p. 262.

1. John Schindler, *Isonzo: The Forgotten Sacrifice of the Great War* (Westport, Conn.: Praeger, 2001), p. 47.
2. I am grateful to Vanda Wilcox for permitting me to use her paper, "Discipline in the Italian Army, 1915–1918," presented at the Second European Conference in First World War Studies, University of Oxford, England, June 23, 2003.
3. Schindler, *Isonzo,* p. 109.
4. Erich von Falkenhayn, *General Headquarters, 1914–1916, and Its Critical Decisions* (New York: Dodd, Mead, 1920), pp. 209–211.
5. Falkenhayn quoted in Alistair Horne, *The Price of Glory: Verdun, 1916* (London: Penguin, 1962), p. 36.
6. Ibid.,, p. 40.
7. Anthony Clayton, *Paths of Glory: The French Army, 1914–1918* (London: Cassell, 2003), pp. 100, 104.
8. Herr quoted in Horne, *The Price of Glory,* p. 51.
9. Joffre quoted in C. R. M. F. Crutwell, *A History of the Great War, 1914–1918* (Oxford: Clarendon Press, 1934), p. 243.
10. Bruce Gudmundsson, *Stormtroop Tactics: Innovation in the German Army, 1914–1918* (Westport, Conn.: Praeger, 1989), pp. 50–60.
11. Pierre Miquel, *Les Poilus: La France Sacrifiée* (Paris: Plon, 2000), p. 270.

12. See Robert Bruce, "To the Limits of Their Strength: The French Army and the Logistics of Attrition at the Battle of Verdun, 21 February–18 December 1916," *Army History* 45 (Summer 1998): 9–21.

13. Quoted in Miquel, *Les Poilus*, p. 287.

14. Bruce, "To the Limits of Their Strength," p. 18.

15. Horne, *The Price of Glory*, p. 316.

16. Quoted in Miquel, *Les Poilus*, p. 292.

17. See Paul Ferguson and Michael Neiberg, "America's Expatriate Aviators," *Military History Quarterly* 14, no. 4 (Summer 2002): 58–63.

18. Pétain quoted in John Morrow, *The Great War in the Air* (Washington, D.C.: Smithsonian Press, 1993), p. 199.

7. A War against Civilization

The epigraph is from Philip Gibbs, *The Battles of the Somme* (New York: George H. Doran, 1917), p. 26.

1. John Schindler, *Isonzo: The Forgotten Sacrifice of the Great War* (Westport, Conn.: Praeger, 2001), p. 139.

2. Conrad quoted in Holger Herwig, *The First World War: Germany and Austria-Hungary, 1914–1918* (London: Edward Arnold, 1997), p. 209.

3. Conrad quoted in ibid., p. 211.

4. Brusilov quoted in Norman Stone, *The Eastern Front, 1914–1917* (London: Penguin, 1975), p. 257.

5. Alexei Brusilov, *A Soldier's Notebook, 1914–1918* (Westport, Conn.: Greenwood Press, 1930; 1971), p. 243.

6. Ibid., p. 257.

7. Roger Chickering, *Imperial Germany and the Great War, 1914–1918* (Cambridge: Cambridge University Press, 1998) pp. 142–143.

8. Herwig, *The First World War*, p. 215.

9. William Philpott, "Why the British Were Really on the Somme: A Reply to Elizabeth Greenhalgh," *War in History* 9 (2002): pp. 446–471, quotation at p. 447.

10. Philip Gibbs, *The Battles of the Somme* (New York: George H. Doran, 1917), p. 43.

11. Winston Churchill, *The World Crisis,* vol. 3 (New York: Scribner's, 1931), p. 171.

12. Gibbs, *The Battles of the Somme,* p. xi.

13. Foch quoted in Jean Autin, *Foch* (Paris: Perrin, 1987), p. 179.

14. Gibbs, *The Battles of the Somme,* p. 30.

15. One of the footballs somehow survived and can be seen today in the National Army Museum in Chelsea Barracks, London.

16. Gary Sheffield, *Forgotten Victory: The First World War, Myths and Realities* (London: Headline, 2001), p. 137.

17. See Albert Palazzo, *Seeking Victory on the Western Front: The British Army and Chemical Warfare in World War I* (Lincoln: University of Nebraska Press, 2000), p. 93.

18. Gary Sheffield, *The Somme* (London: Cassell, 2003), p. 40.

19. Ibid., p. 65.

20. Ministère de la Guerre, *Les Armées Françaises dans la Grande Guerre,* series 4, vol. 2 (Paris: Imprimerie Nationale, 1933), p. 233.

21. Sheffield, *The Somme,* p. 101.

22. Gibbs, *The Battles of the Somme,* p. 148.

23. Haig to Joffre, August 16, 1916, Ministère de la Guerre, *Les Armées Françaises,* series 4, vol. 2, appendix 2942.

24. Gibbs, *The Battles of the Somme,* p. 253. "Boche" was a standard French and British term of derision for Germans.

25. Dennis Showalter, "Mastering the Western Front: German, British, and French Approaches," paper presented at the Second European Conference in First World War Studies, University of Oxford, England, June 23, 2003.

26. Falkenhayn quoted in Herwig, *The First World War,* p. 202.

27. C. R. M. F. Cruttwell, *A History of the Great War, 1914–1918* (Oxford: Clarendon Press, 1934), p. 271.

28. Gibbs, *The Battles of the Somme,* p. 287.

29. Ibid., p. 297.

30. Ibid., p. 55.

8. Driving Out the Devil

The epigraph is from a quotation in W. Bruce Lincoln, *Passage through Armageddon: The Russians in War and Revolution, 1914–1918* (New York: Simon and Schuster, 1986), p. 410.

1. Alekseev quoted in C. R. M. F. Cruttwell, *A History of the Great War, 1914–1918* (Oxford: Clarendon Press, 1934), p. 295.

2. Gary Sheffield, *Forgotten Victory: The First World War, Myths and Realities* (London: Headline, 2001), pp. 50–60.

3. Colin Nicolson, *The Longman Companion to the First World War, Europe 1914–1918* (London: Longman, 2001), p. 211.

4. Brusilov quoted in Francis Halsey, *The Literary Digest History of the World War*, vol. 7 (New York: Funk and Wagnalls, 1919), p. 247.

5. Richard Stites, "Days and Nights in Wartime Russia: Cultural Life, 1914–1917," in Aviel Roshwald and Richard Stites, eds., *European Culture in the Great War: The Arts, Entertainment, and Propaganda, 1914–1918* (Cambridge: Cambridge University Press, 1999), pp. 8–31, quotation at pp. 28–29.

6. Quoted in W. Bruce Lincoln, *Passage through Armageddon: The Russians in War and Revolution, 1914–1918* (New York: Simon and Schuster, 1986), p. 315.

7. Norman Stone, *The Eastern Front, 1914–1917* (London: Penguin, 1975), p. 291.

8. Lincoln, *Passage through Armageddon,* p. 404.

9. Holger Herwig, *The First World War: Germany and Austria-Hungary, 1914–1918* (London: Edward Arnold, 1997), p. 334.

10. Alexei Brusilov, *A Soldier's Notebook, 1914–1918* (Westport, Conn.: Greenwood Press, 1930; 1971), pp. 304–305.

11. Brusilov quoted in Lincoln, *Passage through Armageddon,* p. 408.

12. Herwig, *The First World War,* pp. 334–335.

13. Bruce Gudmundsson, *Stormtroop Tactics: Innovation in the German Army, 1914–1918* (Westport, Conn.: Praeger, 1989), pp. 84–87.

14. Ibid., pp. 114–125.

15. Kornilov quoted in Lincoln, *Passage through Armageddon,* p. 417.

16. Trotsky quoted in Lincoln, *Passage through Armageddon,* p. 433.

17. Wilhelm II quoted in Halsey, *History of the World War,* vol. 7, p. 332.

18. Wilhelm II quoted in Herwig, *The First World War,* p. 383.

19. Sokolnikov quoted in Lincoln, *Passage through Armageddon,* p. 502.

20. Tim Travers, "Reply to John Hussey: The Movement of German Divisions to the Western Front, Winter 1917–1918," *War in History* 5, no. 3 (1998): 368. As the exchange in *War in History* between Travers, Hussey, and Giordon Fong shows, this subject remains

controversial. Travers's estimates seem the most reasonable of the three.

21. Herwig, *The First World War*, p. 386.

9. SALVATION AND SACRIFICE

The epigraph is from a quotation in Pierre Miquel, *Le Chemin des Dames: Enquête sur la Plus Effroyable Hécatombe de la Grande Guerre* (Paris: Perrin, 1997), p. 95.

1. Lloyd George quoted in C. R. M. F. Cruttwell, *A History of the Great War, 1914–1918* (Oxford: Clarendon Press, 1934), p. 398.
2. James Marshall-Cornwall, *Haig as Military Commander* (New York: Crane, Russell, and Co., 1973), p. 84.
3. Lloyd George quoted in A. J. P. Taylor, ed., *Lloyd George: A Diary by Frances Stevenson* (New York: Harper and Row, 1971), p. 139.
4. Nivelle quoted in Allain Bernède, "Les Français à l'Assaut du Chemin des Dames, 16 avril 1917," *14–18, Le Magazine de la Grande Guerre* 3 (August–September 2001): 6–15, quotation at p. 9.
5. Lyautey quoted in Anthony Clayton, *Paths of Glory: The French Army, 1914–1918* (London: Cassell, 2003), p. 125. In *The Duchess of Gerolstein,* the title character promotes Private Fritz, her latest lover, to field marshal. The opera lampoons the military and its decision-making processes.
6. Cruttwell, *A History of the Great War*, p. 409.
7. Nivelle quoted in Bernède, "Les Français," pp. 11 and 12.
8. Nivelle quoted in Robert Bruce, *A Fraternity of Arms: America and France in the Great War* (Lawrence: University Press of Kansas, 2003), pp. 32–34. French officers Marquis de Lafayette and Count Jean Baptiste de Rochambeau had both helped the Americans win their war of independence from the British.
9. Ibid.
10. Gary Sheffield, *Forgotten Victory: The First World War, Myths and Realities* (London: Headline, 2001), pp. 162–163.
11. Rupprecht quoted in Cruttwell, *A History of the Great War*, p. 405.
12. Quoted in Bernède, "Les Français," p. 12.
13. Quoted in ibid., p. 12.

14. Quoted in Pierre Miquel, *Le Chemin des Dames: Enquête Sur la Plus Effroyable Hécatombe de la Grande Guerre* (Paris: Perrin, 1997), p. 162.
15. See Leonard Smith, *Between Mutiny and Obedience: The Case of the French Fifth Infantry Division during World War I* (Princeton: Princeton University Press, 1994), pp. 156–168. See also Guy Pédroncini, *Les Mutinieries de 1917* (Paris: PUF, 1974).
16. Quoted in Pierre Miquel, *Les Poilus: La France Sacrifiée* (Paris: Plon, 2000), p. 339.
17. Smith, *Between Mutiny and Obedience,* pp. 162–168.
18. Quoted in Miquel, *Les Poilus,* p. 340. Craonne is one of the largest towns along the Chemin des Dames.
19. Quoted in ibid., pp. 342 and 347.
20. Clayton, *Paths of Glory,* p. 143.
21. John Schindler, *Isonzo: The Forgotten Sacrifice of the Great War* (Westport, Conn.: Praeger, 2001), p. 153.
22. Ibid., p. 237.

10. A FEW MILES OF LIQUID MUD

The epigraph is from a quotation in *Eye-Witness Accounts of the Great War: Guide to Quotations* (Ypres: In Flanders Field Museum, Cloth Hall, Market Square, n.d.), p. 2.

1. Sims quoted in C. M. R. F. Cruttwell, *A History of the Great War, 1914–1918* (Oxford: Clarendon Press, 1934), p. 384.
2. Robertson to Launcelot Kiggell, August 9, 1917, LHCMA Kiggell Papers 3/1–11.
3. Philip Gibbs, *Now It Can Be Told* (New York: Harpers, 1920), p. 477.
4. Robin Prior and Trevor Wilson, *Passchendaele: The Untold Story* (New Haven: Yale University Press, 1996), p. 59.
5. Harington quoted in Gary Sheffield, *Forgotten Victory: The First World War, Myths and Realities* (London: Headline, 2001), p. 169.
6. Holger Herwig, *The First World War: Germany and Austria-Hungary, 1914–1918* (London: Edward Arnold, 1997), p. 330.
7. Martin Gilbert, *The First World War: A Complete History* (New York: Henry Holt, 1994), p. 336. Two mines failed to explode. One was located and intentionally detonated in 1955. The exact location of the

other remains a mystery. Today it still sits undetonated somewhere underneath the Flanders countryside near Ploegsteert Wood.

8. George V quoted in Richard Holmes, *The Little Field Marshal: Sir John French* (London: Jonathan Cape, 1981), p. 182.

9. Philip Warner, *Passchendaele* (Hertfordshire: Wordsworth, 1987), p. 39.

10. Gibbs, *Now It Can Be Told*, pp. 476–477.

11. Prior and Wilson, *Passchendaele*, p. 85.

12. Robertson to Kiggell, July 27, 1917, LHCMA Kiggell Papers 3/1–11.

13. See the recollections of another Haig staff officer, James Marshall-Cornwall, *Haig as Military Commander* (New York: Crane, Russell, and Co., 1973).

14. Gibbs, *Now It Can Be Told*, p. 485.

15. Warner, *Passchendaele*, p. 173.

16. There are many versions of this anecdote. This one comes from Paul Fussell, *The Great War and Modern Memory* (Oxford: Oxford University Press, 1975), p. 84.

17. Prior and Wilson, *Passchendaele*, p. 166.

18. Ibid., p. 131.

19. General Henry Rawlinson quoted in Prior and Wilson, *Passchendaele*, p. 181.

20. Basil Henry Liddell Hart, *The Real War, 1914–1918* (Boston: Little, Brown and Co., 1930), p. 337.

21. Charles Miller, quoted from Memorial at the Irish Peace Park, Messines, Belgium.

22. Herwig, *The First World War*, p. 332.

23. Mario Morselli, *Caporetto, 1917: Victory or Defeat?* (London: Frank Cass, 2001), p. 8. The quotation in the heading of this section is from p. xii.

24. Bruce Gudmundsson, *Stormtroop Tactics: Innovation in the German Army, 1914–1918* (Westport, Conn.: Praeger, 1989), pp. 131–132.

25. Morselli, *Caporetto*, p. 23.

26. John Gooch, quoted in Morselli, *Caporetto*, p. ix.

27. Herwig, *The First World War*, p. 342.

28. Angelo Gatti quoted in Morselli, *Caporetto*, p. 23.

29. Churchill quoted in Martin Gilbert, *The Routledge Atlas of the First World War* (London: Routledge, 2002), p. 93. Emphasis in original.

30. Fuller quoted in Tim Travers, *How the War Was Won: Command and*

Technology in the British Army on the Western Front, 1917–1918 (London: Routledge, 1992), p. 45.

11. NOT WAR AS WE KNEW IT

The epigraph is from Frances Lloyd George, *Lloyd George: A Diary by Frances Stevenson,* ed. A. J. P. Taylor (New York: Harper and Row, 1971), p. 163.

1. J. M. Bourne, *Who's Who in World War One* (London: Routledge, 2001), p. 204.
2. Grant to Lord Rosebery, November 13, 1916, LHCMA Grant papers 2/1/1–41.
3. Henry de Beauvoir de Lisle, "My Narrative of the Great German War," LHCMA, de Lisle papers, vol. 2 [1919], p. 19.
4. Clemenceau quoted in Général Mordacq to Clemenceau, October 9, 1918, SHAT 6N55, Fonds Clemenceau, Dossier Instances.
5. Général Mordacq, *Le Ministère Clemenceau: Journal d'un Témoin* (Paris: Plon, 1936), pp. 203–205.
6. Quoted in John Terraine, *To Win a War: 1918 the Year of Victory* (London: Cassell, 1978; 2003), p. 46.
7. Clemenceau quoted in B. H. Liddell Hart, *Foch: The Man of Orléans* (Boston: Little, Brown and Co., 1932), p. 261.
8. Haig quoted in Terraine, *To Win a War,* p. 47.
9. Figures from Girard McEntee, *Military History of the World War* (New York: Scribner's, 1943), p. 375. The Jellicoe quotation comes from p. 377. For an argument that suggests that British fears were largely unfounded, see Avner Offer, *The First World War: An Agrarian Interpretation* (Oxford: Clarendon Press, 1989).
10. Martin Gilbert, *The First World War: A Complete History* (New York: Henry Holt, 1994), p. 329.
11. Von Holtzendorff quoted in ibid., p. 306.
12. J. J. Collyer, *The Campaign in German Southwest Africa, 1914–1915* (London: Imperial War Museum, 1937), p. 5.
13. Ibid., p. 20.
14. Memoir of J. Elliott, IWM, Elliott Papers 67/256/1, pp. 22–28.
15. Hew Strachan, *The First World War,* vol. 1, *To Arms* (Oxford: Oxford University Press, 2001), p. 545.

16. Collyer, *German Southwest Africa,* p. 5.

17. Report on meeting at Windhoek, German Southwest Africa, December 1, 1915, IWM, R. B. Turner Papers P252.

18. Memoir of J. Elliott, p. 28.

19. Michelle Moyd, "A Uniform of Whiteness: Racisms in the German Officer Corps, 1900–1918," in Jenny Macleod and Pierre Purseigle, eds., *Uncovered Fields: Perspectives in First World War Studies* (Amsterdam: Brill Academic Publishers, 2004), pp. 25–42, quotation at 28.

20. Wilhelm Deist, "The Military Collapse of the German Empire: The Reality behind the Stab-in-the-Back Myth," trans. E. J. Feuchtwanger, *War in History* 3, no. 2 (1996): 187–207, quotation at 195.

12. JERRY'S TURN

The epigraph is from M. F. Gower to Ada Gillett [early April 1918], IWM 88/25/2.

1. Pat Campbell, *The Ebb and Flow of Battle* (Devon: privately published, n.d.), vol. 2, IWM P91, p. 1.

2. Ibid., pp. 11, 13, 17.

3. Ibid., pp. 21–22, 35.

4. Tim Travers, *How the War Was Won: Command and Technology in the British Army on the Western Front, 1917–1918* (London: Routledge, 1992), p. 89; and C. M. R. F. Cruttwell, *A History of the Great War, 1914–1918* (Oxford: Clarendon Press, 1934), p. 512.

5. Cruttwell, *History of the Great War,* p. 502; and Travers, *How the War Was Won,* p. 89.

6. Philip Gibbs, *Now It Can Be Told* (New York: Harpers, 1920), p. 498.

7. Campbell, *Ebb and Flow,* p. 41.

8. Wilhelm II quoted in Holger Herwig, *The First World War: Germany and Austria-Hungary, 1914–1918* (London: Edward Arnold, 1997), p. 406.

9. Clemenceau quoted in Général Mordacq, *Le Ministère Clemenceau: Journal d'un Témoin* (Paris: Plon, 1936), p. 126.

10. Frederick Maurice to Sidney Clive, August 18, 1917, LHCMA Clive Papers I/1/1.

11. Sonnino quoted in Mordacq, *Le Ministère Clemenceau,* p. 125, n. 1.
12. Herwig, *The First World War,* p. 415.
13. Haig quoted in Philip Warner, *Field Marshal Earl Haig* (London: Cassell, 1991), p. 254.
14. Lt. General Sir Henry de Beauvoir de Lisle, "My Narrative of the Great German War," vol. 2 [1919], LHCMA de Lisle Papers, p. 5.
15. Memorandum of March 26, 1918, quoted in Michael Neiberg, *Foch: Supreme Allied Commander in the Great War* (Dulles, Va.: Brassey's, 2003), p. 63.
16. Foch quoted in General Sir Charles Grant, "Notes from a Diary, March 29th to August, 1918," entry for April 9, LHCMA Grant Papers 3/1.
17. Haig quoted in ibid., entry for March 31.
18. Neiberg, *Foch,* p. 65.
19. Ludendorff quoted in Herwig, *The First World War,* p. 400.
20. Crown Prince Rupprecht quoted in Herwig, *The First World War,* p. 410.
21. Medical Officer Stephen Westman quoted in Malcolm Brown, *The Imperial War Museum Book of 1918: Year of Victory* (London: Pan Books, 1998), p. 101.
22. Ludendorff quoted in Everard Wyrall, "The History of the 62nd (West Riding) Division, 1914–1919," vol. 1 [n.d.], pp. 148–149, LHCMA, Leonard Humphreys Papers.
23. See Travers, *How the War Was Won,* pp. 93–99.
24. Haig quoted in Warner, *Field Marshal Earl Haig,* p. 257.
25. General Alexander Godley quoted in Brown, *1918: Year of Victory,* p. 97.
26. Campbell, *Ebb and Flow,* p. 65.
27. Hindenberg quoted in John Terraine, *To Win a War* (London: Cassell, 1978), p. 65.
28. Quoted in Brown, *1918: Year of Victory,* p. 105.
29. Campbell, *Ebb and Flow,* p. 67.
30. Quoted in Herwig, *The First World War,* p. 414.
31. Foch quoted in General Sir Charles Grant, "Some Notes Made at Marshal Foch's Headquarters, August to November, 1918," LHCMA Grant Papers 3/2, p. 5.
32. On doctrine, see Mark Grotelueschen, *Doctrine under Trial: American Artillery Employment in World War I* (Westport, Conn.: Greenwood Press, 2001).

33. Baker quoted in Robert Bruce, *A Fraternity of Arms: America and France in the Great War* (Lawrence: University Press of Kansas, 2003), p. 151.
34. Pershing quoted in John S. D. Eisenhower and Joanne Thompson Eisenhower, *Yanks: The Epic Story of the American Army in World War I* (New York: Free Press, 2001), p. 114.
35. Clemenceau quoted in Bruce, *A Fraternity of Arms,* p. 150.
36. Ibid., p. 105.
37. Report of British mission to AEF, quoted in Grant, "Notes from a Diary," entry for June 24.
38. Quoted in Robert Zieger, *America's Great War* (Lanham, Md.: Rowan and Littlefield, 2000), p. 97.
39. Herwig, *The First World War,* p. 417.
40. Ministère de la Guerre, *Les Armées Françaises dans la Grande Guerre,* series 7, vol. 1 (Paris: Imprimerie Nationale, 1928), p. 266.

13. ONE HUNDRED DAYS TO VICTORY

The epigraph is from Grand Quartier Général, Second Bureau, "Le morale de l'armée allemande," September 4, 1918, in Ministère de la Guerre, *Les Armées Françaises dans la Grande Guerre,* series 7, vol. 1 (Paris: Imprimerie Nationale, 1928), appendix 960.

1. *Historique du 77ᵉ Régiment d'Infanterie* (Nancy: Berger-Levrault, n.d.), SHAT 26N1734, no. 72, carton 16, p. 66.
2. Ministère de la Guerre, *Les Armées Françaises dans la Grande Guerre* (Paris: Imprimerie Nationale, 1928), series 7, vol. 1, appendix 897, table 1.
3. Pétain to Army Commanders, July 20, 1918, in ibid., p. 91.
4. Ibid., p. 370.
5. Holger Herwig, *The First World War: Germany and Austria-Hungary, 1914–1918* (London: Edward Arnold, 1997), p. 419.
6. Ferdinand Foch, *The Memoirs of Marshal Foch,* trans. T. Bentley Mott (Garden City, N.Y.: Doubleday, 1931), p. 366.
7. Haig quoted in Malcolm Brown, *The Imperial War Museum Book of 1918: Year of Victory* (London: Pan Books, 1998), p. 205.
8. John Terraine, *To Win a War: 1918, the Year of Victory* (London: Cassell, 1978), p. 89.

9. Pershing quoted in ibid.
10. Major General Sir Archibald Montgomery, *The Story of the Fourth Army in the Battles of the Hundred Days* [n.d.], LHCMA Archibald Leslie papers, pp. 6–7.
11. Ibid., pp. 15, 23, 30.
12. Gordon Hassell quoted in Brown, *1918: Year of Victory*, p. 204.
13. Quoted in Terraine, *To Win a War*, p. 114.
14. "Répartition des divisions allemandes sur le front occidental à la date du 31 août 1918," September 1, 1918, in *Les Armées Françaises*, series 7, vol. 1, appendix 922.
15. Foch to Allied Armies, August 31, 1918, in ibid., annexe no. 898.
16. Ibid., p. 277.
17. Montgomery, *The Story of the Fourth Army*, p. 107.
18. Robert Bruce, *A Fraternity of Arms: America and France in the Great War* (Lawrence: University Press of Kansas, 2003), pp. 258, 262.
19. Quoted in Montgomery, *The Story of the Fourth Army*, p. 148.
20. Ibid., p. 192.
21. Ludendorff quoted in Mathias Erzberger, "La Débâcle Militaire de l'Allemagne," *Archives de la Grande Guerre* 12 (1922): 385–416, quotation at 394.
22. Clemenceau quoted in Margaret MacMillan, *Peacemakers: The Pais Conference of 1919 and Its Attempt to End War* (London: John Murray, 2001), p. 41.
23. Herwig, *The First World War*, p. 426.
24. Quoted in Montgomery, *The Story of the Fourth Army*, p. 261, n. 3.
25. Foch, *The Memoirs of Marshal Foch*, p. 463.

CONCLUSION

1. Journal des Marches de 171° Régiment d'Infanterie, SHAT 26N708, Carton 708, dossier 11.
2. Mathias Erzberger, "La Débâcle Militaire de l'Allemagne," *Archives de la Grande Guerre* 12 (1922) 385–416, quotation at 399.
3. Ibid., p. 410.
4. Clemenceau to David Lloyd George, Vittorio Orlando, Edward House, and "Belgium," November 11, 1918, 0800, SHAT Fonds Clemenceau 6N70, dossier 1.

PRIMARY SOURCES

IMPERIAL WAR MUSEUM, LONDON

Bullock, A. V. (02/43/1)
Campbell, Pat (P91)
Christie-Miller, Geoffrey (8/4/03 and 80/32/1)
Churchill, E. F. (83/23/1)
Cooke, Frederic Stuart (87/13/1)
Crowsley, S. W. (02/6/1)
Elliott, J. (67/256/1)
Ennor, F. H. (86/28/2)
Gameson, L. (P396)
Gower, M. F. (88/25/1 and 88/25/2)
McIlwain, John (96/29/1)
Reynolds, L. L. C. (74/136/1)
Turner, R. B. (P252)

LIDDELL HART CENTRE FOR MILITARY ARCHIVES, KINGS COLLEGE, LONDON

Clive, Sidney
De Lisle, Henry de Beauvoir
Gracie, Archibald
Grant, Charles
Humphreys, Leonard
Jacobs-Larkcom, Eric
Jones, John Francis
Kiggell, Launcelot
Maze, Paul
Phillips, C. G.

Service Historique de l'Armée de Terre, Château de Vincennes

Fonds 2° D. I. (24N102)
Fonds 11° D. I. (24N210)
Fonds BUAT (6N9)
Fonds Cabinet du Ministère (5N66)
Fonds Clemenceau (6N55)
Fonds Clemenceau (6N70)
Fonds Gouvernement Militaire de Paris (23N20)
Fonds IV° Armée (19N731)
Fonds IX° Armée (19N1539)
Histoire du 171° R. I. (26N1736)
Historique du 65° R. I. (26N1734)
Historique du 77° R. I. (26N1734)
Historique Sommaire du 64° R. I. (26N1734)
Journal des Marches, 171° R. I. (26N708)
Le 1° Régiment de Marche de Zouaves dans la Grande Guerre (26N1742)

ACKNOWLEDGMENTS

I began the writing phase of this book shortly after two experiences energized my thinking. In June 2003 I attended the Second European Conference in First World War Studies at the Maison Française at Oxford. Pierre Purseigle organized and hosted this, the most intellectually stimulating conference I have ever attended. As he and Jenny Macleod had done in Lyon in 2001, Pierre brought together an incredible array of scholars across disciplines and nationalities. I thank Pierre, Jenny, and the attendees of that conference, including Nicolas Ginsburger, Adrian Gregory, Keith Grieves, Heather Jones, Jennifer Keene, Gary Sheffield, Dennis Showalter, Len Smith, Hew Strachan, Jeffrey Verhey, and Vanda Wilcox, for sharing ideas with me.

Shortly after the conference, Dennis Showalter and I drove the western front, starting at Ypres and ending at the American cemetery at Bony on the Hindenburg Line. Since I first met him in 1998, Dennis has been a model teacher, scholar, colleague, and friend. He generously agreed to read this manuscript and provide his unparalleled insights. For all that he has done for me and for a generation of students at Colorado College, the United States Air Force Academy, and the United States Military Academy, I dedicate this book to him with my utmost respect.

Several other World War I scholars helped me put this book together. They include my colleagues John Abbatiello, Bill Astore, and Mark Grotelueschen, with whom I have had the pleasure to teach and work. Robert Bruce and I have had a long-standing e-mail correspondence, which has helped me better understand some finer points of the war. William Philpott and Martin Alexander provided wonderful sounding boards during our shared time in Paris. I also thank Emmanuel Auzais, Virginie Peccavy, and Hugues and Joëlle de Sacy of the French *Armée de l'air;* Bobby

O. Bell of the American Battle Monuments Commission; and Laurent Henninger and André Rakoto for their friendship and gracious hospitality during my stays in France. Other friends who helped me along the way include Jeremy Black, Lisa Budreau, Jeanne Heidler, John Jennings, Michelle Moyd, Betsy Muenger, and John Shy. Thanks also to Debbie Oliner for her work on the maps and to the Rolfe family for sharing a house and a dog in Britain and for providing some of the photographs.

The staffs of the Liddell Hart Centre for Military Archives, the Imperial War Museum, and the Service Historique de l'Armée de Terre at Vincennes were unfailingly helpful. I gratefully acknowledge permission from these institutions to quote from their materials. I am especially grateful to Sabine Ebbols at LHCMA and Stephen Walton and Tony Richards at IWM. Elwood White, John Beardsley, and Marie Nelson provided the same wonderful assistance that I have always known from the Air Force Academy's McDermott Library. This book would not have been possible without the support of Harvard University Press's Kathleen McDermott and my colleagues at the United States Air Force Academy, including my department head, Col. Mark Wells, and deputy department head, Lt. Col. Vance Skarstedt. Holger Herwig and Edward M. Coffman wrote helpful reports that improved the book. I take full responsibility for any mistakes that remain.

As always, my greatest debts are to my family. My wife, Barbara, and my two daughters, Claire and Maya, have cheerfully put up with my dragging them to battlefields and archives, although I think Paris was only a minor hardship. My family, Larry, Phyllis, and Elyssa Neiberg, and my in-laws, John, Sue, Brian, Michele, and Justin Lockley, have provided unfailing support for all of my endeavors. Thank you.

INDEX